It's Your Move

Marge Watters

It's Your Move

A Personal and Practical Guide
to Career Transition and Job Search
for Canadian Managers, Professionals and Executives

HarperCollins*PublishersLtd*

It's Your Move

© 2001, 2004 by Knebel Watters & Associates, Inc. All rights reserved.

Published by HarperCollins Publishers Ltd

First published in paperback by HarperCollins Publishers Ltd 2001.
This edition 2004.

HarperCollins books may be purchased for educational, business, or sales
promotional use through our Special Markets Department.

HarperCollins Publishers Ltd
2 Bloor Street East, 20th Floor
Toronto, Ontario, Canada
M4W 1A8

www.harpercanada.com

Disclaimer: The material in this publication is provided for information
purposes only. Laws, regulations and procedures are constantly changing, and the examples given are intended to be general guidelines only.
This book is sold with the understanding that neither the author nor
the publisher is engaged herein in rendering professional advice. It is
recommended that the personal services of a competent professional
should be sought.

All of the stories and sample documents are composites drawn from
real-life experiences to illustrate various points and themes, but none
refers to a specific individual or company.

The publisher, author and all others directly or indirectly involved
with this publication do not assume any reponsibility or liability, direct
or indirect, to any party for any loss or damage by errors or omissions,
regardless of the cause, as a consequence of using this publication, nor
accept any contractual, tortious or other forms of liability for its contents
or any consequences arising from its use.

National Library of Canada Cataloguing in Publication

Watters, Marge
It's your move : a personal and practical guide to career transition and
job search for Canadian managers, professionals and executives / Marge
Watters. – 2nd ed.

Includes index.
ISBN 0-00-639463-9

1. Career changes. 2. Career development. 3. Job hunting. I. Title.

HF5384.W37 2004   650.14   C2003-905630-9

RRD 9 8 7 6 5 4

Printed and bound in the United States

*This book is dedicated to the many people
I've had the pleasure of helping with their career transitions.
They have inspired me by teaching me
the tremendous resilience of the human spirit.*

*This book is also dedicated to you,
as you begin your journey
toward the work you want.*

Contents

Part Two — Develop Your Strategy   37

Part Three — Gather Your Resources 99

Part Four — Move into Action   219

Part Five — Cross the Finish Line   261

List of Worksheets

What You Need to Know Before You Start

You can't control the wind, but you can adjust the sails.

Finding the work you want is a whole new game! The rules have changed. The game board has been redesigned. The players don't look or act like they did years ago, and doing well requires fresh strategies. Those who play smart and buy into the new rules will learn a lot about themselves and the dynamic environment of today's workplace.

It's a new game and *it's your move!*

If you're like most of the people I meet in my career consulting practice, you already know that you should be managing your own career. You know that job security is a thing of the past and that losing a job, taking an early retirement package or changing jobs by choice are commonplace. Whether you are currently employed or in transition, you need to set goals, take opportunities to update your skills and actively put yourself forward for assignments that will be challenging and rewarding. This is the new world of work. It's exciting, but it's also frightening.

Much has been written about this new work environment. Perhaps one of the best-known books on the subject is *Who Moved My Cheese?* by Spencer Johnson. Johnson tells the delightful tale of two enterprising mice and their less adaptable colleagues, the little people. When the source of the foursome's livelihood is threatened, these characters react with varying degrees of resilience. We can easily identify with the situation and the characters' reactions to it. The point is clear: "It's better to sniff out changes ahead of time and scurry into action, rather than get hemmed in and be left behind."

Barbara Moses, Canada's well-known career consultant, author, columnist and speaker, promotes career activism. In her book *What Next?* she explains that being a career activist means "being prepared to live in an uncertain work world where the only certainty is you: your skills, your flexibility, your capacity to adapt to change." You need to define yourself independently from your organization and take charge of your career choices. Organizations can no longer be expected to take the initiative for you. Your security will come from knowing you are employable in different work settings.

William Bridges, a leading author on the changing workplace, advises in his book *Managing Transitions: Making the Most of Change* that workers need to think of themselves as "a self-contained economic entity." They must identify work that needs to be done and put themselves forward as an organization's best option to get it done.

Not only has the employment contract changed, but individuals are being measured by a "new yard-stick" according to Daniel Goleman, author of *Emotional Intelligence* and *Working with Emotional Intelligence*. Employers want people who are motivated to keep learning and improving in their jobs. Self-awareness, self-confidence and self-control are highly valued traits in the new workplace, and individuals are judged as much by how they handle themselves and their relationships with others as by how they do their jobs.

These insightful analyses of current workplace issues and job market characteristics take you to the threshold of good career management, but they don't fully explain the steps needed to make a positive career change. *It's Your Move* takes that next important step. It offers a logical process and practical tools designed to help you make choices that are right for you. It explores the challenging issues you will face at every stage of the career transition process, and provides proven methods for identifying and landing your next opportunity.

Have a look at the complete picture. The content of the book follows the sequence pictured here. At every step, you will find practical advice accompanied by exercises, guidelines, worksheets, samples, tips and stories from real-life experiences. Resist the temptation to jump in at Step 3 or 4. The wise strategy is to take time for the first two steps before charging ahead.

Throughout the book, you will be invited to complete extensive and thought-provoking exercises. To do the exercises thoroughly you'll need more writing space than I have given you in the book. Set up a three-ring binder or open a new folder on your hard drive, dedicated to your career transition process. Carve out the time and prepare to do some challenging and enlightening work. As you go through the exercises, spend a third of your time recalling your past and describing yourself accurately, a third of your time writing and the balance reflecting on your answers. Look for patterns, themes and consistent factors. It's the reflective process that opens the door for creative thinking about your future.

Before you begin, I want you to understand what I mean by some of the terms and phrases that are used frequently. When I say "career change" I include looking for a job that is very similar to your most recent one, as well as making a dramatic shift into an entirely different occupation or industry. "Career change" can mean looking for a fresh opportunity within your organization, changing employers or going out on your own. Also, I use the terms "career change," "career management" and "career transition" interchangeably. I consistently use the title "career transition consultant" to describe professionals who assist individuals as they go through the career transition and job search process. "Career consultants," "career coaches," "career transition counsellors" and "outplacement counsellors or consultants" all provide the same type of services.

It's a whole new game. Playing well promises the rewards of flexibility, freedom and unlimited possibilities. But, unless you have the opportunity to work with a career consultant, it's also a lonely game, one in which you are your own strategist, marketer, administrator, advocate and friend. That's why I wrote this book. I hope that it will encourage and motivate you, show you where some of the hazards lie and give you the practical help you need to find the work you want.

Part One

Get Your Head in the Game

Winning relies as much on attitude as it does on hard work.

Objectives

Whether you have decided to move on, or the decision has been made for you, this first step involves ending your current employment situation with confidence and professionalism. By taking care of the details of transition and dealing with the emotions you experience, you can make a positive start. The chapters in Part 1 cover:

- Evaluating your readiness to move on.
- Handling the announcement of your departure effectively.
- Reasons for seeking legal advice.
- Financial planning for transition.
- Building a support network.
- Practical strategies for coping with your emotions.

Rules to Follow

- Be committed to moving on. Fence-sitting is not good for you or your career.
- Pay attention to your finances up front. Establish the maximum length of your transition period on the basis of your finances. Set a minimum remuneration requirement for your next opportunity.
- Separate the emotional issues from the legal issues.
- Choose your confidants wisely. Don't bare your soul to anyone and everyone.
- Plan carefully what you will say about why you are making a change.

Moves That Can Set You Back

- Being negative about any organization or person, thereby making you appear unprofessional.
- Sharing your plans for moving on with anyone inside your organization before you are ready to act on them.
- Being dishonest with yourself about the feelings that change brings.

- Ignoring the effects that a career change will have on the significant others in your life, including children of any age.
- Jumping into the job market before taking the time to do a career assessment and create a strategy for finding the work you want.

Chapter 1

Start Here

*Nothing is more important
than your reputation with yourself.*

Getting your head in the game requires that a decision be made about managing your career. If your employment is terminated, the decision is made for you. You probably won't be consulted, and the news can be quite a shock. The quick hit can be devastating at first, but there are advantages; for example, you don't have to suffer the turmoil of indecision or the disappointment of slow rejection by your organization. The decision is made, and you're at the starting-line.

"Working notice" is a common practice, and it isn't always easy to handle. In this situation, your current responsibilities end, often as the result of project completion or restructuring, and you are given the opportunity to conduct an internal job search. Organizations vary in the degree of clarity they provide regarding their processes and the level of assurance they give regarding job availability. Some offer excellent internal support; others, none at all. If you are given working notice, get your head in the game right away and start managing your career.

Early retirement can be good news or bad news. You're off to a great start if you've been waiting for the opportunity and you already have ideas about what you want to do next. However, if you'll be in bad shape financially, or you're unprepared emotionally and psychologically for this news, the phrase "early retirement" can seem like a euphemism for being fired. Regardless of your initial reaction, there are benefits. You will be able to position your leaving as an early retirement, and having some pension income, you probably won't have to replace all your income to stay even.

If the decision to make a career change is entirely yours, being decisive and making time to do it right will be the challenge. Deciding to leave on your own can be the most difficult starting point. It isn't easy to be proactive about making a move when you are spending all your energy keeping up with the demands of your day-to-day responsibilities. Not devoting the time needed to pay attention to your future, however, is one of the greatest errors in good career management. Doing so requires commitment, organization and discipline. Dedicating yourself to this task is something that only you can do.

In any of these circumstances, you can take control and be determined to make the moves that are right for you. Too many people make mistakes with the closing steps of leaving a job because it is such an emotionally loaded decision, regardless of who makes it. Be very careful about what you say and do.

How you handle your departure from a job will affect your reputation, your references and consequently your future.

Are You Ready to Move On?

If the choice is yours, there will be signs telling you when it's time for you to put yourself into the career management game. Sometimes, colleagues and family can see those signs more clearly than you. After a few years in the same job, some people simply find that they need a new challenge. Perhaps your enthusiasm has diminished because you've become too comfortable at what you do, and it's simply a case of "been there, done that." If you are stale, restless or bored, it's time to consider a change.

Relationships can create or destroy satisfying work. Unproductive and unhappy relationships generate some of the most common reasons for making a change. A reconfigured team might generate too many conflicting opinions. It could be that you and the new boss or the new team can't find a way to work together well. If you've genuinely given it your best shot, consider moving. Chances are high that a move is being planned for you, and it may not be one you want.

When you gain significant practical experience or when you complete formal education adding relevant credentials to your résumé, you might be justified in seeking out a more senior role. Surprisingly, some organizations find it difficult to acknowledge the growing capabilities of their own people. You may have to move on to move up.

In bad economic times, downsizing is commonplace. In good times, mergers and acquisitions bring restructuring. In every economic climate, job loss can result from technological advances, process re-engineering, a change in strategic direction or the arrival of a new leader. Do you wait to see if the organizational change will affect your position, or do you become proactive before you are forced to find a new job? If you are still challenged and enthusiastic about your work, and if that work is likely to continue regardless of structural reorganization, stay put. In this era of non-stop change, you might dodge one upheaval only to land in another.

Regardless of your reasons for a career change, decide to get your head in the game. Don't wait for something magical to happen. You won't find out what else is out there until you go out and have a look. Terrific job offers seldom land in people's laps unsolicited. They're not like junk mail! Most people have to generate new opportunities through thoughtful and diligent effort.

Tip: If you feel so trapped or overwhelmed by your responsibilities or personal circumstances that you can't focus on managing your career, getting professional support is probably a smart idea. First, see your family doctor to make sure nothing is physically wrong. Then, find a qualified counsellor or a competent career transition consultant to help you.

As you work through the following guidelines, remember that you are simply making the decision to begin an active career management process. It doesn't necessarily mean that you will change employers. You might find the ideal opportunity within your current organization.

GUIDELINES FOR DECIDING TO MAKE A MOVE

- Fence-sitting is uncomfortable and unproductive. Find some way of making the decision. Make a list of the pros and cons of staying where you are. Evaluate your current job as if it were a new opportunity. Would you take it?
- Think about what it would take to initiate a career change. Can you dedicate the time and effort to doing it right? If not, can you make some lifestyle changes to make this dedication possible?
- Are you reacting to a temporary or recent situation? If you give this situation more time or effort, is there a chance that your discontentment will vanish?
- Do you like the organization overall? Would you be content with another job in your company if one was offered?
- Career transition consultants are skilled at helping people determine whether or not to look for a new job. Ask someone outside your organization to recommend one and make an appointment to see them.
- Be realistic about the benefits of staying where you are if you have long service with your organization. Consider that leaving might significantly reduce your pension and you might forfeit some types of deferred compensation.
- Once you've decided to look for a new opportunity, commit specific blocks of time to carrying out your intention. Become organized and disciplined.
- Do not discuss your thoughts about leaving with anyone in your organization. Deal with points of dissatisfaction about your job as if you fully intended to be part of the long-term solution.
- Do not make direct or veiled threats about leaving. This seldom generates the result that you want, and it usually labels you as a problem.
- Work through confidential channels. Be cautious with your network and find out which search firms are working for your company so that you do not contact them.
- Use private email and voice mail systems to avoid the possibility of having your search discovered.
- Consider getting legal advice before engaging in conversations with any of your employer's competitors.

A senior lending officer found herself increasingly dissatisfied with her work and decided to leave her corporate role to pursue a completely new career that would involve a significant salary reduction. Over the course of several discussions with her boss, she focused on aspects of her role where changes might convince her to stay. At the same time, she planned her exit but did not reveal this to anyone associated with her work. On the morning that she intended to resign, she received an emergency call from her husband. He told her that his employment had been terminated. As a result, she continued to work in the same position for three years before she could pursue her plan. It was a good thing that she had kept her plans to herself.

You've Decided to Resign

Once you know that you are leaving and where you are headed, give the amount of notice required by your employment contract or company policy. Do not announce your departure too far in advance. Deliver the news of your resignation or retirement respectfully. You never know when you might need to return, or when you might have to deal with your boss or co-workers in another setting.

If a counter-offer is presented by your organization, think about it very carefully. If a substantive change in your role or mandate is on the table, weigh it against your external opportunity. However, if the counter-offer is based solely on remuneration, moving on might be wise. Regardless of what is said, employers have a hard time seeing you as a committed team player after they have had to pay a ransom to keep you. Search firms and placement agencies also become significantly less interested in you after you have jilted them by accepting your company's counter-offer.

Think about what you will say to colleagues, senior management, clients and suppliers about your reasons for leaving. Say more about the new opportunity and less about what you're leaving behind. Be truthful in your explanation, but be respectful. Do not disparage your current employer or anyone who works there.

You've Received Working Notice

Your boss has told you that your current role will be ending, and you will have a specific period of time to look for work while your salary continues to be paid. If you are given the option of looking for another job internally, you can sometimes access internal job boards, career centres or telephone hotlines for help. Here are some questions to guide you.

GUIDELINES FOR DEALING WITH WORKING NOTICE

- Is it possible to receive pay in lieu of working notice and leave immediately? If so, would this be preferable to you?
- How much freedom will you have to look for work internally during the notice period? Will you be given the time to plan your next move, make contacts and attend interviews?
- How likely is it that you will find suitable work within the organization? Will your current boss recommend you for other positions?
- If you find a new job internally, will you feel the same way about the organization? Can you be happy staying if you feel you've previously been rejected?
- If you choose to forego the internal job search, how much time can you take to make contacts and look for work externally?
- Is the support of a career transition consultant available during the working notice period, and, if you haven't landed a job within that time, what quality, level and length of career transition support will be provided?
- If you do not land a new position internally, at what point will you be advised of the details of your severance package?
- If you land a new job outside the organization, can you be released before the working notice period is over? Would you receive any portion of the severance package?
- How would either of these early exits affect your benefits, pension and deferred compensation?

A marketing director received working notice when his department was restructured. He had 90 days to find a new job within the organization. He asked to use the services of a career transition consultant right away, and during the 90 days he split his time between doing his job and looking for the next opportunity. He quickly eliminated the internal options and used his network of contacts to pursue outside opportunities. He landed a job at a higher level with more pay, starting two weeks following the end of the 90-day period. He and his wife enjoyed a nice holiday and banked every penny of his lump-sum severance payment.

You've Been Offered Early Retirement

The opportunity to retire early can feel like a long-awaited blessing, or it can be an unwelcome and abrupt end to your years of service. Your reaction depends on both your financial situation and your interest and energy for continuing to work. Increasingly, people are viewing early retirement as an opportunity to find work that is less demanding, but more fulfilling. This usually means less pay, which is often feasible with supplemental income coming from a pension plan. To help you decide what to do, a thorough review of your financial situation is imperative.

If your finances allow you to stop earning an income, don't make hasty decisions about what retirement might be like for you. It's difficult to know how you will fill your time until you are out of the working world and at home with no obligations to an employer. You might be perfectly happy, or you might feel the need to get back to work in some capacity.

If you intend to continue working, consider whether you want to keep up your usual pace, contribute on a reduced basis or do volunteer work. To find the best opportunity for you, approach the career transition process in the same way you would if this were happening earlier in your career.

You've Been Told That Your Services Are No Longer Required

Out of the blue, you've been called into a meeting and informed that your employment has been terminated. In the space of a few minutes, you find yourself out of a job and in the employment market. Even if you anticipated this or wanted it to happen, the emotional impact of the moment can be overwhelming. Here are some guidelines to get you through.

GUIDELINES FOR DEALING WITH A TERMINATION MEETING

- Just listen. You don't have to say anything. All of your comments and questions can come later.
- You should be told clearly what your last day of work is and what is expected of you in leaving the premises. If you are not told, ask!
- Don't expect to be able to absorb the contents of your severance letter during the termination meeting. If you are a long-service employee, a quick glance at the dollar amount can be helpful. Otherwise, wait until you are at home and read the letter in privacy.
- This is not the right time to confront your boss. Probing for explanations won't resolve or change the situation. Your goal is to make a dignified exit.
- Take the time to talk to a career transition consultant if one is there for you. This can give you some breathing room and some understanding of the level of support available to you.

- Cry if you feel the need. No one expects you to be a hero, but avoid creating a scene in front of your co-workers.
- Do not try to say goodbye to all your co-workers before you leave for home. Call them later, or arrange to meet them in a few days when the initial shock has worn off.
- Arrange to pick up your personal belongings later or ask to have them sent to you.
- Give all keys, passwords and company cards to your manager or career transition consultant.
- Do not touch your computer. If you have personal files or email, ask your manager to have them downloaded and sent to you.
- Take time to compose yourself before you leave. There is no rush to be out the door quickly.
- Think carefully about how you will get home. Arrange for a taxi or call someone to accompany you. This may not be the time to be behind the wheel of a car or alone on a long commute.
- Plan how you will break the news to your spouse or partner. Consider whether telling them immediately by telephone or later in person would be best.
- Walk out with dignity.

Informing Family and Others

Telling loved ones and close friends about your job loss, early retirement or working notice will help you come to grips with the reality of the situation. Unless you have very special circumstances, it's important to tell your spouse or partner immediately about what has happened. Withholding the information for any reason will add to the considerable stress of job loss. If you wait, you risk creating the impression that you do not trust your spouse's or partner's ability to cope. You also deny them the opportunity to be supportive.

Your children should also be told as soon as possible. From as early an age as three they will be able to grasp the basic facts, and they deserve to know what is happening. Everyone in the household will be affected by your transition. It's best if both parents agree on the wording and the tone of the message. Make it reassuring and age appropriate.

Inform other immediate family and friends that you are no longer with the organization. It's better for them to hear this directly from you rather than by trying to call you at work. Many people find that telling their parents is very difficult, as their reaction may be influenced by both the dynamics of the relationship and their potentially limited exposure to the realities of the new world of work. Do not let your reluctance keep you from telling them. They might surprise you with their acceptance and understanding.

Think about friends and neighbours. If you have a spouse or partner, it's wise to decide together what you will say. Your spouse should be ready with the same story that you are telling. When people offer to help and support, assure them that you will call on them when you know what you plan to do.

Keep the explanation of your leaving simple, honest and consistent. You don't need to tell every detail, but everything you say must be true and not misleading. Try to depersonalize the story with a very brief explanation of the context for the decision. What you say must be a reasonable match with what your former employer will say.

Finally, consider your contacts from work. As the news of your leaving spreads, you might receive phone calls offering support and assistance from co-workers, colleagues, suppliers, clients and other contacts. What you say to these people can either build bridges to future employment opportunities or sabotage your prospects. It is extremely important to put on your game face, remaining professional and discreet in what you say. Saying less is usually best.

GUIDELINES FOR HANDLING EARLY CONVERSATIONS WITH
BUSINESS CONTACTS

- Decide who you want to contact personally. This might include clients or suppliers with whom you have current dealings. When you call them, be clear that you are making a personal call, not as a representative of your former employer.
- Do not let any anger or bitterness toward your former employer show. Address the facts and try to sound confident in the belief that you will be moving on to better things.
- Respond graciously to non-specific offers of help by assuring the caller that you will be in touch when you are ready.
- Temporarily postpone specific offers to arrange meetings or make introductions for you. You will need this kind of help when your job search is in full swing, but meeting important contacts before you have had the time to think and prepare can do more harm than good.
- Keep a record of names and phone numbers from these early conversations. This list will be invaluable when you start your job search.

If your employment has been terminated, you're at the starting line for career transition whether you like it or not! You're in the game, and *it's your move*. Taking care of yourself, your loved ones and the closing steps come next.

Chapter 2

Take Care of the Closing Steps

Good beginnings start with good endings.

If your employment is terminated, you need to understand your legal rights and financial situation before you agree to the terms of the severance package or sign a release. This kind of analysis requires clear thinking, at a time when you might be in an emotional fog. It is also entirely normal to have strong feelings of anger, fear and sadness. To help yourself through this difficult time, get good, objective advice from professionals. This chapter will help you decide what professional advice you need. Do not rely entirely on your family and friends for this important step.

Saying Goodbye

In the days immediately following the termination of employment most people feel confused and alone. Knowing what to do first is a challenge. These guidelines will help.

GUIDELINES FOR THE DAYS FOLLOWING TERMINATION OF EMPLOYMENT

- Until the news settles in and you're thinking more clearly, do not make any immediate, drastic changes or big decisions. Don't cancel holiday plans or call the real estate agent!
- Do not sign a release or the severance letter until you understand it completely. Check the date for returning the completed forms, and if you need more time, ask for an extension. You might want to have the severance letter reviewed by an employment lawyer, but it is not essential to do so.
- Do not make a round of emotionally loaded calls to your colleagues and business contacts. Diatribes and hasty explanations of future plans can severely diminish their willingness to stay connected. You will need their help once you have decided what you want to do next.
- Do not activate your job search until you have achieved some equanimity. Do not call placement agencies and search firms, even if you have regularly received calls from them. Take the time to think about how you will position your leaving and your future plans.
- Allow yourself some time to recover from the news. Be patient with yourself as you work through the shock and emotional impact.
- If a seemingly perfect job opening presents itself in the early days following your job loss, do your best to respond by getting your résumé together quickly and preparing for interviews. Try

not to pin all your hopes on this single opportunity. Most job searches take a lot of effort and a fair bit of time. There will be other options if this one doesn't work out.
- Remind yourself that losing a job is a normal part of this new world of work. No job is guaranteed for the long term.

....

Tip: If you have been dismissed because you made a mistake or an error in judgment, choose at least one confidant and share the entire story. This could be your lawyer, your career transition consultant or a very close and discreet friend who has no connection to your working life. You will appreciate having a sounding board as you go through the career transition process.

....

Consider Getting Legal Advice

This section is not intended to give you legal advice. It is meant to make you aware of some of the basic legal issues and to encourage you to seek specific advice from an employment lawyer. Most companies, especially larger ones, ensure that they are in compliance with severance regulations. However, you need to feel that you have been treated fairly, especially if you are a long-service employee. One conversation with a competent and caring employment lawyer may be all that you need to resolve the situation directly.

Common misconceptions about severance packages include the notion that a severance payment is a reward for long service or a pay-off to assuage an organization's guilt over an employment termination. This is not the case. *Severance packages are usually required by law to satisfy an employer's obligation to provide an employee with reasonable notice of termination.* Severance will provide at least some financial assistance to an employee while they search for their next employment opportunity. Therefore, a number of subjective elements come into evaluating the fairness of a severance package.

There are two kinds of law that must be considered: statutory law and common law. Statutory law is written and can be found in the relevant federal or provincial act. Knowing the jurisdiction of your former employer, you could go to the library, a government bookstore or the Internet for a copy of the applicable document. However, statutory law is not the complete picture. Common law emerges as cases are heard and judges decide what constitutes fair treatment in specific circumstances. The decisions that are made by judges regarding severance payments take into consideration the economic situation in the area, and the individual's age, skills, length of service, income and level of responsibility. To fully understand your rights under common law, you will need to consult an employment lawyer.

An employment lawyer is the best choice because they specialize in dismissals and compensation, and are current on court decisions in their region. Labour lawyers usually specialize in unionized situations. If you were part of a union, your severance terms may have been pre-negotiated in the collective agreement, in which case your union representative can give you information.

An employment lawyer should help you separate legal issues from emotional ones, construct a list of negotiating points and suggest that you try the first round of negotiations yourself. By handling these discussions directly, you might get what you want without needing to take an adversarial position, incur significant expense or lengthen the time it takes to reach an agreement. Of course, if you are not willing or able to do this, your lawyer will take over and do it for you. Litigation is not the preferred route. However, if you do proceed, leave the case in the hands of your lawyer and try to get on with your life. Don't let unresolved severance issues and the pursuit of a claim hold you back from whole-hearted engagement in career planning and the job search, or unduly affect your family.

Tip: As long as you are making progress, negotiate for yourself with your lawyer's advice guiding the process. Once you ask your lawyer to write a letter to your former organization, the negotiating will most likely be handled between your lawyer and theirs. This will likely increase the expense and the time required for settlement.

GUIDELINES FOR CHOOSING A LAWYER

- Ask for a referral to an employment lawyer from your own lawyer or a career transition consultant, or call your provincial Law Society.
- Ask for a preliminary meeting or consultation by phone or in person, and explain your situation briefly. Ask these questions of a lawyer before you make your choice:
  - Do you have a conflict in representing me against my former employer?
  - How many non-union termination situations have you handled in the past few months?
  - Do you represent both individuals and organizations?
  - What percentage of your cases are settled out of court?
  - Will you support me if I want to do the negotiating myself, or do you think it is important that you handle the negotiations?
  - How much do you charge? Is there a minimum fee?

If you have been offered the services of a career transition consultant, do not hesitate to use this service right away, even while you are negotiating your package. They should not reveal any information about you or your plans to anyone, and they should have only your best interests in mind. Working with them right away can be a significant benefit to you both professionally and personally. They will help you sort through your issues and avoid the common mistakes associated with job search.

Tip: The courts expect you to do everything you can to mitigate your damages by taking steps to find your next employment opportunity. Using a career transition consultant from the earliest moment will help your case. If you are worried about impartiality or confidentiality, talk with your consultant and ask for written assurance.

Often funding for financial counselling is included in the severance package. It might be provided through the career transition firm. If so, use it. Even the most capable managers of family finances usually learn something from a session with a financial professional.

Do a Financial Review

The benefits of undertaking a financial review at the time you leave your job include making the most of tax shelters, considering the life, disability and medical benefits that you and your family need, and developing a realistic budget for the transition period. Your primary goal in doing a financial review is to establish a comfortable timeline for finding your next employment opportunity, and to alleviate some of the anxiety that accompanies job loss. Think of your severance as payment in advance for your career transition work. If you are re-employed before your severance pay runs out, you have earned yourself a bonus.

Start by completing a thorough list of your monthly expenses. You have fixed and discretionary expenses. It is often an eye-opener to see where the money has been going. With accurate information, you and your family can agree on areas for savings if needed. Compare your monthly expenses with your income from your severance package. How many months do you have until you need to be working again?

Next, take an inventory of your assets and liabilities. Have a plan ready to use in case your job search takes longer than your severance package will carry you. Analyze your assets and liabilities to get a picture of your liquidity. If you need them, which assets would you use first? Do you need to make any investment changes now to provide for the possibility of raising more cash in the future? Do you have any liabilities that represent unnecessary luxuries? At what point would you give up those luxuries?

A man who worked for 28 years in one organization made a rather unique financial decision when he lost his job. He and his wife owned a house in the city and a large cabin cruiser that they loved using on a system of lakes several hundred kilometres away. They were tired of the city, and their children were grown and gone. The couple kept the boat, sold the house and rented a small apartment close to her office. He landed a series of contracts and that income, combined with their investment income, allowed them to afford a new lifestyle, tailored entirely to their liking.

Consider your life, disability and health benefits. Make sure that you understand exactly which benefits continue with your former employer and for how long. This will vary depending on the organization's policy. If you have a short time remaining in your group benefits plan, use it to the full. Make appointments with the dentist and doctor for everyone in the family while you still have coverage. Get your prescriptions filled.

Tip: During your transition period make sure that decisions regarding insurance reflect the appropriate risk factors. Life and disability insurance cover catastrophic, long-term needs. Medical and dental insurance assists with short-term cash flow. Where is the greatest risk for you and your dependants?

Check immediately with your spouse or partner to see if you can be covered by their employer's plan. There is usually a time limit involved. Your former organization's life, disability, health and dental insurance might be convertible to an individual plan without requiring evidence of insurability. This is expensive, but it eliminates insurability concerns. If you need to buy your own coverage, there are many good options available for health, dental and life insurance. Fewer options exist for disability insurance, but there are plans available that can be combined with your severance package to protect your ability to earn an income. Independent coverage is more expensive than group insurance, but being unprotected might be too risky. Call an insurance agent or broker for advice.

Use the worksheets that follow to assist in your financial review.

Tip: By completing a budget you may find that you have more time for transition than you thought. Some people discover that they can double the number of months available by careful planning and frugal spending.

WORKSHEET 2.1
Calculate Your Monthly Living Expenses

Rent	_____	Allowances	_____
Mortgage	_____	Pet care	_____
Taxes	_____	Computer equipment	_____
Property insurance	_____	Computer & Internet	
Hydro	_____	services	_____
Gas	_____	Public transportation	_____
Water	_____	Hair cuts & care	_____
Telephone	_____	Club memberships	_____
Cable	_____	Hobbies	_____
Household purchases	_____	Cosmetics, toiletries	_____
Repairs & maintenance	_____	Prescriptions	_____
House cleaning	_____	Dental care	_____
Lawn care & snow removal	_____	Eye care, glasses,	
Auto –Loan or lease	_____	contacts	_____
–Insurance	_____	Tobacco, alcohol	_____
–Plates	_____	Babysitting	_____
–License	_____	Lessons	_____
–Gas	_____	Dry cleaning	_____
–Parking	_____	Entertainment	_____
–Repairs	_____	Magazines, newspapers	_____
Groceries	_____	Donations	_____
Lunch money	_____	Other expenses	_____
Eating out	_____	Other loan payments	_____
Childcare	_____	Credit card payments	_____
Activities & lessons –you	_____	Income tax installments	_____
–spouse	_____		
–children	_____	**Annual Expenses**	_____
Tuition	_____	Gifts	_____
Clothing & shoes –you	_____	Holidays	_____
–spouse	_____	Family celebrations	_____
–children	_____	RRSPs/savings	_____
Insurance (life, disability)	_____		
Insurance (medical, dental)	_____	Total and	_____ ÷12
		monthly equivalent	_____

TOTAL MONTHLY
LIVING EXPENSES   _____

WORKSHEET 2.2
Your Assets and Liabilities

Non-Registered Assets	Owner You/Spouse	Financial Institution	Amount or Market Value	Maturity Date	Monthly Income
Bank accounts					
CSBs & money market funds					
GICs/term deposits/bonds					
Employer savings plans					
Mutual funds					
Stocks					
Cottage					
Residence					
Rental or investment properties					
Life insurance CSV					
Other					
Total					

Registered Assets	Owner You/Spouse/Child	Financial Institution	Amount or Market Value	Maturity Date
RRSPs				
RESPs and trusts				
Total				

Liabilities	Lender	Outstanding Balance	Renewal Date	Rate	Monthly Payment
Mortgage					
Car loan					
Line of credit					
Credit cards					
RRSP loan					
Other debts					
Total					

WORKSHEET 2.3
Your Financial Picture for Transition

Other Sources of Income		**Upcoming, Non-recurring or Contingency Expenses**	
Part time work	_____	Medical	_____
Fees & honorariums	_____	Dental	_____
Maintenance payments	_____	Personal	_____
Investment income	_____	Travel	_____
Rental Income	_____	Education	_____
Disability benefits	_____	Home repairs	_____
Government benefits	_____	Car repairs or purchase	_____
Pension income	_____	Other	_____
Other	_____	Total	_____
Total other income monthly	_____		
		Estimated monthly payments	_____

Transition Budget

Regular monthly expenses	_____
(Minus) Realistic cost-cutting estimate	– _____
(Plus) Monthly payments re: non-recurring expenses	+ _____
Total monthly expenses for the transition period	_____
(Minus) Monthly income from other sources	– _____
Total monthly amount that must be drawn **from the severance package or savings**	_____
Number of months the severance package could last:	_____ **Months**

Important: File your claim for Employment Insurance (EI) within four weeks of your last day of work regardless of your receiving a severance payment. Delaying in filing your claim may cause loss of benefits. File online at www.hrdc-drhc.gc.ca/ae-ei/ or in person at your nearest HRDC office.

Tip: An honest look at how you spend money and a discussion with your spouse or partner early in your transition period can reduce anxiety and prevent problems down the road. Drafting a comprehensive plan now can give you the freedom to take the time you need for a good transition.

Using a professional financial adviser to help you maximize tax shelters and use your severance package to its fullest advantage is a very good idea. Fee-only Certified Financial Planners (CFP) or Registered Financial Planners (RFP) are planners with nationally recognized designations who have completed education and examination requirements, and are required to meet standards for annual continuing education. Other qualified professionals include Fellows of the Canadian Securities Institute (FCSI), Chartered Accountants (CA), Certified Management Accountants (CMA), Certified General Accountants (CGA), Chartered Financial Analysts (CFA) and Certified Public Accountants (CPA). Be sure that the professional you choose operates on a fee-only basis.

Many investment representatives, financial product salespersons and brokers are paid a commission or fee for the products they sell. You may wish to seek advice from them after you have decided how you will allocate your severance monies; however, they may not be an unbiased source of information for you at this point.

GUIDELINES FOR CHOOSING A FINANCIAL PLANNER

- Ask your bank manager or your career transition consultant for a referral to a qualified, fee-only financial planner. You can also be referred through Advocis, The Financial Advisors Association of Canada, either by calling (416-444-5251 or 1-800-563-5822) or visiting their web site (www.advocis.ca), which allows you to search for financial planners by province and type of service.
- Call and explain your situation briefly. Ask these questions before making your choice:
  - What credentials do you have?
  - Do you operate on a fee-only basis? If so, what is your fee?
  - How many meetings do you think we will need? Can we do follow-up by phone?
  - How many clients with severance packages have you advised recently?
  - What should I bring to the meeting?
- Rapport is important. If you don't feel comfortable with the preliminary call, try someone else.

The meeting itself should take between one and two hours. Encourage your spouse or partner to attend the meeting. Hearing the planner's advice first-hand and having an opportunity to ask questions can contribute to their peace of mind. To make the best use of the time with your financial adviser, do some preparation. Complete the worksheets in this book or those provided by your adviser and bring the following to the meeting:

- a detailed list of your assets, including RRSPs, investments and savings
- an itemized list of any outstanding debts, including mortgages and credit-card balances
- your personal monthly household budget with estimates in all categories

- your last income-tax assessment
- a recent pay slip
- your last statement of account for your pension plan and employee savings plan
- a copy of your severance letter
- your current insurance portfolio, including life, disability, medical and dental

Decide on your objectives before the meeting. Are you most concerned about debt reduction, benefit replacement, pension issues, sheltering the severance through RRSPs (tax minimization) or personal budgeting? Any thoughts on what you'll do next provide helpful information to your financial planner. Are you considering early retirement, financing a new business, moving your residence, looking for a similar job, taking some time off or changing direction completely? The more prepared you are going into the meeting, the more focused the information will be that your planner provides.

Build a Support Network

An empathetic and supportive network of family, friends and professionals can help you tremendously during transition. Sometimes a support network evolves naturally as people offer to be a resource. The phrase "Let me know if there's anything I can do" is usually genuinely meant, but it is seldom backed by specific ideas of what might be done. At the appropriate time, you will have to tell them.

Choose your support network wisely. A person who has been through career transition successfully can provide a wealth of first-hand experience. Former co-workers and bosses can give you insightful feedback on your career plans once you've done a thorough assessment. Any colleague with whom you feel comfortable can become an on-going source of encouragement and advice. Be judicious about how you use the support of family and friends; some are more capable than others of helping you carry the burden. Set clear guidelines from the outset by asking them directly how much they want to know. Keep the lines of communication open, but be careful not to lean too heavily on those who are struggling to cope with their own reactions to your career change.

The formation of your own board of advisers is a more strategic and intentional approach to creating a support network. Your board could include four to six people from varied backgrounds who are willing to offer you advice, feedback and encouragement on a regular basis. You might call on your advisers individually or gather them together in an informal session to do some brainstorming on your behalf. The best combination of people will include those who have different perspectives. They will be people who have your best interests at heart. You will need to feel comfortable receiving feedback and constructive suggestions from them. It also helps to include people who have well-developed networks.

A human resources director, whose employment was terminated when her company was acquired, asked six colleagues from different walks of life to act as her board of advisers. She included a recruiter, a lawyer, a colleague from her MBA class of many years past, a politician and two friends from her volunteer work. She sought advice individually for the most part, but she also chose a convenient pub as a venue for the group to meet on the occasional Friday evening. It turned into a welcome opportunity to network, wind-down and help a friend with her job search.

Tip: Begin to think about who might provide references for you when a prospective employer asks. Record the names of those who offer this support. Consider whether this is an appropriate time to broach the topic with others. Some of your references will be an integral part of your support network. For others, you will need their contribution only when an offer of employment is imminent.

Remember that as part of your support network, a career transition consultant can be a tremendous help. If your employment has been terminated and your organization has not provided transition service, ask for it and negotiate the length and quality of service. If this move is your own decision, consider engaging a consultant. Many people think that they don't need this sort of help, but a capable consultant in a firm with a reputation for individualized service can aid your transition process significantly.

GUIDELINES FOR CHOOSING A CAREER TRANSITION CONSULTANT

- Don't let the titles confuse you. Career counsellors, outplacement counsellors, career transition consultants and career coaches all do substantially the same work.
- The industry is not regulated, and there are no specific designations or credentials to ensure competence. The best consultant for you will have a background that you respect. A good consultant should offer a listening ear, challenge you to stretch your thinking, and provide practical advice that is appropriate for you and your industry.
- If your organization has engaged a particular firm for you, stick with it unless you know exactly where you'd rather go or you have a strong dislike for the consultant, the program or the environment. Shopping around for a new firm can open a new round of negotiations with your organization and can significantly delay your engagement in the transition process.
- If you are on your own, ask a human resources professional, your employment lawyer, a financial adviser, or others who have been through the process, who they would recommend. Call the Human Resources Professionals Association in your province and ask for a list of firms.
- Evaluate the service according to the level of expertise it offers and its reputation. Spending three months with a high-quality firm focused on individualized service will probably do more for you than twice that time with a firm that emphasizes group sessions or self-directed tools.
- Call and describe your background and circumstances briefly. Ask these questions before you make a choice:
  - May I come in and meet you and see your facilities?
  - Who will work with me? What is their background? Please give me a general profile of some of the clients this consultant has advised. How senior? What industries?
  - May I have an outline of the programs? What parts of my program would be delivered through workshops or delegated to a junior staff member? (Individualized service supplemented by optional workshops is best.)
  - How often will I meet with my consultant, and what access will I have to consulting support between scheduled appointments?

- What effort will my consultant make to contact me and remain proactively involved with my job search?
- What access will I have to office space? May I see the facilities that I will be using? Are there ever times when I will not have access because the facilities are full?
- Are there organized networking opportunities as part of my program? How often? What are typical backgrounds of the people who attend?
- What level and length of service has the most appropriate content for me and my situation?
- If you are purchasing the service yourself, be sure to ask about fees.

Give Yourself a Time Frame

If you are employed and you've decided it's time to make a move, give yourself a deadline to work toward for finding a new opportunity. Be intentional about the allocation of time to your search so that your busyness does not cause months to pass without effort being directed toward it. Each step in the process is likely to take longer for you because you cannot dedicate your full attention to it. Looking for work can be a full-time job in itself.

If you are not working, the financial review has helped you establish the maximum number of months you have to make this transition. Even if you have the luxury of ample time, it's wise to make an initial estimation of how long it might take you to find work. It will help you determine how urgent it is for you to get going. Be realistic so that you don't get caught short of time.

Taking a temporary break can be an excellent strategic move, especially if you have been working for years without one, or if your last role was particularly stressful. Regardless of what you choose to do during your time off, be clear about how long you intend to delay your search activities. Let your support network and references know when you intend to begin, and be sure to live up to that commitment. Make your time out a purposeful step in the process.

It's very difficult to predict how long your career transition and employment search will take. Talk with your support network and anyone you know who has successfully gone through the process in order to understand the parameters. Most people underestimate the time needed to prepare for entering the marketplace and few realize how time-consuming an active search can be. The factors that will affect your time frame include how radical a career change you plan to make, your degree of flexibility regarding terms of employment, the buoyancy of the market for your skills and how effectively and diligently you work at your search. Last but not least, being in the right place at the right time never hurts.

To get an overview of where you're headed, look at the charts in the appendices. Reference will be made to them many times as you move through the steps in the process. Appendix A offers a strategic view of the career transition and employment search process. Appendix B is a table that sets out your search activities as a project plan with a timeline. Start using the template in Appendix B now by inserting the date by which you would like to begin working in your next role.

Tip: If you choose to take some time off, it is often very helpful to meet with your career transition consultant before doing so. They will help you through the closing steps and introduce you to the transition process. Their input can help you enjoy the time you need with more peace of mind.

Achieve Closure and Move On

Settling the legal and financial aspects of your severance and building a support network will move you toward closure. Saying your goodbyes and offering to help with the transfer of your work to someone else will be of some help but may be difficult emotionally. A huge part of ending well is in how you handle your feelings about leaving your job and facing the future. The next step deals with your emotional well-being.

Chapter 3

Make It Through the Emotional Maze

*What happens to you is less important
than what happens inside you as a result.*

Every change marks the end of something. Endings involve loss. When you lose something important, you have an emotional reaction to that loss and there's nothing wrong with that. Leaving a job, whether by choice or not, carries with it a loss and the accompanying feelings.

What you do to earn a living gives you purpose in many ways. It provides challenges and opportunities to solve problems. It offers the chance to keep you learning. It lets you interact with others, individually and in teams. It offers recognition and status, as well as the means by which you pay the bills and plan for the future. Your job forms part of your identity. Making changes to something this important requires special care. Dealing with your emotions is an important step regardless of who initiated the change.

Reactions to Change and Loss

The nature and intensity of your reaction to loss depends on several factors. Without question, your degree of control over the situation is a major factor. If you made the decision to change jobs, you might feel some sadness about leaving behind colleagues and a familiar environment, but excitement about the opportunity ahead probably outweighs the sadness. Moreover, you will have had time to prepare for your goodbyes.

A young woman who decided to leave a high-powered job in advertising knew that she would greatly miss her colleagues and her team's cohesiveness. In the weeks before she announced her departure, she carried a piece of paper with her. On it were two columns. One was labelled, "Things I'll miss about this place," and the other, "Things I won't miss." To her surprise, when she actually said her goodbyes, a significant amount of her sadness had dissipated through keeping this inventory.

If your employment was terminated suddenly, both the shock and the lack of control will affect the intensity of your reaction. If you were a long-service employee or your organization was your first and only employer, your attachment to it could be very strong. You may have made a number of personal sacrifices in the line of duty to your employer. It could be that over the years you passed up excellent offers to leave for the sake of loyalty. People who have a long history with an organization usually have deep feelings about losing their job.

Another very significant influence on your ability to deal with career change is the other changes that are occurring in your life. Changes in health, family circumstances, finances, personal goals or lifestyle can make change easier to manage or much more difficult. It is noteworthy that people who meet with career transition consultants seldom have only one change to consider. There are usually other personal circumstances that need attention.

It is impossible to predict how an individual will feel about any change, including job loss. There is no right or wrong reaction. Our feelings are just what they are. There's no point in trying to change, ignore or banish them. Good management of your emotions is essential to healthy change management.

Good management starts with understanding. The range of emotions that we experience is enormous. However, most human emotions can be categorized using one of these four words: sad, mad, glad or afraid. Think about it. You might describe your mood as blue, discouraged, gloomy or devastated. These are words meaning "sad." Frustrated, annoyed, disappointed, angry and #!*@#$ are ways of saying "mad." Relief and gratitude are expressions of gladness. Worry denotes fear. Simplifying the range of emotions to a few broad categories might help you achieve clarity regarding your feelings.

Tip: Learning to name your feelings is an important part of good emotional health. Admitting that you're angry puts you in touch with the feeling, gives you clarity and puts you in a position to choose how you will express that feeling.

Feelings often overlap. It's entirely possible to feel sad and afraid at the same time. People who say that they feel depressed are probably sad and angry. With depression, the anger is usually turned inward. Any combination of feelings can be experienced at once.

Use the following worksheet to put some of your feelings down on paper. This exercise might seem unnecessary, but it allows you to identify and air feelings that might otherwise stay bottled up inside. The objective is recognition and good management of your emotions.

WORKSHEET 3.1
Identify Changes and Feelings

Think about the changes that are occurring for you in each of these areas of life. List each situation and all of the accompanying losses. For example, termination of employment could mean the loss of financial security, camaraderie, status, hopes for advancement, business travel, etc.

Name your feelings. Stretch your imagination and list the beginnings that this change might bring.

	What's changed?	What was lost?	How do you feel about each loss?	Possible new beginnings
Work				
Relationships				
Health & Age				
Community/ Society				

The type and intensity of feelings that you experience will fluctuate. Initially, you might feel paralyzed by anger and fear. These feelings may give way to sadness or even relief, and then return. People recovering from a significant loss often describe their experience as being similar to riding a roller coaster. At first the ups and downs are enormous in their contrast. Eventually, the ride evens out, and a sense of control and stability begins to return.

Physical reactions to loss are not unusual. When you are dealing with intense emotions, your body is vulnerable to illness, aches, sleeplessness, excessive fatigue, changes in appetite, confusion and even diminished memory. People often worry about these physical symptoms, thinking that grave illness has accompanied their loss. Usually, your physiological reactions to your emotional state will be temporary.

One senior executive had trouble concentrating in the weeks following his job loss. He would be halfway through a sentence and completely forget what he was saying. This was embarrassing and disconcerting for one so reliant on his thought processes. He decided to treat his problem with honesty and a bit of humour. Simply admitting what was happening helped solve the problem.

When you are coping with loss, take special care of yourself. Rest, exercise and follow a well-balanced diet. Watch your use of addictive substances, including caffeine, alcohol, tobacco and over-the-counter medications. Consult your doctor. Any of the symptoms described above could need medical attention. It would be a mistake to ignore them, assuming that they will go away once you are over your loss.

Important: If you are feeling so low that you think there is no reason to carry on, or that others would be better off without you, STOP! Call your doctor, a clergy person, a counsellor or a crisis line. There are people who care about you and want to help you make it through this difficult time. Reach out for help right away.

A less well-known reaction to loss is the tendency to remember and grieve past losses in the midst of coping with a current situation. People often find themselves shedding tears over an event that happened years ago. If this happens to you, don't worry. It's not unusual to take an emotional inventory of past losses as you work through your feelings about a current loss. It's okay to remember and appropriately express your feelings regarding your divorce, the loss of a loved one, an unwanted move, hopes unfulfilled or any other change from your past.

Be aware that there is a future-oriented aspect to change and loss. Every ending creates a new beginning. You might not be ready to feel optimistic, but it can help you to think about the possibilities that might open up for you.

Why Worry about Feelings?

Nothing sabotages the career transition process more than unresolved feelings of anger, sadness and fear. Anger is the worst culprit. Sadness that spirals downward into a state of gloomy inactivity scores a close second. Fear is usually manageable through focused activity directed at creating a positive outcome. Gladness is a welcome feeling.

If you have lost your job, you are probably angry. This is not a bad thing in itself. What can be destructive is the way in which you choose to express your anger. Spreading your version of the story, complete with blame and bitterness, will only hurt you. There may be a lot of truth in what you say, but saying it indiscriminately is not helpful to your future prospects. Find safe confidants with whom you can vent your anger in privacy.

A manager had the unhappy task of telling a long-service, well-liked subordinate that his employment was terminated because the organization wanted to build a new culture in the division. The employee was devastated. However, only his wife, his closest friends and his career transition consultant heard the full extent of his reaction. Everyone spoke highly of the professional and dignified way in which he handled his departure. His former boss and colleagues made every effort to support his transition.

Email can be a very dangerous thing in the hands of an angry person. There is something about the immediacy and the informality of this medium that tempts people to write regrettable things. Unfortunately, sending a venomous email is worse than saying something in anger, because, while the spoken word is sometimes forgotten, the email lives on in print. If you are angry, don't touch your email!

Anger not only burns bridges between you and the past, it can destroy your best path forward. Your professional community is small. The more senior your position, the smaller the community is. If word gets around that you are openly expressing your bitterness, your contacts will not want to have more than one final conversation with you. If you go into interviews without having your emotions under control, a skilled interviewer will hook you every time. You will not be offered future opportunities if you are perceived as being unable to cope with the past. The fact that you have lost your job is less important to others than how you are perceived to be dealing with it.

Tip: Before talking with your business colleagues and contacts, write down your explanation of your job loss. Practise saying it to a confidant, and be sure that it is completely free of anger and bitterness.

Do not misunderstand this point. It *is* okay to feel angry, sad and afraid. It is *not* okay to express those feelings to anyone and everyone you meet or in ways that are harmful to you or others. To cope well with change, you must find appropriate ways to acknowledge and express your feelings.

Unresolved feelings not only harm your relationships, they drain your energy and rob you of your creativity. To engage in a positive, forward-focused career management process, you must find your way through the maze by dealing with your emotional reactions to loss. You might need several weeks before you start to find your way, and it could take a long time to exit this maze entirely, but you need to be making progress. There is no way over, under or around these feelings. You must move through them to get past them.

It's a Personal Journey

The strategies that work for you in making your way through the narrow passages, hidden intersections and unmarked turns of this emotional maze will be unique to you. No one can predict what will help you and what will set you back. Your support network can offer suggestions and cheer for you, but you are the one who will discover what works for you. The key is to keep trying different tactics until you begin to make progress.

When your feelings are intense, talk is the most reliable healing agent. Even the most introverted individuals find relief in getting their concerns off their chest. This is why so many people make the mistake of saying too much and talking to the wrong audience. You need to talk to a good listener. This will be an objective person who is removed from the situation. It will be someone who won't judge and won't give simplistic or trivial advice. In fact, while you are hurting, no advice is often the best advice. A good listener just listens. They don't turn the conversation to address their own needs, and they won't breathe a word about your talk to anyone else.

When you find such a person, tell them the unabridged story with as much colour commentary as you wish. This is your chance to let it go! Talking through everything allows you to acknowledge the extent of the situation you are handling. Recognize the feelings that accompany each change. Name your feelings. Shout them out, or cry them out if that's helpful. A good listener won't mind. Talking should help you achieve clarity.

Tip: Express your feelings in a safe way. Cry, yell, punch a pillow, go for a long run, play a hard game of tennis, sing at the top of your lungs or clean the house to within an inch of its life. Do whatever works for you without hurting yourself or anyone else.

There are many additional strategies that you can try as you search for ways to progress through the emotional maze. The list that follows offers suggestions. Some of these activities will work for you, and others won't. Try as many as you wish.

GUIDELINES FOR COPING WITH THE EMOTIONS ACCOMPANYING CHANGE AND LOSS

- Do something symbolic to mark what has ended. Go to a goodbye lunch or party if your co-workers want to do this for you. Burn your business cards. Shred a copy of your company's annual report. Pop the champagne. Create your own way of saying goodbye to familiar places and routines.
- Write about your experiences. Sit down at the computer, or buy a spiral notebook and put everything that happened in writing. Consider starting a journal. Tracking your feelings through the career transition process can be enlightening and helpful. Not too long from now, you will be able to see how far you've come.
- Arrange for a temporary time out, preferably at a place that you love. Spend some time on your own to rest, and be reconciled with what has happened. Solitude is often a great healer.

- Pay attention to your health. Eat a balanced diet. Get lots of sleep. Exercise. If you do get sick, be patient and take the time to recover fully without being anxious.
- Lounge in a hot tub, go for a massage, do deep breathing exercises or attend yoga classes. You hold emotions in your body more than you may think possible. Relax your muscles and let your feelings go.
- Do something creative. Work with your hands. Renovate a room, plant a garden, build a deck, paint, knit, cook, do woodcarving, repair things, sculpt or sew. As long as you find it relaxing and fulfilling, do it!
- Rely on your spirituality. Meditate or pray. If you belong to a community of faith, turn to the people who share your beliefs for support.
- Read the biography of someone you admire. There are countless stories of individuals who have coped with overwhelming difficulties, and left a legacy of courage and inspiration.
- Take stock of how you have handled changes in the past. Were you able to get through them without a lot of difficulty? If so, can you use the same strategies this time?
- Take every opportunity to limit the number of changes happening in your life.
- If you are very frightened, sit down and think about the worst possible outcome this situation could bring. Then practise inverse paranoia. Think about the best possible scenario, and visualize it happening. Write down what you would need to do to make it happen. Try to set at least one attainable goal.
- Be serious about having fun. Doing what you truly enjoy is often one of the first things to go when you're faced with difficult times. It may seem frivolous to schedule time for play, but you need to kick back now more than ever.
- Find reasons to laugh. Look for humour everywhere. Rent a comedy from the video store. Invite your most easygoing friends to dinner. Ask people to tell you the best joke they've heard lately.

Help Your Loved Ones Deal with Your Career Change

When you lose your job, you are not the only one who experiences loss. The people who love you and depend on you can feel the loss of everything from financial security to the company convention in Bermuda and the daily chats with your assistant. Compounding this is their inability to control the situation. For them it's like hitting a patch of black ice when they're not behind the wheel.

Loved ones will experience emotions that can be completely different from yours. Your spouse might feel very angry because you have been hurt, while you are filled with fear and sadness. This can cause tension between you unless you understand that those close to you need the freedom to have their own reactions and cope in their own ways. Communication, understanding and support are vitally important for you and everyone who is close to you.

The turmoil of uncertainty plus the varied emotional reactions of loved ones often puts extraordinary stress on relationships. Even if you have been strong for one another initially, the long journey can be a challenge. These basic principles might help:

- First, take good care of yourself and manage your own emotions well.
- Give your loved ones the freedom to have their own reactions and cope in their own ways.

- Establish a plan for communication with each person who needs to be informed of your progress. Agree on a regular time to talk and put some structure around the conversation. This way, you can avoid unwanted, poorly timed interactions that seem like criticism or nagging.

After days of anxiety and conflict, one husband and wife decided to limit the discussion of the job search to once a week. They set aside Thursday evening, and developed a format for their conversation. They each answered these questions in turn without interruption: "What was this week like for you?" "What was encouraging?" "What was discouraging?" "Is there anything I can do to help you?" "What can we do this weekend that's fun?" Suggestions, judgments and advice were not permitted unless specifically requested. No solutions were expected. This process considerably eased the tension between them.

If you have children living at home, don't be surprised if they begin to act out. Fighting with siblings, letting grades slip and defying household rules are some of the ways that children of various ages express their anxiety. If you ask them what's upsetting them, don't expect them to be able to connect their behaviour to your current circumstances. The best response is to acknowledge their feelings and do something special or different to help them handle their specific problem. Children differ in their resilience and reactions. Some behave in surprisingly supportive ways at first, but a prolonged period of stress in the household will present challenges for them.

Very young children will feel the stress regardless of your words. They will be frightened if they witness their parents' tears and tirades. Continue to show your love for them and manage your intense feelings in a healthy way, out of their sight. Children need assurance that they are not the cause of the tension in the house. They will take their emotional cues from you, so keep your messages as upbeat and positive as possible. Young children are interested in their own routines.

They want to know if they will be able to continue their favourite activities like hockey or swimming lessons. Once you tell them what will be different for them while you are looking for work, and assure them that everything will be okay, they are usually very accepting as long as *you* seem okay. Help them with what they will say to their friends and how they will respond to any questions about your circumstances.

Eight- to twelve-year-olds will take most of their reactive cues from you, but they are also forming their own ability to make sense of things. Some preteens will ask very direct questions, and they deserve honest answers. Tell them a bit about how you are feeling, and at the same time assure them that you are in control of the situation. For example, you might say, "I'm a bit scared, but I'm talking to a lot of people to find another job. It will all work out for us." Others at this age might brood or imagine catastrophes. Spend time with them and keep talking to them. If you keep the lines of communication open, you will be better able to address their concerns. The influence of peers can be significant for preteens. Immature and ill-informed ideas might bombard them. It's critical that your children receive your input and frequent reassurance.

Teenagers can be more realistic about the implications of job loss. They can separate the circumstances from their role in it, and they will have their own emotional reaction. They will look to you as a role model. Tell them the facts and ask for their support in whatever way makes sense for your family. Don't allow the classic teenage hyperbole to throw you. The solutions aren't as simple as they might think, and it can be challenging to be patient with their input. On the other hand, some teenagers will respond in remarkably mature ways and offer to make practical contributions. Accept this help with gratitude, but don't let them take on unrealistic responsibilities. Again, communication is the key. Teens will learn a lot from how you handle this situation.

When you are coping well with the emotions accompanying your career transition, it will have a calming effect on your children and everyone close to you. Offer frequent reassurance that everyone in the family is going to get through this tough time. Tell them that you love them. Hug them often.

The Return of Hope

Making it through the emotional maze will take time. There will be ups and downs, progress and setbacks. Give yourself credit for every step forward. Your goal is to remain aware of the dynamics of your emotions and use good coping strategies. Hope will return.

Gradually you will feel like you're back to what's normal for you. You'll find that you can concentrate again and take more interest in what's happening around you. Flashes of creative thinking and short bursts of energy will herald your discovery of the way out of the maze. Keep heading in the right direction and keep noticing how you feel.

The early moves in this game of career transition have been about ending well. With the decision made, the details settled and your journey through the emotional maze under control, it's time to move on.

Part Two

Develop
Your Strategy

What a person does tells you who a person is.

Objectives

This step invites and challenges you to think in-depth about what you've done and what you want to do next. It will help you identify all that you have to offer the marketplace. You will do a thorough analysis of your situation that concludes with a strategic targeting exercise. The chapters in Part 2 cover:
- Career review and personal assessment.
- Identifying your strategic advantage.
- Evaluating the balance between work and the rest of life.
- Options to a traditional job.
- Looking ahead to retirement.
- Identifying the ideal employment opportunity for you.
- Initial assessment of the market.
- Setting targets where you think your potential to contibute coincides with market needs.

Rules to Follow

- The reflective work you will do is pivotal. Allow yourself the time and freedom to fully explore the questions presented in the following chapters.
- If you get stuck at any point, don't try to force the answers. Let the questions remain with you to answer later or to serve as areas for future exploration.
- Once you've completed a section, reread and reflect on what you have written to assess the patterns and themes.
- Use your own style to record your thoughts. Work at your computer, draw diagrams or pictures, use charts, graphs or mind-maps, dictate an audio recording or write longhand.
- Use career assessment tests only after you have done your own reflective work.
- This is personal and private information. You do not need to share this with anyone unless you would find it helpful.

Moves That Can Set You Back

- Dismissing this section as a waste of time.
- Thinking that you'll get back to doing this later and skipping to the résumé section so that you can get into the marketplace quickly.
- Giving only superficial answers.
- Thinking about the questions without recording your thoughts.
- Overlooking jobs that were unsuccessful or unenjoyable for you. There can be tremendous learning in adversity.
- Neglecting to get input from your support network and advisers that can offer you a reality check.
- Allowing the expectations of others to dominate your thinking. This is an opportunity to be yourself.
- Spending an excessive amount of time in this reflective process, resulting in procrastination.

Refer to Appendix A. In Part Two you will work on your situational analysis and strategic targeting.

Chapter 4

Take Time Out for Reflection

All that is past is prologue.

It takes careful self-assessment and good planning to move forward on the career path that is right for you. In the past, you might have followed your organization's prescribed progression through the ranks or responded to a headhunter's call, taking new opportunities as they presented themselves. In that old style of career management, there was often more emphasis on traditional advancement than on doing the work that you wanted and liked to do. In contrast, the new world of work invites you to understand who you are and where you best fit in the workplace.

You are not the same person you were when you started your career. You're not even the same person you were ten years or even five years ago. This is a rare opportunity to evaluate where you've been and where you are today in order to generate options for where you want to go. Take the time to complete the following exercises in detail. Record your thoughts using a method that is comfortable for you. Relax and enjoy the process; it can be very affirming and do wonders to restore a damaged sense of self-worth. You have tremendous value to offer, and all of your experiences count for something.

Tip: If you are considering a major career change, take yourself on a retreat to do this reflective work. Organizations usually send their people to an off-site, facilitated session when long-term strategic thinking is needed. Plan your own off-site! Get away to a place where you feel totally relaxed, and enjoy solitude while you go through this process.

Create Your Timeline

Take a long look into your past by creating a timeline. Start with your earliest memories and work forward chronologically, recording the people and events that have affected your opportunities and shaped your decisions, especially as they relate to your career direction. Divide your history into blocks of time or chapters that have been significant for you. Be sure to include your experiences from outside the workplace. Look at the timeline provided and create your own, using the worksheet. Then follow the guidelines to help you recall how your career direction evolved.

GUIDELINES FOR TIMELINE ANALYSIS
- Answer the following questions for each chapter of your personal history:
  - What was your ambition and career direction at that time?
  - What significant events or experiences influenced your expectations and outlook?
  - Who were your role models?
  - Who provided examples of undesirable behaviours and attitudes?
  - What were the roads taken and not taken?
  - What opportunities did you wish to have and why weren't they available to you?
  - What caused you to close this chapter and move to the next?
  - What did retirement mean to you at this time?
  - If you could re-write parts of your personal history, what would the revised edition say?
  - What elements of your lifelong dreams remain unfulfilled?

An Entrepreneur's Timeline

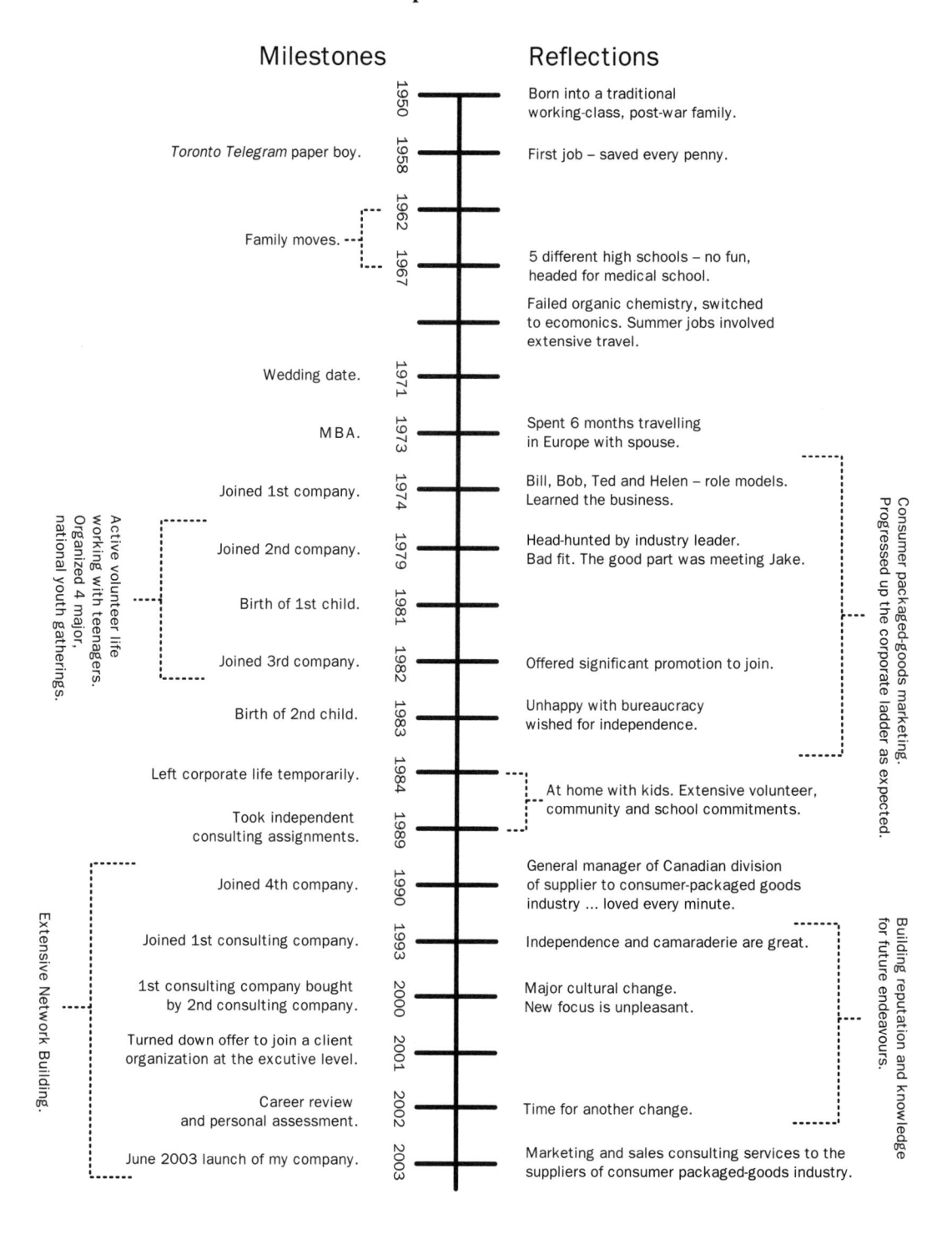

Milestones | Reflections

Year	Milestones	Reflections
1950		Born into a traditional working-class, post-war family.
1958	*Toronto Telegram* paper boy.	First job – saved every penny.
1962	Family moves.	
1967		5 different high schools – no fun, headed for medical school.
		Failed organic chemistry, switched to ecomonics. Summer jobs involved extensive travel.
1971	Wedding date.	
1973	M.B.A.	Spent 6 months travelling in Europe with spouse.
1974	Joined 1st company.	Bill, Bob, Ted and Helen – role models. Learned the business.
1979	Joined 2nd company.	Head-hunted by industry leader. Bad fit. The good part was meeting Jake.
1981	Birth of 1st child.	
1982	Joined 3rd company.	Offered significant promotion to join.
1983	Birth of 2nd child.	Unhappy with bureaucracy wished for independence.
1984	Left corporate life temporarily.	At home with kids. Extensive volunteer, community and school commitments.
1989	Took independent consulting assignments.	
1990	Joined 4th company.	General manager of Canadian division of supplier to consumer-packaged goods industry ... loved every minute.
1993	Joined 1st consulting company.	Independence and camaraderie are great.
2000	1st consulting company bought by 2nd consulting company.	Major cultural change. New focus is unpleasant.
2001	Turned down offer to join a client organization at the excutive level.	
2002	Career review and personal assessment.	Time for another change.
2003	June 2003 launch of my company.	Marketing and sales consulting services to the suppliers of consumer packaged-goods industry.

Active volunteer life working with teenagers. Organized 4 major, national youth gatherings.

Extensive Network Building.

Consumer packaged-goods marketing. Progressed up the corporate ladder as expected.

Building reputation and knowledge for future endeavours.

WORKSHEET 4.1
Your Personal Timeline

Milestones   Reflections

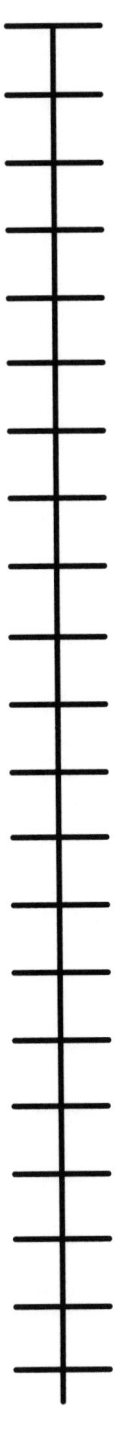

Identify Your Accomplishments

Think back over your career and volunteer history, and recall the times when you had a sense of pride or satisfaction in something you did. The important stories are the ones in which your accomplishments were significant and satisfying to *you*. They might or might not have been part of your job. They could have attracted recognition and reward, or perhaps you were the only one who noticed. They could have taken years to unfold or only a moment's time. Think about this for a while. You are recalling times when you might have said or thought, "It's great to be me, doing what I'm doing." These stories are often called "accomplishment stories" or "peak stories."

Experiences from your personal life, volunteer commitments and community involvement are important for this exercise, but they cannot totally substitute for accomplishments on the job. Keep thinking until you have at least five work-related stories. Stop at ten stories as a maximum to avoid belabouring this exercise. Embedded in these stories are your key skills and core values. Use these guidelines and the following worksheet to record your accomplishments in detail and reflect on them.

Tip: At this point, don't worry about what you are going to do next. Plumb the depths and harvest the riches of your experiences—they contain the clues to your future!

GUIDELINES FOR RECORDING AND ANALYZING YOUR ACCOMPLISHMENTS

- First, relax and simply let the stories from your past surface. Collect as many as you like. Don't edit any out.
- Choose approximately ten stories that mean the most to you. For each of these, record the circumstances, the place and the people who were involved. Note the approximate dates.
- Analyze each story using this formula: Situation—Action—Result:
  - **Situation:** What was happening? What was the challenge, problem or opportunity at hand? What could have resulted without your involvement? Why did this matter to you? What motivated you to act?
  - **Action:** What did you do?
  - **Result:** What resulted from your efforts or activities?
- What common elements are present in your stories? Is it being in charge, advancing your career, making a profit, building a team, solving a problem, helping someone, improving a process, creating something new or shattering the status quo?
- What skills did you use in achieving these accomplishments?
- What themes are emerging?

A human resources manager in a large decentralized company was transferred to the region with the largest employee population. Her mandate was to establish a human resources group that would both contribute to the business strategy and standardize policies and procedures. She began by surveying the needs and expectations of the line managers. Within 18 months, she initiated recruiting and orientation programs that reduced turnover from 34 percent to 18 percent; tied the results of customer satisfaction surveys to group rewards, resulting in a 52 percent improvement in overall ratings; and restructured the ratio of professional staff to customer service staff, generating savings of 21 percent in salaries. Her model was subsequently used across the company.

You might struggle with identifying your accomplishments if your emotions are still heightened or if you have been working in an unsatisfying role for too long. If so, try identifying "rut" experiences— times when you were really frustrated, discouraged or burnt out. These stories will probably illuminate situations in which the skills you enjoy using were not engaged and your most important values were ignored or contravened.

The purpose of this exercise is to put you back in touch with what's important to you and what gives you a sense of being valued. Whether you have come at this renewed awareness by recalling good times or bad, you now have top-of-mind several key stories that demonstrate the best of what you have to contribute.

Tip: Accomplishment stories told using the Situation—Action—Result formula will become the backbone of your communications as you go through the search process. It is a powerful way to make your skills and strengths known to others.

WORKSHEET 4.2
Record Your Accomplishments

List at least five work-related accomplishments plus several from your volunteer commitments, community involvement and personal life.

Sample:

    Situation: Lack of appropriate and effective family support for Alzheimer's patients in chronic care due to inadequate family education.

    Action: Led a committee of physicians, nurses and others to create training and support programs.

    Result: Delivered 36 sessions over an 18-month period resulting in greater understanding and involvement by families, and less pressure on nursing staff to deliver sporadic information.

1. **Situation:**

    Action:

    Result:

2. **Situation:**

    Action:

    Result:

3. **Situation:**

    Action:

    Result:

4. **Situation:**

    Action:

    Result:

5. **Situation:**

    Action:

    Result:

The People in Your Past

Your co-workers and colleagues on the job can make any assignment or situation more enjoyable or more difficult. To do a thorough career review, it's important to reflect on the personalities, styles and skills of the people who were part of your past work experiences. By doing this, you will improve the likelihood of choosing a positive work environment for your next employment opportunity.

Think about past bosses, other superiors, peers, subordinates, clients, suppliers and others from your past. Using Worksheet 4.3 as a guide, list the names of as many individuals as you can recall in each category. Then use the prompting questions to reflect on the characteristics of each person who had a notable influence on your success, development and enjoyment, either positive or negative. Reflecting on bad experiences is often more enlightening than reflecting on the good.

The final prompt in each section of the worksheet invites you to develop a general profile of the sort of people that would create an inviting and energizing work environment for you at this point in your career.

A semi-retired businessman in his seventies works with a mid-sized consulting firm and intentionally seeks assignments with start-up organizations focused on e-business. These organizations tend to be populated with people in their twenties. The exposure to fresh ideas and different expectations keeps this man feeling young and energetic. His clients receive the benefit of wise counsel and access to an extensive network of contacts across many industries. It's a win-win situation!

Tip: There are many books on management and leadership style that could serve as additional guides for your reflection.

	WORKSHEET 4.3 **Reflect on People in the Workplace**
Names to Consider	**Personal Characteristics, Style and Skills**
Bosses and other supervisors	• For those who brought out the best in you, was their delegating style specific and complete or general and more directive? How did they communicate, confront, make decisions and represent you to others in the organization? How did they give recognition and rewards? What were they particularly good at doing? Was it team building, developing subordinates, planning strategy, implementing, organizing, selling or communicating? • Answer the same questions for those who brought out the worst in you. • How have your needs for leadership changed over time? • Develop a composite profile of the ideal boss and other superiors for you at this point in your career.

Names to Consider	Personal Characteristics, Style and Skills
Peers and colleagues	• How would you describe the colleagues and peers with whom you accomplished the most? • Answer the same question for those with whom you accomplished the least. • How would you describe the colleagues and peers whom you enjoyed the most and the least? • What were the usual causes of friction between you and your co-workers? • How has your need for interaction with co-workers changed over time? • How would you describe the ideal group of colleagues and peers for you today?

Names to Consider	Personal Characteristics, Style and Skills
Subordinates	• As a supervisor or manager, what have been your most rewarding experiences? • Who were the subordinates you recall as outstanding? Who were the most challenging? Why? • What were your greatest challenges as a manager? • How do you think your most outstanding and most challenging subordinates would describe your management style? • If you could build a team from the ground up, what characteristics, styles and skills would you seek in your team members? • Do you like managing people?

Names to Consider	Personal Characteristics, Style and Skills
Clients and others outside the organization	• How would you describe the clients and other external contacts with whom you built excellent relationships? • What personality and style issues caused conflict between you and people outside the organization ? • How do you think your key external contacts would describe your personal characteristics and style? • What sorts of people would comprise an ideal group of external contacts for you today?

Organizational Culture

Organizations have unique personalities and characteristics that profoundly affect the way work is done and determine what type of persons will feel comfortable working there. If you are not compatible with the true personality of your workplace, it can be a major struggle for you.

For each organization, separate department or specific team, think about how you reacted to the various aspects of its culture. If your career has taken you into numerous situations, narrow these down to the few that seem most significant. Be careful to identify the difference between the expressed cultural norms and values versus those practised. There is often a large gap.

The charismatic CEO of a small, entrepreneurial financial services company developed a values statement that put customer service at the top of the priority list. He worked hard to ensure that his staff and external contacts heard this message. However, day in and day out, the questions that he would ask his people were, "What deals are you working on?" or "How's the XYZ deal going?" Everyone knew what was truly valued!

Analyzing your fit with various aspects of organizational culture is an important step in deciding what you would like to do next. Use the questions on the following worksheet as a guide for your analysis. Think about past experiences, and determine how each aspect of culture affected your job satisfaction.

Tip: People who have spent all their working lives in one organization find it difficult to predict how they will feel in a different culture. Your network of friends and business colleagues from other organizations can help with this analysis. Ask them to tell you stories exemplifying various aspects of cultures that they have experienced. This can be invaluable for analyzing prospective organizations.

WORSHEET 4.4	
Analyze Your Fit with Organizational Culture	
Areas to Consider	**Questions to Consider**
Size and structure	• How big was the physical size of the facility where you worked? How many departments? How many employees? • Was the structure centralized or decentralized? Were there numerous layers of management, or was the structure flat? • Was the organization global, multinational, regional or local in scope?
Decision-making and communication	• How were decisions made? Did you have ready access to decision-makers? • What was the style of communication? Were important messages delivered in person or in writing? Was information conveyed thoroughly and promptly to the appropriate people? • Were senior individuals in the organization visible to the rank and file? • Was it a secretive environment, or was there an atmosphere of openness? Was the style formal or informal? • Was feedback and constructive criticism given and received in a positive way?
Fit with your values	• Were the policies and procedures rigidly structured or was independence of thought and action required? • What achievements were recognized and rewarded? How would you describe the characteristics of those who got ahead? • What was the track record regarding diversity and equality? • Was the culture one of entitlement, or did you get ahead only by continually making a valuable contribution? • Was there a gap between expressed values and what was actually rewarded and praised? • What made you feel valued?

Education and Professional Development

Is this period of career transition an opportunity for you to return to the classroom? What would you study and how would it add to your strategic advantage? If you are lacking credentials that are expected at the next level in your profession, consider taking the time to get them. Having fresh knowledge of the most current theories and practices is a tremendous benefit in any area. In some fields, training in the leading-edge technologies and processes is essential for making a good move.

If you have any interest in advancing your education, be sure that you have thought through your long-term plans. Mid-career education is very costly. The time commitment and sacrificed earnings will be significant. Choose the institution and the courses wisely. Be certain that you know exactly what will be required of you and how this study can advance your career.

Through your contacts, determine how prospective employers will value the education you intend to pursue. Make an appointment to see the dean or the program director and ask where recent graduates are employed. Interview a few of them, and ask what other institutions they considered, or why they made the choice they made. Ask if they would do anything differently now.

Work Beyond the Workplace

In creating the timeline and identifying your accomplishments, you were encouraged to include experiences from your non-working life. At this point, think about the people that you have gotten to know through these other commitments, experiences and interests. Choose appropriate questions using the worksheets as a guide to reflect on your relationships outside the workplace. The people with whom you have enjoyed working on volunteer and community commitments and other non-work experiences can serve as models for the ideal group of future colleagues.

Look at the organizations where you allocate your time and energy. Are you active in your industry or professional association? Do you help with fundraising or other work for a charity? Are you active in politics? Do you help out at your children's schools? Are you a member of a religious or service organization? Are you on the board of a member-owned sports club? What role do you typically assume in these organizations, and are you happy with what you are doing? Are there other groups or organizations you have considered joining? If yes, why haven't you done so? What roles would you like to fill?

A time of career transition will offer the opportunity to make changes in your volunteer life. Examine what you value and make careful choices as you move forward. Plan to back away from commitments that drain your energies without providing sufficient personal rewards.

Hobbies and Interests

When your time is truly your own, what do you enjoy doing? Even if you haven't had time recently for your hobbies and personal interests, bring them back to mind. While you are moving through the transition process, engaging in your favourite pastimes can help keep your spirits up.

Some people consider turning their hobby into a livelihood. This often depends upon having a pension or some other source of income. It is more often the case that hobbies and interests provide balance in life rather than significant income opportunities. Carving out time for these things is a worthwhile goal as you choose your next employment opportunity.

A research specialist in the insurance industry combined her ability to track down minute bits of infor-mation with her interest in reuniting families. She launched a home-based business that assisted her clients in finding long lost family and friends. Since the business used Internet technology, she was able to move to a small town where the cost of living was lower and the quality of life was more in keeping with her values.

Wrap Up Your Reflections

Ideally, this broad look at your past has generated some fresh ideas for your future. At least it should have helped you remember what you disliked in the past and prefer not to repeat. As a conclusion, answer these questions: If you had to choose a specific period of your past working life and relive it, what would you choose? Why?

The next step in the reflective process will provide you with a snapshot of who you are today.

Tip: You may still feel bogged down or overwhelmed by negative feelings about your last job. Perhaps all you need is more time to move through your feelings; however, the problem could be more complex. Be kind to yourself and get the help you need from a professional counsellor or your doctor.

Chapter 5

Identify Your Strategic Advantage

Compete where you have an advantage.

Play to your strengths. Your point of greatest marketability and highest degree of job satisfaction is found where your style, skills, knowledge, interests and values intersect. It's the unique combination that makes it very difficult for anyone to imitate your approach and contribution. This is your strategic advantage. Don't try to find work where none of these attributes are needed or valued. Take the time to define your strategic advantage precisely and you will have the means to find an employment opportunity that integrates *what you do* with *who you are.*

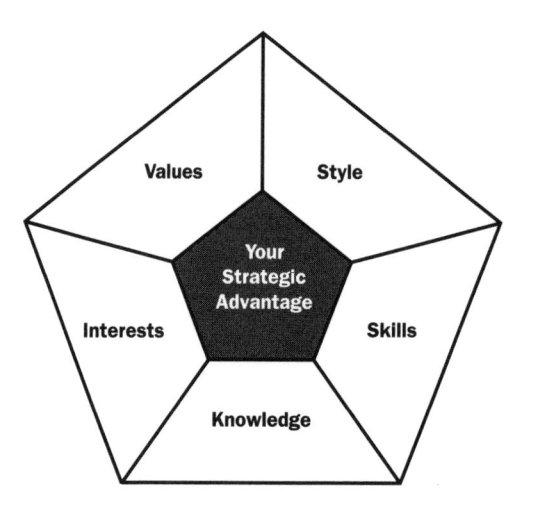

Whether you are considering only a slight shift in focus or a radically new direction, you must take stock of your skills, knowledge and personal style. These are the traditional components of job specifications, and the core attributes on which you can build your future. If you are also able to incorporate your interests and values in your next employment opportunity, you will have made the most of this transition.

Tip: Don't look for a career assessment test that will circumvent this work. No test can tell you who you are and exactly what you should do. Complete your own reflective process first. You know yourself well. It might take time for the picture of your ideal career to come into focus, but it's on your radar screen somewhere.

As you work through the following sections, take notes. You will use your notes to develop a description of yourself that is specific, factual and businesslike. It will become invaluable to you as you move through the career transition process.

Your Personal Style

Your personal style is the summation of your distinguishing qualities. It describes the characteristics and attributes that you bring to your work and your interaction with others. It governs how you work. When you understand your personal style, you have the option to choose tasks and relationships that will engage your strengths. You can avoid unsuitable situations and adjust your style to accommodate circumstances where your strengths will not be helpful.

You are likely to be aware of your dominant characteristics. You know yourself, and you have been praised for your strengths and criticized for your weaknesses. The more subtle aspects of your style will be somewhat hidden from you. Look for clues in past performance reviews and informal feedback. Ask trusted colleagues to help you with this exercise.

A young woman described herself to a career transition consultant by talking about what she enjoyed doing in high school, in university and in summer jobs. It was obvious that she was creative, quiet, intellectual, unconventional and spontaneous. No wonder she was very unhappy as the manager of a large operations department in the back offices of a huge bureaucratic organization.

If you are considering a major career change, your personal style stays with you even if you leave everything else behind. In fact, it is often a person's most striking personal characteristics that lead the way into new territory. For example, an altruistic, pragmatic manager with a persuasive communication style might use his skills to run a charitable foundation.

To develop a description of your style, use the following worksheet and choose words that are appropriate for you in each category. A list of descriptive words is included to prompt your thinking.

WORKSHEET 5.1
Describe Your Personal Style

Choose a few words, or write a very short phrase, to describe yourself in each of the following areas. Do not limit your choices to the examples given; use the inventory of adjectives on the next page for ideas.

Thinking style   This is the way that you approach a problem or opportunity. Descriptors might include realistic, visionary, strategic, analytical, logical, perceptive, concrete, etc. There are many others.

Communication style   This might elicit words such as enthusiastic, cautious, comprehensive, persuasive, inspiring, reserved, straightforward, etc.

Management style   Here you might describe yourself as fair-minded, authoritative, caring, democratic or non-directive. You might write, "I delegate tasks and give minimal specific direction."

Subordinate style   How do you like to be managed? Are you self-reliant, consultative, a conscientious task implementer, a questioner or a loyal follower?

Team style   What role or task usually falls to you? Are you the innovator, the detail monitor, the implementer, the communicator, the relationship caretaker, the organizer or the leader?

Work style   Are you highly organized, spontaneous, meticulous, flexible, process-oriented, a team player, a loner, results-focused, decisive or a perfectionist?

Resilience   How are you hard-wired? Are you a worrier or are you relaxed? Do you take things too personally? Are you critical or accepting, optimistic or pessimistic, driven to achieve or non-competitive?

Think of a story from your past to exemplify each of the words that you used to describe yourself. Is the picture accurate and complete? What else should be added?

Inventory of Adjectives

accepting	consultative	forward-thinking	opportunistic	sensible
accommodating	cooperative	friendly	optimistic	sensitive
accurate	creative	future-oriented	organized	serious
achieving	credible	generous	outgoing	shrewd
adaptable	customer-focused	hands-off	participative	sincere
affirming	deadline-driven	hands-on	patient	skillful
aggressive	decisive	hard-working	people-oriented	sophisticated
agreeable	dedicated	helpful	perceptive	spontaneous
altruistic	deliberate	high-impact	perfectionist	straightforward
ambitious	demanding	high-potential	persevering	strategic
analytical	democratic	honest	persistent	strong
articulate	dependable	humorous	personable	subtle
artistic	detail-oriented	imaginative	persuasive	successful
aspiring	determined	impressive	philosophical	supportive
assertive	diligent	incisive	poised	sympathetic
assured	diplomatic	independent	positive	tactful
astute	direct	individualistic	powerful	tasteful
authoritative	discerning	industrious	practical	team builder
aware	disciplined	ingenious	pragmatic	team leader
believable	discreet	initiating	process-oriented	team player
calm	dynamic	innovative	productive	technical
candid	easygoing	insightful	professional	tenacious
capable	effective	inspiring	proficient	thorough
careful	efficient	intelligent	project-oriented	thoughtful
caring	eloquent	intense	punctual	tolerant
cautious	empathetic	intuitive	quality-driven	top performer
charismatic	empowering	investigative	quick	top producer
cheerful	energetic	judicious	quiet	tough-minded
clever	engaging	kind	realistic	troubleshooter
collaborative	enterprising	knowledgeable	reasonable	trustworthy
committed	enthusiastic	logical	refined	truthful
communicative	entrepreneurial	market-driven	reflective	unconventional
competent	ethical	methodical	reliable	understanding
competitive	experienced	meticulous	reserved	unrelenting
compliant	expressive	motivated	resilient	upbeat
comprehensive	facilitating	multi-talented	resourceful	versatile
composed	fair-minded	non-competitive	respected	visionary
conceptual	far-sighted	non-conforming	responsible	well-balanced
concerned	firm	non-directive	results-focused	well-spoken
concrete	flexible	objective	results-oriented	willing
confident	focused	observant	risk taker	
conscientious	formal	open	savvy	
consistent	forthright	open-minded	self-reliant	

Your Key Skills

This part of your strategic advantage comprises the professional credentials and technical skills you have acquired through formal education and training plus the functional skills that have grown out of your practical experience. Skills constitute what you do.

To create a complete inventory, start by recording all of your credentials and core skills. Include any processes, methodologies, systems or programs in which you are qualified or where you have substantial experience. Add your functional skills, which are most easily identified by considering the areas of responsibility where you have gained expertise. Include the skills you have acquired in your volunteer and community work as well. Use the samples as a guide.

Tip: Many skill sets cross boundaries and provide the credibility to move from one industry to another. Focusing on your skills gives you an independent identity based on your capabilities. You no longer need to describe yourself only as a former employee of an organization.

Samples of Professional Credentials

CHRP	Certified Human Resource Professional
RN	Registered Nurse
CFRE	Certified Fund Raising Executive
P Eng	Professional Engineer
CMC	Certified Management Consultant
CFA	Chartered Financial Analyst
CMA	Certified Management Accountant
CFP	Certified Financial Planner
FLMI	Fellow of the Life Management Institute

Samples of Technical Skills

Human Resources Information Systems
ISO quality registration
Six Sigma
Quality Circles
Project Management
Alternate Dispute Resolution
Systems Applications
Programming Languages
Databases

Samples of Functional Skills by Occupation

CEO	vision, strategy, marketing, operations, finance, corporate governance, selection and communication
CFO	strategy, corporate governance, budget control, reporting, risk management, finance, taxation, raising capital and communication
CIO	strategy, business process improvement, systems architecture, data integrity and security, infrastructure management, business alignment and technology solutions and communication
CHRO	strategy, organizational design, change management, leadership development and communication
Account Manager	sales forecasting, territory management, client relations and business development

Controller	financial planning, budgeting, treasury, cash management, auditing, and financial reporting and analysis
General Manager	team leadership, strategic planning, managing processes and systems, business development and customer relations
Health Care Director	management of staffing, volunteers, patient care and facilities, admissions and discharge planning, budgeting and proposals
Human Resources Manager	recruiting and selection, compensation and benefits, training and development, performance management and labour relations
Journalist	writing, editing, interviewing, research, layout and design
Lending Officer	business development, credit analysis, asset recovery and portfolio management
Marketing	product development, pricing, distribution and promotion
Property Management	building systems, tenant relations, maintenance and upgrading, leasing and staffing
Plant Operations	team leadership, project management, logistics, resource allocation, quality control and continuous process improvement
Retail Operations	merchandising, promotions, inventory and cost control, staff training and development

---

WORKSHEET 5.2
Your Skills Inventory

Professional credentials:

Technical skills:

Functional skills:

When your list is complete, think about which skills you enjoy using and which ones you'd rather leave behind. Being good at doing something does not automatically mean that you like doing it. Many people enter the workforce without a clear idea of where their interests lie. They develop expertise in an area that is not a good fit and stay in a role because the cost of change is too high.

Tip: If you are serious about walking away from your current set of technical and functional skills, be prepared for a longer search, the possible need to re-train, a significant orientation period and a cut in pay. To do this, plan your finances, get your support network in place, muster your courage and go for it! You are making a courageous decision.

Your Knowledge Base

Your knowledge can be separate and distinct from your formal education and your professional skills. It consists of everything you have learned about everything! It includes your understanding of various industries, companies, products, market segments, regions, regulations, cultures, special interest groups, etc. It is the combination of information, exposure, experience, savvy and acumen about people, places, things, activities and ideas.

You have gained knowledge about many things that can be useful to other people and organizations. In some instances, a confidentiality or non-compete agreement will restrict you from sharing what you know. This is clear evidence of the value of this knowledge. Your integrity depends on respecting these agreements, but you will also have a large amount of unrestricted knowledge that you will be able to contribute to your next employment opportunity.

Use the worksheet to surface some of your most significant points of knowledge. Think expansively. Do not be restricted by the categories listed.

Tip: Every industry segments its market in some way. Organizations adjust their product and service offerings to better serve targeted groups. Your knowledge of specific market segments will be a valuable transferable asset.

WORKSHEET 5.3
Your Knowledge Inventory

List the industries you know well. Which ones do you know marginally?
  E.g., advertising, health care, telecommunications

In addition to your previous employer, what companies or organizations do you know well?
  E.g., competitor A, supplier B

What products do you understand in depth?
  E.g., derivatives, home appliances, small engines, wine

In which types of transactions or strategic initiatives do you have experience?
  E.g., acquisitions, outsourcing, re-engineering, turnarounds, collective bargaining

List the market segments you know well.
  E.g., institutions, retail, high income, business travellers, women

List the regional markets or geographical areas where you have expertise.
  E.g., South America, Atlantic Canada, Asia

List the languages you speak fluently or conversationally.
  E.g., French, Spanish

Include other knowledge that you have accumulated that will make a contribution to a future employer.
  E.g., Succession planning for small family business owners.

Your Interests

Your interests can be a significant component of your strategic advantage. If your work allows you to be involved with something that genuinely fascinates you, you are fortunate. People who are curious and passionate about their product, service or market have a natural enthusiasm that is unmistakable. If you can, expand your work to include your interests. For people considering a career change, your interests can be a guide to ideal employment opportunities.

Some people have no trouble identifying their interests, while others find it surprisingly difficult. If you have been working too hard or you are under too much stress for any reason, your interests might have been pushed so far into the background that you can't think of what they really are. On the other hand, if you are one who is curious by nature, you might have so many interests that it's impossible for you to identify the ones that could be incorporated into your working life.

What are your interests? Think beyond your hobbies and athletic pursuits. Interests include ideas or issues and philosophies that fascinate and attract you. Some may be lifelong interests; others may be emerging and evolving. Your interests are a large part of what makes you unique. If the answers are obvious to you, jot them down. If not, the worksheet and the inventory of interests are designed to help you.

Tip: Many people who have the option to retire early focus on their interests when choosing their next endeavour.

A nurse who had moved into an administrative role lost her job when her hospital amalgamated with another. While she was in transition, her 82-year old mother had a stroke and became in need of a chronic-care facility. As she went through the time-consuming and difficult process of arranging for her mother's care, she realized how daunting it could be for people who knew very little about the health care system to find and gain entry to a facility that would meet the needs of both the family and their loved one. She parlayed her interest into full-time work by offering her knowledge and skills on a consulting basis to families in similar situations.

WORKSHEET 5.4
Assessing Your Interests

What social, environmental, cultural, health-related, religious, judicial, political or business issues do you find the most compelling?

On the job, when you choose a course or read an article in a trade or professional journal, what topics attract your attention because you are truly curious?

In the workplace, what departments, roles, projects and activities seem appealing?

What magazines, books, TV shows, movies or Internet sites interest you?

Who are your role models and heroes?

How do you like to spend your time outside the workplace?

At social events, what topics of conversation do you welcome?

If you were to return to school, what would you study even if it had no obvious practical application?

If money were not an issue, how would you spend your time?

If you need more input, look at the following list to prompt your thinking.

Inventory of Interests

accounting
acting
adolescent issues
alternative
   medicine
amateur theatre
antiques
archeology
art
biotechnology
boards of directors
boating
branding
carpentry
catering
charitable
   foundations
chemistry
children's causes
coaching
collecting
community issues
communications
competitive
   intelligence
computer
   programming

conservation
counselling
criminology
decorating
designing
disaster recovery
e-commerce
education
environmental
   issues
ethics
event coordinating
fashion
film
financial planning
fishing
fitness
flying
forensics
franchises
fundraising
gardening
genealogy
gerontology
geriatric care
global issues
golf

gourmet cooking
graphic design
health issues
history
home restoration
horticulture
hospitality
   industry
human resources
human rights
information
   technology
interior decorating
international
   development
investments
journalism
judicial system
keynote speaking
labour relations
landscaping
languages
law
leadership
   development
literature
marketing

market research
martial arts
massage therapy
media
mentoring
merchandising
organizational
   behaviour
organizational
   design
philosophy
photography
physics
poetry
political issues
politics
process re-
   engineering
product
   development
psychology
public relations
quality control
research
recruiting
real estate
religion

retail business
risk management
sales
security
small business
   adviser
snowmobiling
special interest
   groups
spirituality
sports
strategic planning
stock market
teaching
tennis
theatre
travel
university courses
web site design
wilderness
   adventuring
women's issues
woodworking
writing
yoga

Your Values and Motivators

Values are your personal guideposts. They go hand-in-hand with the motivators that drive you. Ideally, these principles exert enormous influence over your choices regarding work. They are informed by your upbringing, role models, expectations and experiences, and comprise your unique inner rationale. Following them generates a sense of fulfillment. If you are in a situation that continually requires you to act against your principles, you will become unhappy, unduly stressed or burnt out.

Thinking about values and motivators is very important to the career transition process. They can be a powerful part of your strategic advantage. The highest degree of job satisfaction is found where your principles align closely with the requirements of your role and the expectations of your organization. Success on the job usually follows. "Know thyself" is a proverb that is often quoted because it's so important.

Tip: Values and motivators are not necessarily lofty ideals. For example, being an expert in your field is a value held by many. The desire to earn a lot of money can be a powerful motivator. Be honest with yourself, and be clear about your priorities at this time in your career and life.

It may be difficult to maintain a grasp on your values and motivators for two reasons. First, they change and evolve as you move along your career path and through different stages of life. Second, they are often conflicted within you, and with those of people who are important to you. Some people spend a lot of time contemplating these aspects of their lives, while others are less concerned.

To gain some clarity, consider your preferences and needs in the workplace separately from the responsibilities and values in your personal life. For the purposes of identifying your strategic advantage, first consider only what is important to you in the work that you do. Think of your present needs and expectations as they pertain to your work. You will be invited to bring the rest of your life into the picture in the next chapter.

WORKSHEET 5.5
Prioritize What's Important in the Workplace

Prioritize the following list by identifying each statement as A (primary importance), B (secondary importance) or C (little or no importance). Feel free to add anything else of importance in regard to your work and include these in your ranking. Next, review your A list and identify no more than three non-negotiable needs that will drive any decision regarding your next employment opportunity. Then develop a secondary list of things you would like to have.

_____ Performing work that contributes to the good of society

_____ Helping or caring for individuals and adding value to their lives

_____ Having bottom-line accountability and being responsible for results

_____ Working in a competitive environment, having a chance to win at something

_____ Having stability and security at work through a structured environment

_____ Having an opportunity to bring change to an organization

_____ Having an opportunity to preserve tradition and protect proven processes

_____ Being free of bureaucracy and entrenched policies, a more entrepreneurial approach

_____ Defining your own work schedule, having flexibility

_____ Mentoring or training other individuals either formally or informally

_____ Managing a group of people, building an effective team, being the leader

_____ Having freedom from management responsibilities

_____ Being acknowledged as an expert in a technique, field or specialty

_____ Developing a strong industry profile and gaining the recognition of peers

_____ Working for an organization that is recognized as best-in-class

_____ Having opportunities to travel or work outside the office

_____ Having direct contact with people outside the organization such as customers and suppliers

_____ Using and developing presentation skills by speaking to small and large groups

_____ Having lots of contact with people during the day

_____ Having plenty of time alone to think, write or work on a task

_____ Working with intelligent co-workers who are experts in their field

_____ Being part of a closely knit team where challenges, opportunities and credit are shared

_____ Being part of a cross-functional team that touches every part of the organization

_____ Being able to work independently, deciding on your own how to achieve objectives

_____ Working with a group who enjoy social activities and have fun together

_____   Having clear, step-by-step direction and supervision

_____   Solving new and complex problems that challenge your thinking and use your skills

_____   Being responsible for implementation of ideas created by others

_____   Exercising your creativity to develop new ideas, solutions and products

_____   Enjoying variety and regular change in the mandate or job content

_____   Having a stable, predictable routine month after month

_____   Enjoying access to the latest technology

_____   Being offered opportunities for further training and development

_____   Being offered potential for career advancement, a ladder to climb

_____   Working in a fast-paced environment with a rush of urgency and a demanding schedule

_____   Having opportunities to work with people who are ahead of you in job title and status

_____   Having a job title and status

_____   Being recognized for work well done, receiving awards, verbal praise, commendations

_____   Building a sense of personal and professional growth

_____   Having an opportunity to make a lot of money through bonuses, commissions or stock options

_____   _____

_____   _____

_____   _____

Do not confuse this exercise by adding things like time for the family, location or a minimum level of remuneration. Stay with what you need from the work itself.

What work have you done that truly reflected your values?

What work have you done that was contrary to your values?

List your non-negotiable criteria for being satisfied and motivated in your work.

List the values and motivators that are desirable but could be traded off.

Career Assessment Testing

Now that you have done a thorough self-assessment, consider taking advantage of the many career assessment tests that are available. These tests can affirm your thinking and bring to the surface things that you have not considered. They cannot tell you exactly what to do with your career. They categorize the interests, abilities and attributes that you report, and provide lists of the careers in which people with similar profiles report success and satisfaction. The more sophisticated tests explain the reasons why specific careers match your profile. Don't expect miraculous revelations. Expect a helpful analysis that complements your own work.

It's best to work with a professional, such as a career transition consultant, psychologist, executive coach or therapist, who is qualified to administer the testing. They will help you understand the results and integrate them with your self-assessment work. However, you can do this on your own, using tests that are available in books or on the Internet. The resources section of this book provides lists. The following guidelines should help you through the process.

GUIDELINES FOR CHOOSING CAREER ASSESSMENT TESTS
- Tests alone cannot tell you what to do with your career. Consider the results of career assessment testing as another step in the process.
- Determine if testing is for you. If you are comfortable with your self-assessment and know exactly what you want to do, or if you have been through the testing process numerous times with the same results, it may not be worth your while.
- There is no one test that is more conclusive or gives better results than another. Each one has a unique approach, so it's best to use several.
- Much-used and well-respected tests that look at career choice include the Myers Briggs Type Indicator, the Strong Interest Inventories, the Campbell Interest & Skill Survey and the 16PF. Each of these has a cost associated and should be administered by a qualified professional. Look at samples of different reports to see if the type of data generated is what you need.
- If you are working with a career transition consultant, counsellor or coach, ask if the feedback session can be audiotaped for you. This is very helpful for your subsequent review.
- Don't expect a definitive answer. Sometimes there are discrepancies between test results. You might also get results that don't seem to fit your self-image. Remember to put the testing in context. Talk this over with your career transition consultant or your support network. Your own analysis and feedback from people who know you should take precedence.

Get Input from Others

At this point, go back to your support network, board of advisers or references for input. You might be overlooking some of your most significant strengths because you don't think of these qualities and abilities as anything extraordinary. Your colleagues from the workplace and anyone from your volunteer and community endeavours will most likely have valuable insights. Gather a group together or approach each person individually, provide them with a summary of your notes, and ask for their views using the following guidelines.

GUIDELINES FOR REQUESTING AND RECEIVING INPUT

- Choose your input providers wisely. Relatives and close friends might be good choices, but they probably haven't seen you in the workplace. Include some people from your work environment.
- Choose people who will be honest in their responses but sensitive to your situation. This might not be the best time for you to hear too much negative feedback.
- Decide how you will record their responses. Usually allocating time for taking notes following the conversation will be sufficient. If you're getting a group together, appoint a recorder. If what's said is not written down, you might forget it.
- Ask questions such as:
  - What are my most natural talents, skills and abilities?
  - How would you describe my style for each category on Worksheet 5.1, "Describe Your Personal Style"?
  - In what areas do you recognize me as particularly knowledgeable?
  - In your opinion, what are my three greatest strengths?
  - Do you think that I overuse any of my strengths? In what way?
  - What skills do I need to develop?
  - From your perspective, what do I appear to value highly?
  - What are the kinds of jobs or roles that you think I would do well in and like doing?
- Try to receive this input without defensiveness. Just listen. Asking for clarification and examples is a good way to increase your understanding of what is being said.
- Remember to thank these people with a written note.

Tip: The most significant input is often that which you don't expect.

Put It All Together for Presentation

With all of the data that you've collected in thinking about your strategic advantage, it might be a challenge to narrow it down and explain it clearly, but it's worth the effort. Presenting yourself in terms of your skills, knowledge, style, interests and values is a powerful way to communicate to the marketplace. A verbal synopsis of your strategic advantage breaks away from the use of titles and names of previous employers, expanding the possibilities for your future. It responds to the invitation of the new world of work to position yourself as an individual with a unique and independent set of talents and attributes, seeking opportunities to add value.

To create your script, select a few key points from each component of your strategic advantage and think about how you want to present them. Use this example as a template for putting it together. It packs a lot of information into very few words.

I'm a retail operations executive with extensive experience in managing a nationwide chain of over 100 franchise stores selling specialty kitchen items. My particular strengths include inventory and cost control, merchandising and the provision of training and development support for store managers. I understand the challenges facing small retail franchise owners in Canada. I am at my best when handed a mandate and the flexibility to do it my way. I am a manager, not an innovator. My creativity emerges in finding solutions to very practical problems.

Your strategic advantage brings together who you are with what you do, what you know and what you care about. Once it is clearly identified, this powerful combination can give you the leverage to find an employment opportunity that meets your needs.

Tip: Don't confuse your strategic advantage with passion. If you view your work only as a means of making a living, don't think there's anything wrong with that! What you care about and enjoy most may never have anything to do with your work. Have confidence in being who you are!

Chapter 6

What Really Matters to You?

Life is all about choices.

What you value in your work and the things that motivate you on the job rightfully have a powerful influence on your career choices. However, you have responsibilities to your family, friends, community and volunteer commitments. You also have personal needs and dreams. All of these compete for your time, energy and talents. Their importance to you must be considered as you plan your next career move.

There's more to think about regarding employment. The analysis of work-related values and motivators that you did in Chapter 5 covers only a part of the picture. The work environment, your terms of employment and market factors beyond your control can significantly affect your ability to achieve the balance that's right for you. This chapter invites you to examine these things as both a reality check and an opportunity to re-set your priorities.

Write a Toast to You for Your 90th Birthday

Imagine that you are turning 90. Your friends and family are planning a big party to which guests from every phase and sphere of your life have been invited. A toast will be offered to you and you have the privilege of writing it. What would you like it to say? Use the worksheet on the next page to create it.

WORKSHEET 6.1
A Toast to You

Here's to [*You*]_____.

Your friends and family appreciate you for

_____

_____

_____

Professionally, you are known for _____, and made significant
contributions to _____

You are dedicated to (a cause, organization, group, activity, hobby, spiritual practice)
_____ which has inspired or influenced you to

_____

Everyone here knows that you can always be counted on to _____

_____

Please join us on this very special occasion in a toast to [*You*]_____.

Tip: There is no better time than the present to make the things that truly matter to you your priority!

Personal Needs and Aspirations

Are you satisfied with the vitality of your body, mind, emotions and spirit? Feeling completely balanced with regard to your own well-being is elusive. Most people either neglect self-care or become obsessed with one facet of it to the detriment of others. A temporary period of unemployment offers the opportunity to review your priorities and reclaim healthy practices and good habits that you have allowed to lapse. It also allows you the time to form new ones.

Use the following worksheet to reflect on your personal needs. Make some realistic commitments to yourself.

Tip: Life is a gift. Good health is an extra blessing. Are you living with an appropriate sense of gratitude?

WORSHEET 6.2 **Evaluate Your Priorities Regarding Yourself**	

Physical health *Your body is the only permanent home you have!*	Are you comfortable with your physical condition and appearance? Is this affecting your career in any way? Can you make a realistic commitment to change without creating impossible hurdles? Are you putting inordinate importance on this aspect of your well-being?
Intellectual stimulation *If you don't use it, you'll lose it!*	What do you do to keep your mind active? Are you dependent on your job for intellectual challenge? If you have been either bored or out of your depth at work, how does this inform your career choice? What level of additional formal education would you be willing to pursue to assist you in achieving your career goals? Is more education an accessible, affordable and attractive prospect for you?
Emotional balance *Are you competent in managing yourself and handling relationships?*	Self-awareness, self-control, self-esteem and emotional stability are very important for success on the job. Have you experienced difficulties in these areas that have affected your job performance? What are you prepared to do about making changes?
Spiritual well-being *Religion is cultural. Spirituality is universal.*	What spiritual practice helps you cope with challenges and appreciate good fortune? For example: • Enjoying nature, art or music • Solitude • Meditation or prayer • Yoga or Tai Chi • Following the practices of a religious denomination • Reading inspirational works If you would like to devote more time to your spiritual well-being, what are you prepared to give up?

Commitment to Your Family, Friends and Community

Where do you draw the line between the time and energy you put into your own well-being, your work and time devoted to loved ones? If you have responsibility for small children, adolescents or aging parents you are probably performing a difficult balancing act. You could always work more at the expense of the family, or do more caregiving at the expense of the job. Volunteer commitments and community activities could soak up every spare moment if you were to allow it. Finding a compromise is challenging.

On the following worksheet, use the sections that are relevant to you as a guide for your reflections on your commitments to others.

WORKSHEET 6.3	
Evaluate Your Responsibilities and Priorities Regarding Family, Friends and Community	
Spouse or partner	Is your spouse or partner financially dependent on you?
	Does your spouse or partner have special needs?
	Do you have responsibilities associated with his or her work?
	How does his or her career influence your career choices?
	How supportive of your career plans is he or she likely to be?
Children	At their ages, what do they need from you?
	Do any of them have special needs?
	How much support do you get from their other parent, extended family members or paid child care?
	What lifestyle do you want for them?
Parents	Are they dependent on you in any way?
	Do they live close by or far away and does this influence your career choice?
Friends and neighbours	Do you have obligations or interests involving friends and neighbours that are important to you and require your time and attention?
	How much of a priority is this?
Volunteer commitments **Community responsibilities** **Service or religious affiliations**	How much time do you devote to these types of activities?
	Are you satisfied with your choice of activities and level of involvement?
	How will your career choice affect your involvement?

A woman in her late forties lost her management job with a large retailer when it was acquired by a competitor. She had never liked working in a business environment, but because she carried responsibility for her large extended family, she had persevered. Her love was working with children. Having none of her own, she volunteered at camps on her holidays, taught church school and worked occasionally at a local daycare centre. When her employment was terminated, she decided to use her severance to return to school and obtain a certificate in Early Childhood Education. Upon graduation, she landed a job and now manages programs for several centres while enjoying working with children.

Work Environment and Terms of Employment

In Chapter 5 you analyzed what is important to you in the workplace, looking at the content of the work, relationships, autonomy, responsibility and advancement potential. There is much more to consider. Many people willingly trade some aspects of job satisfaction for a more favourable work environment or more suitable terms of employment, such as a shorter commute or flexible hours. Use the worksheet to focus your thinking on these issues. Your responses will begin to clarify the strategic targets you will define in Chapter 8.

WORKSHEET 6.4 **Evaluate Your Priorities Regarding Work Environment and Terms of Employment**	
Remuneration	What is the minimum income that you must earn to maintain the lifestyle you want and to take care of your dependants? How much of it needs to be base salary, and how much can come from variable pay such as bonuses, profit sharing, stock options or commissions?
Mobility	Are you willing and able to relocate? Would your spouse and children be willing and able to relocate? If so, what would be your preferred location?
Commuting	How much time and expense will you tolerate? What mode of transportation is available and acceptable? Will you commute by car, bus, subway or train? Would you like to work from a home office? How much of the time would you be willing to spend there?

Benefits	Do you need full insurance and health benefits from an employer or can you purchase what you need independently?
Physical environment	How important is the style and quality of your physical surroundings? Do you need to work in a private office or is a cubicle acceptable? Do you need any special accommodations?
Travel	What amount of job-related travel is possible for you? Do you like to travel for your work? What destinations are acceptable and desirable?
Vacation	Are you accustomed to long, uninterrupted vacation periods? Are you willing to take fewer vacation days?
Schedule	Do you work in the evenings and on the weekends? Are there peak periods in the year? Do you carry a pager? Would you like flexible work hours or job-sharing? How many hours are you willing to work every week or month? Is part-time or seasonal work an option for you?
Your future	How many more years will you be working? What are the steps to retirement for you? Can you make short-term sacrifices for long-term gains? What would that mean for you?

Other Factors That Influence Career Choice

Freedom to make career choices is often limited not only by personal priorities and circumstances, but also by market factors beyond your control. Markets evolve, governments bring in decisions, political influences shift and economic conditions change. Many roles require specific professional credentials, and graduate-level education is a prerequisite for advancement to senior roles in some organizations. Age and gender can be unofficial, but real barriers. Let's face it, the law protects you, but you can't become a ballerina or make the NHL at age 56.

It is crucial to be realistic about these factors. Direct your energy toward choices that have no barriers for you. Resist becoming overly pessimistic during tough economic times or unduly optimistic when market conditions are good. Many cycles are temporary and simply require you to wait it out. Some trends are permanent and recognizing them as such is wise. Accepting ongoing change is part of good career management.

Tip: There is opportunity in every situation. It takes resilience, creativity and often perseverance to find it.

WORKSHEET 6.5 **Consider the Realities That Affect Career Choice**	
Economic and regional determinants	What economic conditions and regional factors will influence your search for employment?
Industries in transition	What are the current and future prospects of your industry? What industries are advancing? Which ones are contracting?
Government initiatives	Is your work dependent on government funding, protective tariffs or specific government-driven initiatives?
Educational requirements	What professional credentials or level of education is required for further advancement in your field or entry into a new field?
Age	How will your age affect your employment prospects?

In the late 1990s when the federal government balanced the budget for the first time in years, there were devastating implications for individuals who worked in the fixed-income securities market. Because there were no more new issues of government bonds, a number of traders and salespeople lost their jobs. One young trader decided to take a step down in remuneration in order to make the switch to an analyst's role. A seasoned salesman moved into selling retail investment products and joined a franchise operation that was establishing offices in Canada. A woman with young children took the opportunity to stay at home with her family for a while. She also recognized that her true interest lay in working with physically disabled children. She enrolled in a Master's program part-time to pursue her ultimate career goal.

A Realistic Look at Values

How do personal priorities and other circumstances affect your career choices? For many people, very significant and limiting factors exist, making a major career shift unthinkable. If this is true for you, make your goal the revitalization of your career through a change of venue or focus. By transferring current skills and knowledge to a similar role in another organization or by identifying a role that requires a variation on well-known themes, many achieve a renewed sense of interest and energy in their work.

Your challenge is to incorporate as much of what you value into a realistic career plan.

Tip: Most people are free to make choices as long as they are willing to make sacrifices. You can't have it all, but you can aim to have what's most important to you.

Chapter 7

*Consider Alternatives
to a Traditional Job*

You could be the CEO of "You, Inc."

Do you want another full-time, permanent job, or will you consider alternatives? Have you thought about striking out on your own and working independently? Could you start or buy a business? Is retirement on the horizon and would you like to ease into it gradually? What work arrangement would best suit your current lifestyle, and what do you think the future holds?

The new world of work is characterized by non-traditional work arrangements. Organizations see the benefit of just-in-time workers, and there is an increasing willingness to hire outside expertise and assistance for specific non-core tasks and projects. This has created a large market for occasional, variable and part-time employment. Interim executives, contract workers and consultants are frequently engaged. Think about the options this provides for you, each with its benefits and drawbacks.

In a traditional job, you trade your skills and knowledge for remuneration, title and status, development opportunities and a modicum of job security. In non-traditional employment relationships, you negotiate flexible, time-limited terms under which you exchange your skills and knowledge for remuneration. With a business, you deliver products and services to the marketplace under your own banner and employ others to assist you. This diagram illustrates a range of options:

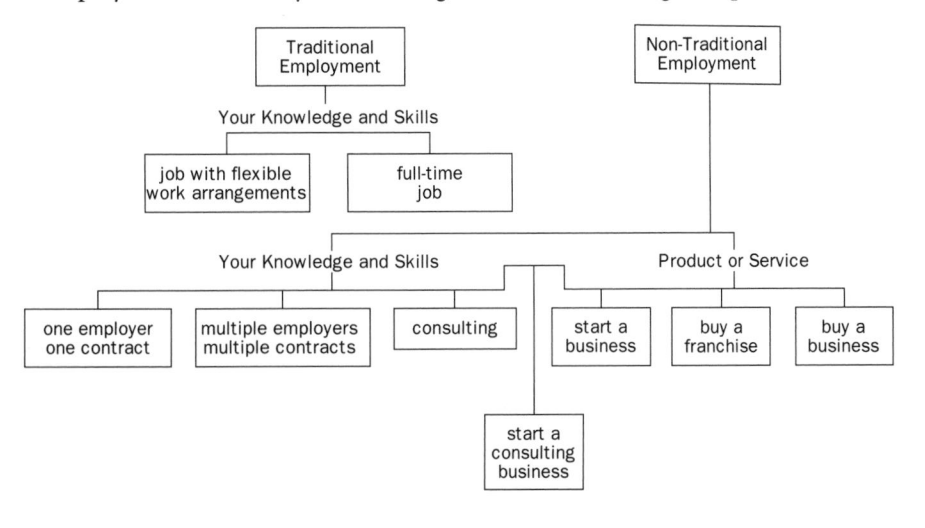

Traditional Employment—Flexible Work Arrangements

Flexible hours and telecommuting have created the opportunity for many employees to have some of the advantages of working independently while staying in a traditional job. It is increasingly common for executives, professionals and managers to regularly work from home, or organize their hours in the office according to their personal priorities. Job-sharing is gradually gaining acceptance in the executive ranks, but only where the work lends itself, the participants are suitable and the organization's culture accepts the arrangement. Part-time opportunities at the executive level are few and far between, but they can be the answer for people who want to improve the balance between work and personal interests. Seasonal work is a possibility for some professionals such as accountants.

The new world of work has created flexibility that works extremely well for some, but the trade-off can include lower earnings, no benefits, limited professional development opportunities, difficulty maintaining a sense of belonging and less chance of upward mobility within an organization.

Contract Work

Contract work usually involves joining the ranks of an organization for a short time. The contract assignment might be related to a specific project or a peak in the organization's business. Alternatively, the contract worker fills the shoes of a permanent employee who is on temporary leave. The length of contracts can extend from a few weeks to months and even to years. The work might be full- or part-time. You could be paid as an employee, or submit invoices as an independent supplier.

Tip: To be able to claim self-employment status, you must exercise control over the way your work is done, the schedule and the location. You must bring your own tools and materials to the job, provide a service that is not an integral part of the organization's core business and bear some financial risk in the contract. Check www.ccra-ardc.gc.ca for details. Consult your accountant for tax advice and your lawyer for help with contracts.

There are several ways that contract work can fit into your plans. One is as a stop-gap. This involves taking contract opportunities that come along while you are looking for a full-time position. Doing this keeps your skills sharp, broadens your experience, adds new contacts to your network and generates income in the process. Many organizations use contract assignments as a way of evaluating a candidate's skills and fit before making a permanent hiring decision. The downside of taking a full-time contract is that you will be much less active in the job market, leaving you with little or no time to market yourself.

Tip: Expressing interest in non-traditional employment can provide the quickest route to re-employment. It can also open a door that eventually leads to permanent employment.

Contract work can also be a career choice. Either as an independent or working for an organization that supplies contract workers to its many clients, you have the benefit of constant change in your work environment. This option usually involves some business development responsibility. If you strike out on your own, the challenge of finding the next assignment will always be with you.

Some people use contract work as a step toward retirement. It's not unusual for employers, suppliers or competitors to ask a recently retired individual to accept a contract position. These people often find that being valued in a completely new culture is one of the most affirming things that has happened in years. You might be surprised to find that you become busier than ever, pushing the notion of retirement far into the future.

A senior manager who accepted an early retirement package from a major financial institution decided to continue deploying his skills and interest in internal auditing by seeking contract work. He had been on the leading edge in using business intelligence and data-mining technology to eliminate the hit-and-miss sampling technique common to audit procedures. His ability to apply software built for market research to other business solutions quickly caught the attention of several financial institutions, and his venture into the arena of contract work soon took precedence over his plans for having more leisure time.

Consulting

Consulting refers to the process of offering information and recommendations at a strategic level to the managers of an organization or to an individual. Implementation is usually left to the client. Consultants are typically engaged when something is going wrong, when existing processes and systems are inadequate or when changes are needed or being anticipated. They are expected to bring to their clients the best practices in their areas of expertise. An expert consultant will review the situation, identify the issues and make suggestions for interventions and change, with practical advice for implementation. The process consultant will facilitate the client's learning, planning or decision-making process. Often both specific expertise and process facilitation are involved.

To become established as a consultant, you usually need to have recognized expertise in your field, good contacts and strong marketing, negotiating and facilitation skills. It also helps to have the appropriate professional designations and formal education at the graduate level. Consultants can choose to work independently, in association or partnership with other professionals or with a consulting firm. To be successful, independent consultants must have the ability to originate business.

Tip: When you work independently, you need to pay attention to your record-keeping and tax status. Don't use the shoebox-of-receipts method of accounting! Falling behind with tax remittances incurs penalties and can give you a false sense of how well you are doing financially. Purchase and use a software package for bookkeeping. Hire a Chartered Accountant to get you set up, and to do your annual statements and tax filing.

GUIDELINES FOR EVALUATING YOUR READINESS FOR CONTRACT OR
CONSULTING WORK

- Even when no one in your target market is hiring, opportunities for contract or consulting work probably exist. Organizations frequently fill their staffing needs in non-traditional ways during a hiring freeze.
- Be prepared to confidently present your skills and knowledge as the means of solving a problem, completing a project or making a meaningful contribution to your prospective clients or employer.
- Plan how you will manage a fluctuating income stream.
- Research the availability of life and disability insurance plus medical and dental benefits for yourself and your dependants at a reasonable cost.

Tip: Insurance and medical and dental benefits may be available through your professional association or the Association of Independent Consultants. Check their web site at www.aiconsult.ca.

Independent contractors and consultants are free from the infrastructure of an organization. They may be able to work from their home offices and perhaps employ family members or sub-contractors. Often they handle more than one assignment at a time, providing variety, breadth of exposure and an ever-increasing knowledge base built on experience. Independence can be exhilarating.

The allure of self-employment also includes the perception of having freedom to work when you want, for whom you want and at what you want. It seldom turns out to be utopia. To replace an employer's demands, your clients will have ill-timed crises and unrealistic deadlines. In the absence of workplace politics, you will have the challenge of balancing your clients' expectations with your actual ability to perform miracles. However, with hard work, these options to a traditional job can be made to fit your interests and needs.

After managing three acquisition integrations, a senior human resources professional decided to establish herself as an independent consultant. To augment her MBA, she became a Certified Management Consultant and contacted her broad network of business colleagues to solicit assignments. After two years of building her practice, she works long hours and weekends to meet the needs of her ever-growing list of demanding clients. Her expertise in managing people through times of significant organizational change has generated great success and a frenetic lifestyle.

Tip: Starting a business from your home only works if you have the right facilities and an environment that suits the business. Having your toddler crying in the background while you're on the phone might work for a babysitting service, but it will damage the credibility of a market research company.

Small Business Ownership

The thought of owning and operating a small business has appeal for those who want to be in charge of an enterprise. The impetus is usually the recognition of a niche market. This could be a new product or service, or the need for improvement on what is currently available. Whatever the inspiration, you can look at building a business from scratch or buying an existing business or franchise.

Before investing too much time and money in the start-up phase, use the guidelines above to test your readiness. Then write a thorough business plan. Financial institutions provide excellent templates, and many are available on the Internet. Your plan must include a full description of your product or service, including its features and competitive advantages. Establish pricing and calculate the cost of sales. Do a thorough market analysis.

A couple decided to start a small business providing computer software training programs. To begin the venture, they needed to lease office space with training facilities, purchase furniture and equipment, and hire administrative staff. They constructed a plan that calculated the precise point where they would have to abandon the venture without leaving their family's finances in irreparable ruins. They each knew how they would orchestrate a quick return to paid employment. Once the plan was in place, they took an optimistic and tenacious approach to building the business without second-guessing their strategy.

Decide how much you can afford to invest without a financial partner. Don't expect financial institutions to provide funding for your business without collateral or your personal guarantee backed by solid assets such as your house. Get financial and legal advice before you start.

Tip: Choosing the appropriate form of business is critical. Incorporating, establishing a partnership or operating as a registered or unregistered sole proprietor are your choices. Each carries advantages, risks and costs. Ask your professional advisers which is best for you.

To build or buy a small business, you can go it alone, team up with one or more colleagues or get the backing of an existing organization that has interests matching yours. On the surface it might seem that going it alone is the most risky option, but that's not always true. Partners with an investment and interest in your business should add ideas, effort and support. It could turn out that their priorities and abilities are not as advertised.

A would-be entrepreneur decided that his skills in internal communications and employee relations would work well in the field of diversity training. He was introduced to a potential partner who was working as an executive coach and had a similar interest. The pair incorporated, entered into a complex shareholders' agreement, leased an office and developed a model for their service before either one focused on their target market and how they would actually bring business in the door. As time passed, one partner kept himself so busy with his coaching practice that he was unable to generate leads for the joint effort. The other lacked contacts and the confidence to develop them. After much expense, their venture had to be wound down.

Another route to business ownership is buying rather than building. The simplest and safest approach is buying a franchise. Reputable franchise vendors have done most of the groundwork for you. They know the product or service and the market very well. There should be an established formula for operating the business as well as training and support to get you started. Your ongoing fees pay for marketing and advertising, and there may be preferential supplier arrangements negotiated for you. The downside includes the potentially staggering cost of purchase and the reality that you will probably have to work morning, noon and night for limited potential earnings. It's crucial that you like the sort of work that you'll be doing, and thrive in structured situations. Buying a franchise is not a good idea for people with high needs for independence and variety.

Tip: Before buying a franchise, do your research and planning as if you were going to build the business from scratch. Your bank manager and the Canadian Franchise Association are reliable sources of advice and caution.

Buying an existing business is another story altogether. The best advice here is "buyer beware." Make sure that you know and have confidence in the current owners' reason for selling, and do not proceed unless you get a clear and thorough answer to every question you ask. As with building a business, you need to understand the product or service well and have a grasp of the market. Look at the financial situation with a critical eye, and most importantly, look at the people who work in the business. You need to be confident that the team will rally around you and do their best to take things forward.

Tip: If you are considering buying an existing business, surround yourself with a team of qualified professionals. Even if the entity is very small and you think you know it well, hire help! You will need a lawyer, an accountant and, ideally, a business broker, venture capitalist or co-investor to look over your shoulder. Do not try to do this alone.

GUIDELINES FOR EVALUATING YOUR PROSPECTS FOR SMALL BUSINESS OWNERSHIP

- Before considering starting or buying a business, answer these questions:
  - What product or service will you offer? Define it clearly and specifically.
  - What amount can you invest and what other sources of funding are available to you? How much financial risk you are prepared to take?

- • Who will buy your product or service? Where is the market? Do you have access to it? Why would customers choose your product or service over your competitors'?
- Think about what this will mean for your family. Building a business is nearly always an all-consuming task. If you aren't working at it, you're thinking about it. The stress on relationships can be great. Make sure that you have your family's support.
- Think about all of the skills that will be needed for a successful operation. You cannot supply everything personally. It won't do any good to bring in the sales if you can't discipline yourself to do the invoicing. Decide how you will fill the gaps and plan to set up properly from the start.
- Talk with all the entrepreneurs you can find. The closer their product or service is to yours, the better. Be careful that you don't mislead prospective competitors. After hearing their stories, be honest with yourself about why you want to own your own business.

An experienced general manager learned that a small office furniture manufacturing company was for sale. He asked a neighbour who owned his own small manufacturing business to accompany him on a fact-finding visit to the target company. After two hours of looking at the financials, touring the plant and interviewing the owner, the two men left to ponder their findings. The asking price was $750,000. On the way home, the small business owner said, "For that much money, I'd just as soon start up fresh. I can make a lot of mistakes for $750,000." The decision was made, and the purchase was not!

WORKSHEET 7.1
Evaluate Your Entrepreneurial Qualities

From the items listed below, choose the five that describe your strongest abilities or qualities. Take some time with this. You might find that all of the terms describe you somewhat and identifying the top five is a challenge. Make note of the five runners-up. The answer key is printed upside down at the bottom of the page.

__ Perseverance

__ Desire and willingness to take the initiative

__ Competitiveness

__ Self-reliance

__ A strong need to achieve

__ Self-confidence

__ Good physical health

__ A willingness to take risks

__ A high energy level

__ An ability to get along with employees

__ Versatility

__ A desire to create

__ Ability to be innovative

__ Ability to lead effectively

__ A willingness to tolerate uncertainty

__ A strong desire for money

__ Patience

__ Good organizational skills

__ A need for power

__ A need to closely associate with others

Worksheet Key
The list on the worksheet is arranged in order of the importance attributed by successful entrepreneurs to these abilities and qualities. Perseverance has the highest ranking and a need for association has the lowest. There is no scoring system attached to this exercise because you are not to assume that success as an entrepreneur is dependent upon how you ranked yourself. Many things might have influenced your answers. The purpose of the exercise is to give you more food for thought as you consider the option of self-employment.

Steps to Retirement

The new employment model with its wide range of non-traditional employment relationships has had a profound impact on retirement issues. Today, remaining with one company long enough to claim a gold watch and the accompanying pension is unlikely. As a result, traditional retirement with unlimited leisure time and no further paid work is less prevalent. Financial needs motivate many people to continue working past traditional retirement age, and others choose to stay employed to avoid boredom, especially if their spouse or partner has not yet retired. Increasingly, retirement has become a gradual process rather than an event.

Ideally, the new retirement model involves four steps:
- strategic career management
- pre-retirement planning
- semi-retirement
- full retirement

Emphasizing strategic career management throughout your working life is the best insurance that retiring will be a welcome and satisfying process. People who keep their skills up to date and their knowledge fresh will have more options when they want to move into part-time or contract work. If you intentionally take on assignments and projects that genuinely interest you and raise your profile with like-minded colleagues and contacts, you are laying a foundation for opportunities to become available when you want to work less and enjoy it more. Strategic career management might require sacrifices, including reduced remuneration at earlier stages in your career, as you make choices based on other priorities. However, if you would like to do more of what you love as you move toward retirement, it will be worth it.

Pre-retirement planning is often initiated by other life transitions. An empty nest, a health warning or the simple passing of a milestone birthday can shift your focus to thoughts of working less or not at all. This is the time to establish a financial plan that is based on your needs and expectations for the future. It is also an excellent time to do a thorough career assessment as a means of expanding your horizons beyond the confines of your current role. Start your research on retirement possibilities by talking with people who are in the process and observing how various organizations employ semi-retired individuals. At the same time, consider which aspects of your skills and knowledge might lead to interesting semi-retirement opportunities, and watch for market niches that could be filled by someone with your experience.

Semi-retirement is an increasingly popular and productive career phase. It is usually characterized by the need for less pay, as a result of having at least a partial pension or investment income. This phase might be initiated by an early retirement package from your long-standing employer or simply by your desire to gear down. Even individuals who have recived a package often return to their former employer on a contract basis to do a special project or to fill a temporary vacancy. Many build second careers in related fields. Former bankers become certified financial planners; an accountant may teach CPA courses or keep the books for a charitable organization; an executive from the hospitality industry might buy a small inn.

Progressing from semi-retirement to full retirement can be an abrupt action or a gradual process taking a number of years. Scaling back the frequency of contracts, the volume of clients or the number of days worked typifies a wind-down. Leaving paid work behind is often accompanied by other lifestyle changes such as a move, health concerns or the desire to spend more time travelling, playing tennis or with the grandchildren. In full retirement, community or volunteer work can offer continued opportunities to use your skills and make a contribution without the constraint of a fixed schedule or unwanted responsibilities. Having an interest in others and a sense of purpose can give you vitality throughout your later years.

The choices are yours. Decide what's most important to you and make this transition a good one.

Chapter 8

Set Your Targets

*Where does your ability to contribute
coincide with market needs?*

You've reviewed your career history, gathered your accomplishment stories, identified your strategic advantage and reflected on your values. Now it's time to pull all of this together into a vision statement of the ideal employment opportunity for you. Next, have a preliminary look at the marketplace and consider industries and sectors where you could make a contribution. Combine this with your preferred terms of employment, and your strategic targets are set. These targets are working hypotheses that will give your search focus and direction. This diagram illustrates the targeting process.

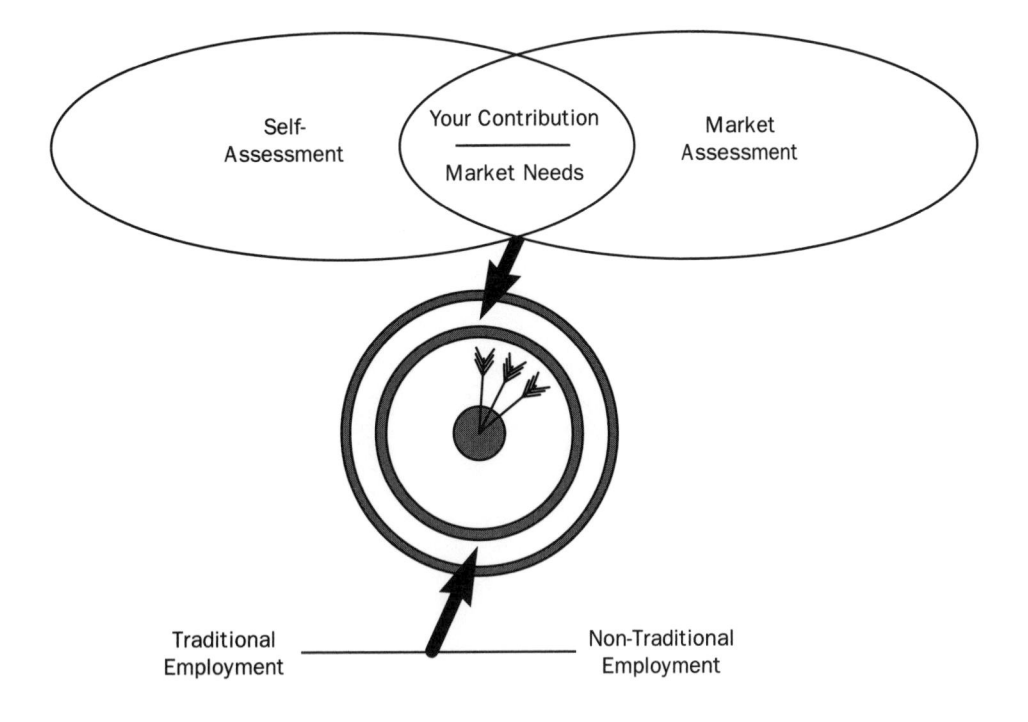

Self-Assessment

Your Contribution
———————
Market Needs

Market Assessment

Traditional Employment ——————————— Non-Traditional Employment

Self-Assessment—The Ideal Employment Opportunity for You

To summarize the self-assessment work you have done using Chapters 4–7, create a vision statement of the ideal work for you. It will describe the activities or functions to which you are best suited and the types of cultures or environments you prefer. It will not name specific job titles or organizations. This vision statement will be forward-looking, yet grounded in the realities of your talents and experience. As you progress through your search for work, use it as a touchstone to keep you on the right track.

Use the following worksheet to create your vision statement. Share it with your support network. Ask if they think it's an accurate description of you. Have you missed anything that is key?

A top-performing salesman had spent the most recent two years of his career working on the implementation of new sales support technology. This detail-driven, internal role left him feeling burnt out and out of touch with his key skills. As he recalled accomplishment stories from earlier years and identified his strategic advantage, he described himself as charismatic and competitive. He claimed to understand the emotional dynamics of successful sales. Sales management held little interest for him, but achieving higher monetary rewards was important. He wanted variety and travel opportunities in his next role. After sharing his vision statement with his support network, it was suggested to him that he become a motivational speaker. After taking a few courses, he succeeded in getting on the speakers' circuit, and now makes his living addressing sales conferences and conventions for a variety of organizations.

WORKSHEET 8.1
Self-Assessment—Your Vision of the Ideal Employment Opportunity for You

List the elements of your strategic advantage (Chapter 5) that you will take to your next role.

- Skills

- Style

- Knowledge

- Interests

- Values and motivators

What roles or functions align with your strategic advantage?

Describe the type of people with whom you most want to associate in your work (Chapter 4).

Identify the culture and type of organization that most appeals to you (Chapter 4).

What other personal values, obligations and priorities will affect your career decisions (Chapter 6)?

What are your remuneration requirements?

What is your preferred geographical location?

On what terms will you accept a non-traditional employment arrangement (Chapter 7)?

How will your next career step move you toward your long-term goals?

Market Assessment

Begin the process of assessing industries and sectors where your skills and knowledge might be used. The sector in which you have worked most recently will probably be the one that you know best. You may already have a clear picture of your employment prospects there. For less well-known sectors, do some very preliminary research. Check a few web sites and talk only with your close contacts. Later in the search process you will do in-depth research that will include reaching out to knowledgeable people who are not in your immediate support network. Research and networking will provide answers to the questions that are forming now. At this point in the exercise you are making assumptions to help clarify your thoughts and organize your search. As you progress you will learn more about the markets that interest you. You will likely return to this market assessment exercise many times.

First, take a realistic look at the market where you have been working most recently. Use the following worksheet to record your analysis. Next, explore several other industries or sectors in which you think you might like to work and complete a separate market-assessment worksheet for each of them.

Tip: For your first round of market assessments, consult only with your support network and, if appropriate, your references. While you are setting your initial targets and before you have gathered your resources, you are not fully prepared to be actively networking.

Refer to Appendix A and review the diagram to see where you are. Once you have completed the market assessments, your situational analysis is done and you are ready to set your targets.

WORKSHEET 8.2
Market Assessment

Market, industry or sector _____

Who are the players? This is your top-of-mind list. You will expand it later.

Organizations   _____   _____
                 _____   _____
                 _____   _____

Key People   _____   _____
                 _____   _____
                 _____   _____

What does the playing field look like?

   Which organizations are best-in-class? Are acquisitions or mergers expected? Will there be new entrants to the market? Which organizations are the most successful—on what basis and in whose opinion?

   What are the current trends? What issues or challenges does the market face? What does the future seem to hold for the industry or sector? What skills are in demand?

   How large is the market? How much time will it take you to explore employment opportunities in it? Is it large enough to sustain a full-time search? Which organizations are hiring?

What are the rules?

   What background and education or professional credentials are required? Do they hire from outside the industry?

   How do they recruit? Public advertisements of all opportunities? Postings on corporate web sites? Search firms and placement agencies—which ones? Primarily word-of-mouth or networking?

Strategic Targeting

To set a target, either choose one market and surmise how its needs might coincide with the key elements of your ideal employment vision statement, or choose one role that suits you and consider how it might be useful in various industry sectors. The possibilities are: stay in your current market or move to a new one; fill a role that is the same or similar to your most recent one, or shift to a new role. For this exercise consider the word *market* to be synonymous with sector or industry.

Your targets will fall into one of these quadrants:

higher pay
shorter search

Same role Different market	Same role Same market
Different role Different market	Different role Same market

less pay
longer search

If remaining in the same market and role is an attractive and viable option for you, you will likely succeed more quickly and with better remuneration than with any of the other three options. While, the top right quadrant of the model represents what is often the optimum route to quick re-employment, this is not always the case. People who worked in the IT and telecom sectors in the late 90s or are veterans of the amalgamation of corporate and investment banks know better. Many of these individuals eventually sought opportunities in different roles in different markets. They found success by moving to the bottom left quadrant of the model, the one that represents the most challenging career transition. It takes the most time and often requires a step down in remuneration, but it can be the beginning of a refreshing new chapter of your work experience.

Tip: If landing comfortably in the top right quadrant of the model is not going to be easy for you or you are looking for a major career change, this targeting exercise will help you identify other options that may be plausible.

Set one target at a time using the following worksheet. For each target, keep the variables to a minimum by considering either one market and multiple roles, or one role and multiple markets. If you put too many possibilities on one target, you will sacrifice the clarity that this exercise is intended to achieve.

Stop when you have identified your key questions for each target. Prioritizing and setting time frames is covered in Chapter 14 as part of the planning process.

Once you have set at least three strategic targets, you have completed the second phase illustrated in Appendix A. You are ready to move on to the next step, which is gathering your resources. Your targets will influence the content of your marketing resources. As you write your résumé and prepare your verbal pitch for interviewing and networking, keep a specific target in mind. You will return to these targets when you are fully prepared to move into action.

A human resources professional from the consumer packaged-goods industry set three targets at the outset of her career transition experience. She felt confident that she could land a more senior human resources role in a smaller packaged-goods company. She also considered applying for a human resources job at her current level in the health care industry. Her interest in health care arose from her dedication to helping her niece who had special needs. She also wanted to explore the possibility of moving into the non-profit sector as an executive director of an organization where she could contribute more directly to helping children with exceptional health-related issues. Having these three targets gave her search a distinct focus and clear direction.

WORKSHEET 8.3
Your Strategic Targets

Industry(ies) or sector(s):

Size and scope of target organizations within the sector:

Possible role(s), function(s) or title(s) in relation to size and scope of target organzation(s):

Remuneration: Preferred _____   Minimum _____

Geographical boundaries of search: Preferred _____
                                      Acceptable _____

Possible terms of employment:

How do you think your ability to contribute coincides with the needs of this market?

What is most compelling about this target for you?

What key questions will help you determine the pragmatism of this target?

Target priority ranking (A, B or C):

Rationale for this priority ranking:

Search Activities Project Plan

Target time frame:	Revised time frame:	Revised time frame:
Start date _____	Start date _____	Start date _____
Assess and revise by:	Assess and revise by:	Assess and revise by:
Date _____	Date _____	Date _____
Time and energy allocation:	Time and energy allocation:	Time and energy allocation:
% of weekly activity _____	% of weekly activity _____	% of weekly activity _____
Hours/week _____	Hours/week _____	Hours/week _____

Wrap-Up

There has been much to consider during this time out for reflection. Congratulations for staying with the process. You're headed in the right direction if you're building on what's best from your past and unique about you today, then moving toward what's right for your future. Regardless of which employment opportunity you take next, the assessment and planning that you have just completed ought to help guide your decisions for years to come.

Now you need to acquire or refresh your self-marketing and search skills in order to move into action.

Part Three

Gather Your Resources

The brilliance is in the details.

Objectives

This section helps you create the materials and develop the skills you'll need to conduct an active search. It offers detailed explanations and numerous samples to guide you. This is the most painstaking, detailed work you'll do. The chapters in Part 3 cover:

- Why research is an essential part of your job search.
- Researching industries, trends and companies.
- Establishing a good record-keeping system.
- Writing a résumé that markets your skills and supports your intended direction.
- Developing additional materials, biographies and brochures.
- Creating five sound bites as a foundation for excellent interviews.
- Preparing for interviews.
- Understanding the various interview formats.
- Writing effective correspondence.

Rules to Follow

- Use a variety of research mediums, including print, the Internet and your network of contacts.
- Make sure that your résumé supports your intended career direction.
- Write an accomplishment-focused résumé, not a reiteration of your job description.
- Include quantified results in the accomplishment statements on your résumé wherever possible.
- Rehearse your answers to the most difficult interview questions.
- Tailor every piece of correspondence to the specific circumstances and the recipient.

Moves That Can Set You Back

- Rushing through the résumé-writing process in an effort to get into the market quickly.
- Going into interviews without thorough preparation.
- Being less than straightforward about your reasons for leaving your last job.

- Approaching companies before you have sufficient background information on them.
- Conducting superficial research without digging into the real issues.
- Neglecting to write thank-you letters.
- Spending an excessive amount of time developing marketing materials you don't really need.

Chapter 9

Research

Information is power.

Most people who embark on a career change begin with a limited amount of information about the options that might be available to them. Not knowing what's happening beyond the walls of your organization or the boundaries of your industry is a common deterrent to exploring new opportunities, and yet, access to a vast amount of information is readily available. Almost everything you need to know to find the work you want can be learned through purposeful research.

....

Tip: It may have been a long time since you've done the kind of in-depth research necessary for a job search. Most positions don't require it, and people in more senior roles usually delegate research tasks. Don't let lack of familiarity hold you back. You'll probably enjoy doing research once you get started.

....

The Value of Research for the Job Search

Research is a primary tool for implementing and advancing your search plan. You will narrow, broaden, revise or eliminate your targets by finding out as much as possible about the roles, organizations, industries and trends that interest you. Every piece of information you set out to find should be focused on pursuing your targets. When you think of research as one of the most important means to your goal, your job search activities will broaden significantly, going well beyond looking for ads and job postings that sound as if they might match your interests and skills.

A financial services executive set one target that involved finding work that would enable him to use his expertise in fraud prevention and risk management. His research focused on finding organizations with a record of increasing fraud losses and insurance claims. After identifying 40 organizations representing four industries, he found out who had responsibility for these areas. This generated a list of over 95 names for his networking initiatives. Through this research he expanded his search horizons and gathered reading material to help him form meaningful questions for discussion in networking meetings. He had no difficulty landing opportunities for contract work.

Your research will also improve your ability to compose pertinent and persuasive written materials. As you dig for information, you will become more familiar with the issues that are relevant to the people you will be contacting. You will also learn how different organizations and industries use and interpret various words and phrases. This will help you choose keywords for your résumé and use current industry jargon in your letters, making you sound knowledgeable and drawing the attention you want.

Research is also crucial to interview preparation. You need to learn everything you can about an organization before presenting yourself as a candidate for employment. Knowledge of the market, the industry and the people who are influential in the organization and the industry sector is important. You should read all the relevant publicly available information and talk with your advisers and networking contacts about the company before going to the interview.

Networking involves research in two important ways. First, research prepares you for networking calls and meetings, and second, research is the subject of networking. More is said about this in later chapters, but note that seeking information is the credible reason for contacting and meeting with people who can advance your search. Furthermore, information that you have obtained can often be of interest or assistance to the individuals you meet in the networking process.

Tip: By doing thorough research and sharing what you've discovered, you will be perceived as exceptionally knowledgeable and up-to-date. Prospective employers will want you working for them, not the competition.

Perhaps the greatest value of research is that it keeps you active in the market, learning more and meeting more people. While you are seeking to follow trends, understand industries, evaluate organizations and discover the names of decision-makers, you will come across new ideas that will expand your search and keep you thinking creatively. You will also meet people who can give you valuable insights and possibly open doors that you never knew existed.

Research Is a Four-Step Process

Like any other skill or ability, the value of research increases dramatically if it is executed well and used wisely. Give yourself credit for having done a good job once you've completed these four steps:

Collect the information:
- Be focused. Clearly define what you want to know, form your key questions and stay on topic.
- Be open to finding information where you don't expect it.
- Use a wide variety of resources.
- Consider people to be a primary research resource.
- Be creative in tracking down information. Think like a private investigator.

Organize it:

- At the outset, establish a meticulous filing and record-keeping system using electronic or hard-copy files.
- Create a system of cross-references for efficient retrieval of information.
- Record the date, page number and name of the publication on every clipping or print-out.
- Keep Internet bookmarks organized efficiently.

Assimilate it:

- An active thought process is the most important element in making research useful.
- Look for patterns and trends. Make connections and note contradictions. Let additional questions arise.
- As one idea leads to another, record off-topic ideas for future research.
- Form hypotheses. Draw conclusions.
- Make notes as your thoughts evolve.

Use it:

- Share your research with your board of advisers, support group and networking contacts.
- Become an information distributor, armed with reprints of articles, web addresses and tips on sources of information, including the names of knowledgeable people.
- Discuss what you've gleaned from your research with everyone possible, asking for their opinions and related ideas.
- Use research as an essential preparation tool for networking and interviewing.
- Look for opportunities to mention points from your research in networking meetings and interviews.
- Let research play a key role in evaluating employment opportunities.

Tip: A complete job search record-keeping system requires a calendar or diary, a database for contact information, correspondence files organized by name and cross-referenced to organizations, and separate files for information and articles on people, organizations, industries and trends. Detailed records allow efficient retrieval of information and prevent embarrassing duplications.

People Are the Best Research Resources

People are the best providers and interpreters of information. Most people enjoy being asked for their opinions, advice and help, especially when your questions are specific and thoughtful. You can ask the same questions of a large number of people, even when you are certain that you have uncovered every possible fact and opinion on a topic. People are flattered to have been asked, and you never know when your questions will elicit a new idea.

The variety of ideas and viewpoints that you gather from your networking contacts gives you an invaluable word-on-the-street perspective that no amount of formal research can match. You usually discover the truly interesting and useful information only from individuals who are willing to speak candidly and off-the-record. If you want to know what it's really like to work at Your Target Co., ask around; don't rely exclusively on press releases or what the analysts and business reporters say. There could be some critical points of view that you will only discover by talking to other people.

Arranging an opportunity to job shadow is an excellent way to get first-hand information, especially if you are considering a significant change of occupation. Of course, the nature of the work, type of organization and seniority of the role must be conducive to an observer's presence.

A commercial banker was considering changing careers after over 26 years working for the same organization. He was interested in teaching business courses, and had done his research regarding the additional education that he would need at both the high school and community college level. To help him with his decision, he asked a neighbour who taught at the local high school if he would consider allowing him to tag along for a week. The arrangements were made and the commercial banker got a very realistic job preview. He decided to teach part-time at a community college as an interim step.

Tip: Your research questions give you reasons to contact the people in your network. A quick phone call or email with a specific question keeps you in touch and brings your networking contacts up-to-date with your search.

How to Focus Your Research

The best way to focus your research is by forming targeted questions. Throughout the job search, there are four topics that will require your research skills: trends, industries, organizations and people. Use the following questions as guides.

Questions for Researching a Trend
- What is meant by the terms commonly used to describe the trend (e.g., "compliance")?
- What industries are being affected by the trend? How?
- Is there a social, cultural, political, demographic, geographic, technological or ethical factor involved?
- What books, articles, studies or government inquiries have been published?
- Is legislative change involved?
- Who stands to gain from this trend and who stands to lose? In what ways?
- What is the range of opinion on this trend? Who is saying what?
- What occupations are becoming obsolete and what new opportunities are opening up as a result of the trend?
- What sort of education or training is becoming valuable in response to this trend?
- How do you think it will affect your career change?

Questions for Researching an Industry

- What factors have affected the development of the industry?
- What are some of the current trends?
- Are there any factors limiting growth?
- Has any recent legislation affected the industry? Is there any pending?
- What environmental factors are affecting the industry?
- What new products or services are influencing the way business is being done?
- How has the use of technology impacted on the industry?
- Are there any specific lobbies or consumer groups that are influencing the industry?
- Are there any global factors that may affect the health of the industry?
- Who are the respected industry analysts? What are they saying?
- What skills are in demand? What skills or occupations are in decline?
- What organizations lead the industry?
- Who are the industry gurus?

A pharmaceutical laboratory researcher with an interest in nutrition and naturopathy wanted to find out more about the field of biotechnology. First she checked universities and community colleges for biotech training programs and found a one-year course available at a reasonable cost. Then she chose a search engine, www.yahoo.ca, and entered the word "biotechnology," which generated 235 category matches and 811 web site matches. Since she intended to stay in Canada, she hit "search Canada only" and narrowed this down to 19 categories and 49 web site matches. She followed up on interesting and relevant links to other sites. Next she chose the HRDC (Human Resources Development Canada) Strategis web site, www.strategis.ic.gc.ca, and clicked on "Business Information by Sector." Using the alphabetized sorter, she pulled up "biotechnology" and perused the links. This research helped her narrow her search to the fields of food technology and nutritional supplements and yielded the names of over 30 organizations.

Next, she checked www.canadiancareers.com, and, clicking on "Career Info," she found the Sector Specific Career Resources section including occupations in biotechnology. This yielded a number of organization and industry association names that had not come up in her previous search. In the Biotechnology sections, she looked at the BHRC (Biotechnology Human Resource Council) job bank, which listed 50 opportunities. Under the Alternative Medicine sections she looked at the Canadian Naturopathic Association web site. As a final step she went to www.monster.ca and www.workopolis.com to see what type of positions were being posted in this field and located 57 opportunities to explore out of a total of 231 lisings across the biotechnology and pharmaceutical sectors. All together, a few hours of research on the Internet gave her a realistic picture of a viable career option.

Tip: If your keywords generate too much information, narrow your search by adding additional parameters. For example, "biotechnology" and "trends" and "Vancouver" will give better-focused responses than just "biotechnology" or "trends." If no responses are generated by your search, it's too narrow. Eliminate words or revise the combination of keywords until the type of information you want is generated.

Tip: Even if you are at the executive level, pursuing your research as if you were a student entering the field will yield keywords, names of organizations, industry associations and current information that will advance and expand your search.

Questions for Researching an Organization

- Is it owned publicly or privately? What can you find out about the owners?
- Has there been a recent change of ownership or is a change pending or predicted?
- How is it structured? Does it have subsidiaries, divisions, branches, decentralized offices, etc.?
- How many employees does it have? In what locations?
- Who are the principals? Who is on the board of directors?
- What is the history of the organization? Has it grown or contracted by acquisition, divestiture or internal initiative?
- What is its financial situation?
- What are its products and services? (If they are available in the retail market, try them.)
- Who are the customers and why do they choose to do business with this organization?
- Who are the main competitors and what differentiates this organization from them?
- How does it market its products or services?
- Have there been any recent press releases or articles about the company?
- What new ventures is the company planning?
- How do people describe the culture of the organization?
- What is its reputation for how it treats employees, customers and suppliers?
- What charities does the organization support?
- What attracts you to this organization? Would you be interested in joining it?
- What would be the negatives about working there?

Information to Gather about People

- Contact information, including proper spelling of the name, current title, address, phone number, etc.
- Do some research on their organization and industry.
- What is their background, including previous jobs, achievements and education?
- Have they been published? What press coverage have they had?
- What are their interests, concerns, personal goals?
- Who referred you to them? Why were you referred?
- What information do you expect them to have?

In this age of information, there is an enormous variety and quantity of research resources available. The following pages will help direct you to some good starting points. As you gather information in your area of interest many more doors will open, and you will find excellent resources—far more than can be listed here.

If you are a novice at doing research on the Internet, these two web sites provide excellent introductions:
- Bare Bones at www.sc.edu/beaufort/library/bones.html
- WebTeacher at www.webteacher.org

For resources that are not accessible on the Internet, go to a reference or business library and ask the librarian. Most of them delight in directing you to the appropriate resources.

The following pages offer a selection of research resources.

An Inventory of Research Resources

Directories

Where the directory is available on the Internet, the web address is given. Others are available at reference and business libraries.

General Business / Trade Directories
- Blue Book of Canadian Business (www.cbr.ca)
- Canadian Key Business Directory
- Dun's Regional Business Directory
- Financial Post Survey of Industrials
- Who Owns Whom: North America
- Canadian Trade Index (www.ctidirectory.com)
- Fraser's Canadian Trade Directory (www.frasers.com)
- Industry Canada Company Directories (www.strategis.ic.gc.ca)
- Scott's Canadian Business Directories (www.scottsinfo.com)

Specific Sector Directories
- Directory of Canadian Management Consultants
- Directory of Retail Chains
- Career Directory
- Financial Services Canada
- Contact Toronto—Toronto Board of Trade (www.bot.com)

Associations Directories
- Canada's Information Resource—web hotlinks for online Associations and Financial Services directory (circ.micromedia.ca/hotlinks/associations/main.htm)
- Canadian Sourcebook

Online Telephone Directories
- Canada 411 (canada411.ca)
- Yellow Pages (www.yellowpages.ca)
- Yellow.ca (www.yellow.ca)

Organizations' Web Sites
Information such as the organization's history, structure, principals, financial data, products and services can often be found on their web site. This information has been written by the organization. To locate web addresses use directories or search engines:
- www.yahoo.ca
- www.yahoo.com
- www.altavistacanada.com
- www.altavista.com
- www.google.com
- www.lycos.com

Annual Reports
- Report Gallery (www.reportgallery.com)—online library of financial reports
- TSX Group (www.tsx.com)
- SEDAR—System for Electronic Document Analysis and Retrieval (www.sedar.com)
- U.S. Securities & Exchange Commission (www.sec.gov)

Business Links
- Bloomberg (www.bloomberg.com)
- Globe and Mail Investor Web Site (www.globeinvestor.com)
- Hoover's Online (www.hoovers.com)
- StockHouse Canada (www.stockhouse.ca)
- Web 100—Big Business on the Web (www.metamoney.com/w100)
- Advice for Investors (www.adviceforinvestors.com)
- Wright Investors' Service (www.corporateinformation.com)

Industry Profiles
- Industry Canada (www.ic.gc.ca) provides a wealth of government information, including the Strategis database (strategis.ic.gc.ca).
- Ontario Economic Development (www.2ontario.com) details a variety of industry sectors.
- Statistics Canada (www.statcan.ca/) publishes a wide variety of information on economic and social conditions in Canada. Some free census data is also available.
- GDSourcing Research and Retrieval (www.gdsourcing.com) assists in finding free Canadian statistical information.
- Business publications that list top companies by sales, assets and number of employees.
  - *Canadian Business*—i500/tech 100 (www.canadianbusiness.com)

- *Profit 100* (www.profitguide.com/profit100/)
- *Report on Business* (top1000.robmagazine.com)
- *Fortune 500* (www.fortune.com/fortune/fortune500)

Online Magazine Indexes
Searching is free—document delivery charges apply
- *Canada One* (www.canadaone.com)
- *Electric Library Canada* (www.elibrary.ca)

Online Newspapers, Trade Publications and Magazines
- *Bizlink—Business Information Group* (www.bizlink.com)
- *Media Link*—directory of experts for journalists (www.medialin.com)
- *JournalismNet* (www.journalismnet.com)
- *Online Guide to Canadian Newspapers* (www.cna-acj.ca)
- *The Globe and Mail* (www.globeandmail.com)
- *Report on Business* (www.robmagazine.com)
- *Financial Post* (www.nationalpost.com/financialpost)
- *Fast Company* (www.fastcompany.com)
- *Ivey Business Journal Online* (www.iveybusinessjournal.com)

Tip: Full-text newspaper and magazine information databases with efficient search capabilities can often be accessed through your public library.

News Wire Services
- BusinessWire (www.businesswire.com)
- Canada NewsWire Ltd. (www.newswire.ca)
- PR Newswire (www.prnewswire.com)
- Reuters Online (www.reuters.com and www.reuters.ca)

Directories and Portals
These are access points for a large volume of pre-organized information.
- CEO Express (www.ceoexpress.com)—business portal for executives
- Dow Jones Web Links (www.dowjones.com/index_directory.htm)
- Maple Square: Canada's Internet Directory (www.maplesquare.com)
- Business.com—the business search engine (www.business.com)
- Canada Online (canadaonline.miningco.com)
- Canadiana—the Canadian resource page (www-2.cs.cmu.edu/Unofficial/Canadiana)

Tip: Industry Canada's business information web site, Strategis (www.strategis.ic.gc.ca), provides current information on specific industry sectors, export opportunities, company capabilities, international intelligence and business contacts, new technologies and processes, management experts, market services, government economic research and statistics, micro-economics and more. It's a researcher's gold mine!

Chapter 10

Write an Effective Résumé

*The quality of the result is proportionate
to the quality of the effort.*

Having a well-thought-out and carefully prepared résumé is essential for responding to interesting opportunities. A good résumé presents your experience and qualifications clearly and concisely to a potential employer, and helps to persuade them that you have unique value. The amount of planning, energy and strategic thinking you invest in developing your résumé is important to your ultimate success.

Before you begin your résumé, list and describe the skills you would like to use in your next employment opportunity, the kinds of roles you would find interesting and where you believe your talents could be well used. This might seem overwhelming if you skipped to this chapter without working on your career review or identifying your strategic advantage. Investing some time in those topics now would be wise if you have not already done so. However, if you know your key skills and where you're headed, carry on with writing your résumé.

Rule number one is to write it yourself! There are any number of services that will take this task off your hands, but crafting your résumé enables you to become totally comfortable with the points you want to discuss in your interviews and the ways in which you want to express them. Find someone to offer suggestions and reliable feedback, but make the content your own. You know yourself best and you will do the best job of reflecting and emphasizing the most important aspects of your background, achievements and employment interests.

Tip: One of the primary benefits of having a résumé is what you learn in the process of writing it. Spending time reviewing your career and developing your accomplishment statements are the best ways to put your experience at the top of your mind so that you can readily talk about your achievements, skills and strengths in an interview or networking situation.

There are many pitfalls in writing a résumé. Use the following guidelines to direct your approach to the process.

GUIDELINES FOR WRITING YOUR RÉSUMÉ

- Don't expect to be able to dash off your résumé in an hour or two. Putting together a good résumé takes time, often days. You want the quality of your résumé to be top-notch.
- If you have an old résumé, it is often a good idea to get a fresh start by beginning again. You can use your previous résumé as a reference.
- Create a résumé that truly reflects your expertise and strengths. The original version of your résumé may be sufficient to address a number of your targets (see Chapter 8) when accompanied by a well-written cover letter that focuses on specific market characteristics or position requirements.
- You may need to write different versions of your résumé, aimed at different targets. However, it is wise to minimize the number of résumés you have.
- More than roles and responsibilities, your résumé must talk about your accomplishments. Write about problems and issues you have addressed, actions you have taken and outcomes you have achieved.
- Quantify the results of your accomplishments wherever possible. A compelling case is created with data such as "achieved savings of $2 million annually" or "decreased staff turnover from 20% to 12%."
- Every statement that you make on your résumé must be factual and true. Your résumé forms part of the basis for a legal agreement and a good-faith relationship with your employer. If false representations are made, the consequences could be very embarrassing and costly to your career.
- Employers might be looking through hundreds of résumés for each of their advertised or posted positions. Yours must spark interest quickly. Your key skills, experience and style must come through in a clear and concise way.
- Limit the length of your résumé to two pages, three at the most. In a few employment sectors such as IT, science, medicine or university teaching, longer and more detailed résumés are expected. If you have written articles, had works published, completed significant transactions or made professional presentations, list these on a separate page.
- Appearance is important. Pay attention to the format and layout along with spelling and grammar. Use high-quality paper and a laser-quality printer.
- Don't be fooled into thinking that good appearance will make up for poor content.
- Proofread your résumé carefully and ask at least two other people to proofread it for you.
- Remember that your résumé is not your most important marketing tool—you are! Your résumé will help you get an interview and provide documentation to support what you say in the interview, but hiring decisions are based on personal interactions and the chemistry established between you and the people you meet.

As you begin to write, there are several formatting decisions that need to be made. The first involves the arrangement of your data, and the second, font and spacing. The best advice is to keep it simple.

Format the Résumé

Chronological Format

The chronological résumé is the accepted standard for organizing your information. This format describes your work experience in reverse chronological order, with the most recent job listed first. It emphasizes the names of employers, dates, job titles and primary responsibilities along with your key accomplishments. It displays your employment history sequentially and, where you have a record of increasing responsibilities and promotions with no major employment gaps, this is clearly an advantage.

Executive search and human resources professionals have a strong preference for chronological résumés. They are used to reading them, and they can find what they're looking for fairly quickly.

Functional/Chronological Format

An alternative to the chronological format is a combination functional/chronological résumé, which is organized according to the key areas of your work experience (also called "functional activities"). The chronological section of this combination format either precedes or follows the functional section and outlines the traditional information, including names of employers, dates, titles and additional information. It should be no more than one page. Résumé Sample #3 at the end of this chapter illustrates this format.

The functional/chronological résumé enables you to bring out the underlying themes running through your various positions and experiences, which can be particularly advantageous when some of your key accomplishments occurred several years in the past. By using this format you can also establish the transferability of your skills and accomplishments, which can be a real asset when you're planning to change career paths. Due to their nonlinear format, gaps in your experience may not be as apparent. This is one reason they are less favoured by human resources professionals.

Tip: An exclusively functional format is not recommended. This type may include the names of employers but gives no dates. It merely outlines experience by functional area. A functional résumé that contains no chronological data gives the impression that you have something to hide.

Other details to consider include font, spacing and layout. Simplicity in these areas is more conducive to scanning and emailing. An 11- or 12-point type using either the Times New Roman or Arial font is recommended. Margins should be no less than 3/4 of an inch at the left and right, and no less than 1 inch at the top and bottom. The choice of layout is somewhat restricted by the need to put a lot of information in a small space. The creative use of columns and bullet points can make information stand out but reduces the amount of space you have for content. Leave as much white space as possible and take care to be consistent. This includes text fonts, heading fonts, underlining, bolding, spacing between lines, paragraphs and sections. Use white or off-white paper.

The samples in this chapter illustrate various formatting options.

An Outline of the Résumé

The Heading

Use one of the samples as a template for formatting the heading, and begin with your name, address and contact information. Use the familiar form of your name, and drop the middle initial unless you use it regularly. Include relevant degrees or professional designations after your name, but don't overdo it. You want to be perceived as qualified and competent, not a braggart.

Make sure that your email is reliable and that you are comfortable using your software. By including an email address on your résumé, you are committing to checking for messages regularly. If your email is likely to be intercepted by your administrative assistant at work or your teenager at home, you might decide to get another email address and use it exclusively for your job search.

The profile statement follows the heading. However, since it summarizes the information contained in the résumé, it's best to write it last. Directions for writing the profile statement are given later in this chapter.

Career History and Accomplishments

The body of your résumé contains a review of your employment history. The primary objective of this section is to convey substantive evidence of your abilities and talents. A second objective is to demonstrate your level of expertise and achievement in the various functional areas that are relevant to your profession.

Tip: Information that dates back more than about 10–12 years won't capture much attention. If you have significant accomplishments that you want to highlight from earlier years, consider using the combination functional/chronological format.

There are many options for the title of this section. They include professional experience, business background, career highlights, background and achievements, selected accomplishments, etc. The choice is yours. Create an outline by listing all past employers, position titles and dates in reverse chronological order. Use copies of previous job descriptions and performance appraisals for reference.

Return to your career review and consider the accomplishments that you identified there. Sit back and reflect on each period of your career and identify what gave you the greatest sense of pride. Be sure to think about the challenging times when you learned a lot or were stretched to do more than you thought you could. Try to come up with at least 12 to 15 career accomplishments or highlights, and five that are recent.

In the body of the résumé, include these career highlights in the form of accomplishment statements, which are concise descriptions of a specific situation or challenge. They describe your actions and results, and are far more interesting to read than simple descriptions of duties and responsibilities. Accomplishment statements make your skills and interests come alive for the reader by creating a verbal picture of you doing the work that you are good at doing.

It's tempting to transfer phrases from a job description to your résumé, but try to resist doing this. The contrast between accomplishment statements and standard job description jargon is striking. For example:

• Responsible for business development and customer service in the Lower Mainland.

becomes:

• Recognized the need for a more focused approach to attracting new business through a revised customer referral program. Worked with a team of five retail managers and developed the *Convenience Plus Program* to promote a full range of products and services. Achieved a 15% increase in sales in the Lower Mainland territory within the first six months.

This second version tells the reader much more about what you can do than the first statement.

To write accomplishment statements use the Situation—Action—Result formula (see Chapter 4):

• Describe the **Situation** or context of the work including the obstacles, problems or challenges you faced.
• Detail the **Actions** you took or directed others to take.
• Highlight and quantify the **Results** of your actions.

Begin each accomplishment statement with an appropriate verb (consult "Inventory of Verbs" that follows, to generate ideas). Tell your story in a few short, declarative sentences. Use the past tense and a newspaper reporting style of writing. Do not use the word "I." Add depth and detail to each accomplishment statement by quantifying wherever possible. Note size, volumes, percentages, dollar values and timelines. This allows your reader to gain an understanding of the level of responsibility you've achieved. When unsure of an exact number, use qualifying words such as:

approaching	less than
approximately	over
in excess of	ranging from ___ to ___

You do not need to claim all the glory in your accomplishment statements. Where appropriate, use phrases such as:

assisted with	participated in
contributed to	shared in the success of
in support of	worked with ___ to

Prospective employers want to know that you can produce results. The implication is that if you have done it once, you can do it again. Describe and quantify the results of your efforts by including statements such as:

achieved sales targets

avoided a potential problem

avoided potential losses

boosted staff morale

contributed to team effectiveness

created client awareness

created positive public relations

decreased staff costs

delivered on time

delivered under budget

developed new markets

eliminated capital costs

formed a strategic alliance

generated new business

generated savings of $__

identified new market opportunities

improved a reporting process

improved accuracy

improved client relations

improved customer service

improved product knowledge

improved product performance

improved profit margins by __%

improved recovery rate

improved retention

improved service delivery

increased customer satisfaction

increased/improved efficiency

increased market share

increased sales by __%

increased shareholder value

leveraged existing resources

met an urgent/demanding deadline

met company goals

organized better procedures

preserved a competitive edge

provided a tax advantage

provided more accurate information

reduced costs

reduced customer complaints

reduced downtime

reduced errors

reduced inventories

reduced processing time

reduced turnaround time

reduced turnover

resolved problems

secured government support

streamlined administration

streamlined operations

turned around a difficult situation

won an award for

Once you have written your accomplishment statements, decide which ones best support your intended career direction. Within the relevant position, put them first. Include accomplishment statements to cover every functional area in which you were involved and the full range of responsibilities you carried. Review your analysis of your strategic advantage (Chapter 5) and be sure that your accomplishment statements exemplify it.

There is no other element of a person's résumé that will have as high an impact on job search success as the *identification of key accomplishments*. It is crucial for you to put a great deal of thought and effort into this component of your résumé.

Tip: Do not overcrowd your résumé. Cramming too much on two pages, or expanding the résumé to four or five pages, will not necessarily impress the reader. Dense and lengthy résumés will not be read in detail.

An Inventory of Verbs

Achieving results
accelerated
accomplished
achieved
acquired
advanced
authorized
boosted
built
captured
delivered
drove
established
exceeded
expanded
improved
increased
introduced
launched
met
outperformed
overcame
pioneered
procured
produced
reduced
re-engineered
repositioned
resolved
restored
restructured
safeguarded
secured
solidified
solved
streamlined
sustained
systematized
surpassed
transformed

unified
united
won

Managing
analyzed
assigned
attained
capitalized
chaired
coached
consolidated
contracted
coordinated
delegated
developed
directed
enlisted
evaluated
executed
generated
guided
improved
inspired
led
managed
mentored
mobilized
motivated
normalized
officiated
orchestrated
organized
oriented
outsourced
oversaw
planned
prioritized
produced
recommended

recruited
rejuvenated
reviewed
scheduled
selected
set goals
solved
strengthened
supervised
trained

Selling
booked
campaigned
closed
cold-called
convinced
cross-sold
developed
explained
gained
generated
increased
influenced
launched
marketed
merchandized
met targets
negotiated
persuaded
proposed
positioned
sold
targeted
up-sold

Creating
changed
created
customized

designed
developed
directed
energized
envisioned
established
fashioned
founded
generated
illustrated
initiated
instituted
integrated
introduced
invented
originated
personalized
rebuilt
redesigned
reorganized
replaced
revamped
revitalized
shaped
structured

Communicating
addressed
advised
advocated
arbitrated
authored
briefed
clarified
collaborated
communicated
confirmed
corresponded
critiqued
crystalized

defused
developed
directed
drafted
edited
educated
formulated
influenced
informed
interpreted
interviewed
investigated
judged
lectured
listened
mediated
moderated
negotiated
oriented
persuaded
presented
promoted
proved
publicized
qualified
questioned
realized
recognized
recommended
reconciled
reinforced
related
relayed
represented
responded
resolved
spoke
transcribed
translated

verbalized
wrote

Performing tasks
adapted
administered
allocated
analyzed
applied
appraised
arranged
audited
balanced
budgeted
calculated
catalogued
charted
classified
collected
compiled
computed
developed
dispatched
documented
executed
finalized
forecast
generated
implemented
inspected
maintained
manufactured
modified
monitored
operated
organized
perfected
performed
planned

prepared
processed
produced
programmed
projected
reconciled
recorded
regulated
retrieved
reviewed
scheduled
screened
served
specified
structured
validated
verified
worked with

Teaching
adapted
advised
clarified
coached
communicated
developed
educated
enabled
encouraged
evaluated
explained
facilitated
guided
informed
instructed
led
stimulated
taught
trained

Serving customers
followed up
handled
listened
merchandized
met
processed
promoted
resolved
responded
satisfied
serviced

Researching
collected
investigated
located
mapped out
master-minded
networked
observed
piloted
pinpointed
predicted
rated
recorded
retrieved
reviewed
simplified
summarized
surveyed
systematized
tabulated
tested
translated
understood
verified

Tip: Be ruthless in your editing. Clear, concise copy is not easy to write. Eliminate repetitious words and phrases and look for ideas that can be combined.

Additional Information

At the end of your résumé, list other relevant information. This includes the following categories:

Education:

List the degrees or diplomas you hold and the name of each institution. Dates are optional. Their inclusion is a matter of choice, depending upon your willingness to disclose your age. If you have not yet completed the course, use the term "in progress" or "currently enrolled."

Languages:

Use "fluent in," "conversational" or "written and spoken" to describe your level of expertise in other languages.

Professional Development:

Indicate the name of the course provider, title of the course and date completed. Include any in-house courses provided by former employers that are relevant to your future direction. Don't go overboard and list every training session you have ever attended.

Professional Affiliations/Memberships:

Use the full name of the organization to which you belong; then note its abbreviated form if appropriate. Indicate any offices you have held. If you have taken a key role in events or conventions hosted by your organization, note them as well.

Community Involvement:

Include any volunteer work or fund-raising activities in which you have participated in the last few years. Make special note of positions you have held.

Computer Skills:

List only the programs and languages that are integral to your professional work. Unless there is a specific reason for doing so, you need not list standard software packages like Word or Excel.

Awards:

Awards show that you have been recognized for excellence. They are an important addition to your résumé. Include both professional and volunteer awards, and the reasons they were given.

Publications:

Publications include any articles, columns or books you have authored, you have co-authored or to which you have contributed.

Interests:

Including interests is optional, especially at more senior levels. If you include them, list hobbies, physical activities, outdoor activities, intellectual pursuits, unique interests and pastimes. These will identify you as a well-rounded person who manages stress and leads a balanced, active life. Interviewers may also refer to your interests at the beginning of your meeting as a way of breaking the ice and putting you both at ease.

Profile Statement

The last piece of your résumé to be created, and perhaps the most important, is the profile statement. As an advertising and positioning statement, your profile should immediately grab the reader's attention by summarizing the skill sets and themes found in the body of your résumé. Ideally, it should define what differentiates you and state your strategic advantage. It is as unique as your thumbprint and should be an accurate overview of your abilities, experience and personal style. Give it some marketing sizzle to make it compelling.

The terms "profile statement" and "objective statement" are sometimes used synonymously. However, an objective statement usually describes the job title or role being sought. In years past it was common practice to have an objective statement at the beginning of the résumé. For most people, an objective statement would be either so vague as to be meaningless or so specific that it would limit the range of possible employment options.

Tip: In addition to profiles, career or job objectives are customary for IT and technical positions.

Since your profile statement is a summary, writing it will likely be more challenging than writing your accomplishment statements. Take your time and get it right. Employers tend to read this section first, and a well-written profile statement can make a strong impression. Despite the time and effort required, many people find that completing this section of the résumé crystallizes their thinking, raises their confidence and convinces them of their marketability.

Tip: Your profile statement makes claims about you and what you can contribute to an organization. Your accomplishment statements provide the proof.

Your profile statement lets the reader know the professional category in which you place yourself. Are you a human resources professional or a labour relations specialist? Are you a project manager or a business developer? This choice is very important because it either limits or expands the number of different roles for which you might be considered.

The profile statement should also give the reader a clear picture of:
- the industries in which you have experience
- how long you have been working (optional)
- the level of seniority you have attained
- your key strengths or skills
- some features of your interpersonal style

Here's an example:

A senior manager with expertise in applying leading-edge technologies to common business problems. Experienced in leading cross-functional project teams with the mandate to increase operational efficiency and /or reduce costs in a variety of areas, including internal audit, quality assurance and operations. Excellent credentials and 25 years' experience in financial services and manufacturing organizations. Able to motivate diverse specialists to contribute to a team effort in a collaborative and proactive working environment.

Use the following template to create a first draft of your profile.

A (adjective, e.g., results-oriented, focused) **title or professional category** (descriptive title for your professional area, e.g., lawyer, marketing manager, financial services executive, senior manager) with over (total number) **years' experience in** (type of work, e.g., financial analysis, recruiting or managing operations) **within the** (be specific, e.g., financial services) **industry. Key strength**s include (name three, e.g., cost reduction, developing new business and building teams). **Committed to** (comment on management, interpersonal or leadership style).

If your title or professional category seems misleading or inadequate for your purpose, substitute a more generic self-descriptor such as:

business leader	innovator	project manager
change agent	manager	risk-taker
communicator	motivator	self-starter
contributor	negotiator	specialist
executive	organizer	strategist
expert	planner	team builder
generalist	problem-solver	team leader
implementer	professional	troubleshooter

Additional ways to lead into strengths include:

able to	demonstrates	readily undertakes
adept in	emphasizes	skilled in
brings a _____ approach to	excellent knowledge of	solid grasp of
can be counted on to	excels in	takes pride in
capable of	experienced in	thrives on
combines (this) with (that)	expertise in	track record of
committed to	focused on	understands the value of
creates value by	proven ability to	willing to

You must be comfortable with every word and phrase in your profile statement. Ensure that your accomplishment statements substantiate it, and be prepared with an experiential story to illustrate every point.

Tip: Test your profile statement by sharing it verbally with someone who knows you and your industry. It should be a clear and appropriate description of you.

---

eRésumés and Other Technologies

When you apply for advertised positions, you will forward your résumé to prospective employers online or by email more often than not. There is protocol to follow regarding the format of your résumé. If you are an Internet neophyte, or have used it only for email messaging, don't panic. There are many excellent resources that explain everything you need to know in order to create eRésumés, including exactly how to use your computer technology. Thankfully, they are written for the layperson.

Tip: For detailed, step-by-step instructions on formatting and dispatching your eRésumé see *The Riley Guide* www.rileyguide.com, and go to the section entitled, "Preparing Your Résumé for the Internet and Posting It Online." The book *eResumes,* by Susan Britton Whitcomb and Pat Kendall (McGraw-Hill), is also an excellent, comprehensive resource.

The term "eRésumé" is used broadly to describe a number of Internet-ready variations of a résumé created in MS Word or WordPerfect. You do not need new or different content for your eRésumé. Your original word-processed document can easily be formatted for dispatching online.

The simplest form of eRésumé is an ASCII (pronounced "ask-ee") version. It is impervious to computer viruses and compatible with the retrieval, search and filtering technology used by many hiring organizations, search firms and Internet job boards. It is the most commonly requested eRésumé. More advanced forms of eRésumés include personal web pages and web portfolios. Their usefulness for an employment search is discussed in Chapter 11.

eRésumé Format Options

There are a variety of formatting options for eRésumés. The simplest and most common option, and one that you have probably already used with ease, is to send your original word-processed document as an email attachment. This is acceptable only for sending your résumé to a specific person who is expecting to receive it as a result of a conversation or meeting with you. With the thousands of résumés currently blasting through cyberspace and the high risk of attachments containing a virus, an MS Word or Word-Perfect document attached to an email and arriving unannounced is likely to be deleted immediately.

Recruiters and Internet job boards usually specify exactly how they want to receive your information. You must follow their instructions precisely. Failure to do so will cause your résumé to be discarded before it is ever seen by a human being. The various formats are described on the chart that follows.

eRésumé Formatting Options

Type	File Extension	Description, Advantages and Limitations	Uses
ASCII text résumé emailable pasteable plain-text simple-text text-only unformatted	.txt (text)	• Résumé stripped of all formatting enhancements that can be pasted into email messages or Internet eforms. • Compatible with all computer systems. • Cannot contain computer viruses. • Easily searched. • Adheres to the recipient's default font settings, making it impossible to control the appearance once it leaves your computer. • Loses original line breaks when recipient forwards it to others. • Plain in appearance.	• Responding to a posting that states, "email your résumé." • When online, the "apply here" button opens your email program. • When using eforms on a job board, or at an agency's or organization's web site. • To solve system incompatibility.
Rich text résumé formatted printer-friendly rich text format RTF	.rtf	• Résumé in ASCII format but retaining formatting such as bold, italic, indentations and other style elements. • Sent as an attachment to an email message • Compatible with all computer systems. • Somewhat impervious to viruses. Safer than a Word or WordPerfect document as an attachment. • Looks better than the ASCII format.	• When a recruiter requests a formatted document. • To solve system incompatibility. • Only when an attachment is acceptable.
PDF résumé Acrobat file digital imaging printable format printer-friendly	.pdf	• Résumé, saved in PDF (Adobe Corporation's Portable Document Format) that can be posted on the Web, emailed, viewed, printed, searched or saved. • Compatible with all computer systems. • Retains résumé formatting and looks good. • Free of viruses. • You must have PDF Writer software. • Recipient must download Adobe Acrobat Reader or PDF viewer.	• Only when recipient specifies that PDF is acceptable. • In combination with an emailable résumé. • As an optional download on your web site.

Type	File Extension	Description, Advantages and Limitations	Uses
Posted Résumé My online résumé Internet résumé Web-based résumé	Site specific record site	• Résumé submitted to a web site, usually an Internet job board or an organization's web site. • Typically password-protected access, using technology that allows you to make changes, copy, paste, email to employers and delete. • Usually text-only, resulting in poor appearance. • Often forces you to use a rigid, pre-defined format. • Raises privacy issues. Your confidentiality may be compromised and your information might stay online indefinitely. Cases of identity theft have occurred.	• On Internet job boards. • On some organization's web sites and on some search firm databases. • Niche sites such as industry specific or professional association web sites.
Web Résumé or Portfolio HTML résumé Internet résumé Online résumé Résumé web page	.html .htm .xml or .xhtml	• Résumé that resides on the Internet with its own URL (web address). Accessible 24/7 to anyone online. • A web portfolio is comparable to a small commercial web site. Can have virtually unlimited content. Should have clear navigation tools. • Both can contain hyperlinks, graphics, audio files, video clips and photos. • Can include other formats of your information as down-loadable options (e.g., PDF, MS Word). • Compatible with all computer systems. • Free of viruses. • Privacy is foregone unless you protect the site with a password. • Requires knowledge of web site development soft-ware—you may have to hire a developer.	• Essential for small businesses and some consultants and contract workers. • When delivery of non-print information is needed, e.g., audio and video material. • When projecting a cyber-savvy image is crucial.

Scannable Résumés

eRésumés are automatically scannable. Special instructions for producing a scannable résumé refer only to word-processed documents sent by either surface mail or fax that are then scanned manually or automatically by OCR (optical character recognition) technology into an applicant-tracking system.

A scannable résumé must be very plain. It can have bold text and bulleted lists, but those are the only style and design elements. Depending upon the sophistication of the recipient's technology, everything from columns to vertical lines, slashes, hollow bullets, italicized text, ampersands, percent signs and foreign characters may not translate properly. If you send your résumé to an employer who might want to scan it, do not staple or fold the résumé.

Tip: Unless otherwise specified, always choose email over fax or snail mail when responding to a posting or sending your résumé to a search firm or placement agency. Saving an email document is far easier for recruiters than using OCR technology to record information.

CD-ROM and Video Résumés

CD burners have become standard equipment in many households and offices. It's easy to save your résumé on to a CD in any size or shape if you have the technology. Although the standard round disk is the most commonly used, you can also produce CDs to resemble business cards, insert them into clear holders and hand them out as you would a regular card. A lot of information can be stored on them, including graphics and photos. CDs are more costly than paper and rely upon the recipient having sufficient interest in you to put the disk into their computer, open it and read it.

Tip: A survey of Canada's top executive search firms indicates a strong preference for eRésumés over CD-ROMs. The extra steps required to open and read the information on a CD are a nuisance and the large volume of extra information that is often included merely slows the process.

Video résumés have recently surfaced as an option. These are used when an employer hires a third party host to film job candidates as they respond, unrehearsed to a series of basic selection questions. The short video is reviewed by the employer who has the benefit of listening to the candidate's responses and assessing such non-verbal clues as appearance, body language and tone of voice prior to making the decision to conduct a face-to-face interview.

CD-ROM and video résumés are still novelties, and it will be interesting to see if they move further into the mainstream.

Keywords

Keywords are a crucial component of your résumé, regardless of its format. If you have developed a convincing, accomplishment-focused résumé, all the keywords pertinent to you and your targets should already be included. Nevertheless, it's a good idea to double-check.

GUIDELINES FOR CAPTURING KEYWORDS

- Include words that are specific to your industry or profession. Use functional descriptors and industry jargon, e.g., risk management, arbitration, procurement, market cap, ROI, JIT and MRPS.
- Use the language of managerial and leadership excellence. If your organization has a list of competencies or stated leadership principles borrow from it. Go back to Chapter 5 and ensure that the words you used to describe your style, skills and knowledge appear in your résumé.
- List your academic and professional credentials with your name at the top of your résumé.
- If you are bilingual or multi-lingual, name the specific languages.
- Scour job advertisements for keywords as you prepare your application. Revise your résumé to include any missing words that apply to you and repeat some of them in your cover letter.

Although computer searches will pick up keywords anywhere in a document, it's wise to position the most important ones front and centre, or otherwise make them stand out in every way possible. See Résumé Sample #4 for an example.

Your Next Move

Once you're satisfied with your résumé, ask people in your support network or your references to review it and offer feedback. Use good judgment when deciding whether to take or dismiss suggestions. Don't let résumé revisions become the focus of your efforts.

A training and development specialist made the mistake of asking 15 people to review his résumé. While spending weeks trying to incorporate all the feedback, he was so engrossed that he stopped check-ing job postings. He almost missed an excellent opportunity while he was revising his résumé.

That's it. With a final edit and careful proofreading of your résumé, you're ready to move on. If you've followed the steps, you should have an outstanding marketing document that describes in concise and compelling terms where you've been and where you want to go.

One of the real advantages of working through the résumé process is the tremendous psychological boost it gives as you begin to see, often for the first time, how much you have achieved and how marketable you are. Use this positive energy and enthusiasm to introduce your résumé to the outside world. Remember that however excellent your résumé may be, it still must get to the right people!

Sample Résumés

Key points to note as you read Sample Résumé #1

President, CEO and Director
Food Service Industry, Franchising
- The profile is concise and powerful. The reader is immediately aware of the writer's level of leadership, area of expertise and scope of experience.
- This is a chronological résumé with an effective variation on the standard format. The selected achievements are arranged in an order that exactly matches the chronological data. Brand names are mentioned in all but one point. Even though the dates of the achievements are not specifically indicated, it is immediately obvious to the reader which achievement relates to each position.
- At the CEO level, results tell the story. A one-page résumé is sufficient to relate the necessary information.
- The Situation—Action—Result formula is implicit in each achievement statement. The use of percentages implies the "before" picture.
- The style and formatting of this résumé is uncluttered. The use of bold type makes the impressive results stand out.
- Information on education and interests is omitted. With a track record such as this, added information is unnecessary.

Sample Résumé #1

NAME

Address
City, Province
Canada Postal Code

Bus.: 000-000-0000
Cell: 000-000-0000
Email: mail@isp.ca

Leader, Persuader, Entrepreneur
A pioneer of franchising in Canada

Reputation for:
Successful multi-store business acquisition and restructuring
Excellent knowledge of Canadian, U.S. and international fast food industry

FAST CHINESE FOOD, LTD.   1998–2004
    President, Chief Executive Officer and Director
OFFICE SERVICES UNLIMITED, INC.   1996–1998
    President, Chief Executive Officer and Director
SUB SENSATIONS—MEGA FOOD SERVICES, INC.   1992–1996
    President, Chief Executive Officer and Director
BIG BURGER CORPORATION, LTD.   1989–1992
    Executive Vice President, Chief Operating Officer and Director
MAJOR MULTINATIONAL, INC.   1986–1989
    Vice President and General Manager, Franchising Division
STURDY TAIL PIPES, INC.   1975–1986
    Vice President, General Manager and Director

SELECTED ACHIEVEMENTS

Repositioned, energized and expanded FAST CHINESE FOOD restaurant chain in Canada (590 stores, $150 million sales, 5000 employees)—**increased sales 72% and doubled the net profit**

Developed and expanded an international chain of service centres for small business owners through franchising—**realized increase in sales of 60% and net profit of 400%**

Expanded Sub Sensations restaurant chain in Canada (65 to 110 units) and in the United States (50 to 142 units). Opened 6 units in the UK—i**ncreased sales 517% in the United States and 70% in Canada over four years**

Led the merger of four fast food outlet companies with distinct corporate cultures into Sub Sensations— international chain with $75 million in sales and 185 units

Launched Big Burger franchises in Taiwan, South Korea, Hong Kong, Philippines, Singapore, Malaysia, Thailand and Australia and opened units in the United Kingdom

Pioneered Sturdy Tail Pipes in Canada at 20 years of age. Led development from one storefront operation to 910 nationally with $48 million in sales by 1986

DIRECTORSHIPS

Relevant Industry Association	Canadian Franchise Association
Refrigerated Hauling, Inc.	Children's Charity
Fancy Fries Corporation, London, England	Jones International Limited, Hong Kong

Key points to note as you read Sample Résumé #2

Executive Vice President and COO
Hospitality Sector, Travel and Tourism Industry

- The profile lets the reader know in a few words the level of seniority, breadth of experience and leadership qualities of the writer. The marks of an extensive and distinguished career are unmistakable. The claims made in the profile are substantiated by achievements in the body of the résumé.
- A role description is given immediately below the title, "Executive Vice President and Chief Operating Officer." It is more of a high-level strategy statement, which is very effective for understanding the organization and the seniority of the role.
- This is a chronological résumé.
- Achievements are at the strategic level. Accountability for results is a consistent theme and is often expressed in percentage increases, demonstrating a focus on the bottom line.
- The third bullet point confirms the extent of this individual's team-building activities.
- Because Eastview Management Ltd. would not be widely recognized, a one-line description of the company's business is included. The role description gives the well-known names of the hotels.
- Although it is clear that this individual joined Eastview Management Ltd. in 1975, specific dates are not mentioned for roles prior to 1984. The writer has not disclosed his age, but rather given the reader evidence of longstanding international experience.
- Roles prior to 1984 have been summarized by title and location on the last page of the résumé. This indicates that the individual's early experience was progressive in nature and laid a foundation for the senior roles that followed.

Sample Résumé #2

Name, *C.H.A.*

Address • **City, Province** • **Postal Code** • **Res:** • **Email:**

Profile

An international hotelier with extensive experience in operations and strategic development at the executive level of two of the largest, global, multi-brand hotel chains. Achieved excellent results in portfolio growth, successfully developed strong brand relationships, substantially improved financial performance and selected and built outstanding management teams. An industry-wide reputation for integrity in all dealings with investment groups, developers, owners, franchise companies and joint venture partners. Mentor to many successful hospitality professionals.

Professional Experience

International Hospitality Inc.   *1997–2004*

Executive Vice President & Chief Operating Officer

Directed the development and growth of the company's portfolio of full-service hotels under a variety of brands. $300 million revenue, 8,000 rooms, 3,500 staff.

- Negotiated conditions of the franchise agreement and management contract for the company's first Luxury Hotel in Canada. Produced higher margin incremental income with no equity investment by the company and laid the foundation for future development of Luxury brands in Canada.
- Established and nurtured a long-standing relationship with Distinguished Hotels & Resorts (Travel Suites, Royal Hotel and Squire Lodge) to secure the most attractive franchise terms and conditions.
- Raised the calibre of management at all levels throughout the organization. Selected and led a corporate executive team which included Senior Vice President, Operations; seven Regional Vice Presidents; Vice President, Sales & Marketing; Vice President, Food & Beverage and Directors of Revenue Management, Human Resources and Property Management. Recruited the best-in-class hotel managers throughout the portfolio.
- Developed a comprehensive five-year capital plan for all hotels to include pay-back analysis on all major capital investments, achieving aggressive corporate ROI targets.
- Directed sales and marketing activities of a multi-brand portfolio to achieve a 10% premium in market share over the competitive set.
- Increased division occupancy, Average Rate and RevPar by over 14% in both 1997 and 1998 contributing to gross operating margins and profits being consistently ahead of national industry averages over the past four years.
- Established Regional Operations Vice Presidential role to more effectively support and coach hotel managers in every region of the company's operations.
- Initiated audits to benchmark every hotel's Food & Beverage operation and identify opportunities for increasing revenues and profitability.

Eastview Management Ltd.   *1975–1997*

North America's largest independently owned, multi-brand hotel management company.

Senior Vice President & Chief Operating Officer   *1984–1997*

Directed the development of the company's portfolio of 56 hotels under a wide variety of brands in Canada, the U.S. and Europe, including Caribbean Inns, Vacation Hotels, Guest Plaza, Les Suites du Roi and Independents and Resort Hotel Properties.

- Directed an executive team, which included four Regional Vice Presidents, three Regional Sales Coordinators, two National Directors of Sales & Marketing, two Directors of Design Services, a Director of Purchasing and two Food and Beverage Coordinators.

- Developed new contracts for the company, negotiated terms and conditions of all hotel management contracts and nurtured ongoing relationships with all owners, securing 27 new hotels contracts in a 10-year period.
- Developed relationships within the financial and real estate communities and acted as liaison for international hotel chains, potential joint venture partners, hotel owners and investment groups, creating an extensive network of investors for future growth opportunities.
- Formulated, developed and executed the operational decentralization of the company from a central hierarchy to four self-sufficient regions.
- Introduced effective ongoing strategic planning to cover all aspects of the company's growth including a national purchasing program, an awards recognition program and the introduction of executive floors in all full-service hotels.
- Introduced Food and Beverage troubleshooters to develop new concepts and turn around low-margin operations.
- Developed Regional Sales Coordinators' roles to maximize sales potential on a regional basis.

Additional Senior Roles Included:

Vice President, Western/Pacific Region, Eastview Management Ltd.
General Manager, Relaxation Inns Central Region
General Manager, Paradise Hotel, Hong Kong
General Manager, Revita House, Madrid
Senior Restaurant Manager, Premier Resort Corporation of California
Restaurant Manager, Stone Manor, London

Business/Community Affiliations

Director of a Number of Committees and Organizations Including:
Tourism Industry Association of North America.
Committee Member of International Association Luxury Hotels.
King Suites Promotion Committee.
California Hotel Association.
Eastern Seaboard Hotel Association.
Tourism Association of England.
Hotel Association of Canada.

Education

Catering Training College, Zurich, Switzerland.
Management Development Program, Paris, France.
C.H.A. (Certified Hotel Administrator), Educational Institute, AH & MA.
Luxury Hotel University Management Training Programs.

Interests

Skiing, Cycling, Cooking, Gardening, Live Theatre, Tennis, Travel.

Key points to note as you read Sample Résumé #3

Vice President
Retail and Franchise Store Operations
- To illustrate capability in a breadth of functional areas, this individual chose the combination chronological/functional format.
- Notice the short description of the two companies. If your organization is not well known, or you want to emphasize the size and nature of the business, this is a good way to do it. Using bold type for the description keeps it as part of the heading.
- The description of your mandate or role provides a context for the reader. Results stand out against the backdrop of the mandate. In this example, the seniority of the role is explained simply by the statement, "Reported to the Chairman."
- If you are including one, the mandate or role description should be placed directly under your position title.
- Using bold type for the headings of the functions within each role allows the reader to scan for information and grasp the key components of each position quickly.
- This résumé is packed with quantified results. The writer's ability to deliver is unmistakable.
- At the end of the background section of the résumé, using the phrase "Roles Prior to 1986 …" alludes to greater experience without extending the résumé or giving away the writer's age. In such a statement, you can mention position title, companies, functional areas or any combination thereof.

Sample Résumé #3

NAME
Address
City, Province Postal Code
Office: **Cell:**   **Email:**

PROFILE

A high-energy, strategic and bottom-line-oriented retail professional. Over 20 years of hands-on executive experience in store operations, merchandising, marketing and human resources. A motivator and team builder working with corporate and franchise managers and staff to develop and implement innovative programs for customer service and in-store merchandising.

BUSINESS BACKGROUND

WELL-KNOWN KIOSK CO.   **2001–2004**

The licensed operator for Sightlines Inc. managing 80 optical stores across Canada: 52 corporate stores and 28 franchised.

VICE PRESIDENT

Mandate: Plan and direct a reversed strategy for marketing and operations to return ABC Company to profitability within 18 months. Established proper staffing and service levels to ensure all stores achieved sales potential. Reported to the Chairman.

OPERATIONS

- Established sales, gross margin and salary budgets. Labour costs were reduced by 14.2%, sales increased 7.1% and gross margin increased 2.4%. Within first year of mandate, store contribution results were positive despite a significant loss in the previous year. Second year store contribution results increased 34.7%.
- Reduced lab "redos" by 25% and instituted quality control procedures at the lab by conducting random daily eyewear checks before shipping.
- Renegotiated terms and costs with most suppliers, resulting in a cost reduction of 25%, increase in terms to 180 days and new consignment deals. Cash flow improved as a result of honouring payment terms and commitments.
- Developed a Store Manager's Operations Manual and In-Store Checklist to increase efficiency and streamline administration.

PROGRAM INITIATIVES

- Set up a proto-store to test-market new strategies and serve as a merchandising model in order to standardize the planning process for promotional events and future expansion.
- Instituted a Store-Front Marketing Program to book doctor's appointments. Launched supplier Trunk Shows that doubled sales on event days. Used Board Management System strategy to merchandise the mix of frames on the boards.
- Began Monthly Payment Plan and Deferred Payment Plan for customers, in coordination with Sightlines Inc.'s legal, advertising, and credit departments.
- Developed marketing and operations strategies to introduce Laser Vision Correction procedures.

DECORAMA LTD.   1979–2001

A national paint, wallcovering and hard window coverings specialty Canadian retail chain of 145 stores: 85 Corporate and 60 Franchised. Divisions included paint manufacturing facilities, wallpaper wholesale and warehouse. Sales in excess of $100 million with over 1,000 employees.

VICE PRESIDENT, OPERATIONS   1993–2001

Mandate: Manage all retail operations, providing leadership and direction to two Senior Regional District Managers, six District Managers, Manager Human Resources, Public Relations Consultant, Trainers, Payroll Department, six Shop-at-Home Sales Reps., and approximately 1,000 employees (including franchise stores). Reported to the Chairman.

PROFITABILITY AND COST CONTROL

- Identified the need to reduce out-of-stocks at store level to prevent lost sales. Created auto shipment program based on store volume, to anticipate peak sales periods and reduce out-of-stocks.
- Conducted research analysis and determined that average sales increased 10% when franchise stores were converted to corporate stores. Recommended and managed the conversion of 30 stores.
- Identified the need to create payroll system to control costs of $6 million. Developed methodology to measure stores with similar sales volume. Wage costs reduced 14%.

MERCHANDISING / MARKETING

- Identified need to improve general appearance of stores, store layout and merchandising practices. Executed monthly sales promotions and improved consistency and accuracy of information given to stores by District Managers. Sales increased 10%.
- Introduced merchandising programs, weekly manager meetings and bi-monthly videos to review current promotions: created standard displays, implemented checklists for customer service, general housekeeping, and merchandising, and developed photo albums for District Managers to take to stores.
- Developed long-term strategy to restructure and decentralize store operations to create an environment for stores to operate more independently, reducing the number of District Managers. Established communications systems such as photos and inter-store communiqués to ensure maintenance of a consistent information flow.
- Developed optical scanning technology that simplified the wallcovering selection process.

INFORMATION SYSTEMS

- Developed long-term information systems strategy that introduced a point-of-sale system to implement the following:
  - improve customer service by allowing inventory checking between stores
  - create an imaging system to restructure Head Office purchasing function
  - identify top sellers in each department
  - balance inventories within corporate stores

CUSTOMER SERVICE

- Identified the need to improve staff productivity and service levels. Instituted a "Customer Approach in 10 Seconds or Less" program.
- Identified with managers and staff, policies and procedures that were not customer friendly. Empowered staff to deal with customer complaints directly. Established new refund policy, instituted Head Office Policy of "Customer Complaints Handled Within 24 Hours."

TRAINING AND DEVELOPMENT

- Created a more effective method of training sales staff, store managers and owners, focusing on product knowledge, selling skills, and decorating advice to ensure that customers were always treated in a knowledgeable and courteous manner.
- Designed a Manager Trainee Training Program and produced educational videotapes to provide ongoing staff development.

VICE-PRESIDENT, HUMAN RESOURCES   1986–1993

- Implemented and directed all personnel policies including compensation and benefit programs for stores, office, distribution centre and manufacturing division.
- Directed labour relations for 450 warehouse and factory personnel. Negotiated contracts and planned and coordinated strike coverage to prevent business interruption.

ROLES PRIOR TO 1986 INCLUDED DIRECTOR OF HUMAN RESOURCES, MANAGER OF HUMAN RESOURCES AND TRAINING COORDINATOR.

EDUCATION

University of Alberta, B.A., Economics & Sociology

INTERESTS

Basketball, karate, tennis, classical music

Key points to note as you read Sample Résumé #4

Human Resources Manager

Health Care

- This résumé uses keywords at the beginning of each accomplishment statement to accommodate computer scanning technology and to draw attention to each area of expertise. This will also facilitate quick and efficient reading.
- While some of the keywords are used only once (e.g., communications and department administration), many repeat (e.g., training and development, and HRIS).
- Human resources accomplishments are typically difficult to quantify since they often deal with processes. In this case, including the number of staff and association members gives the reader an idea of the size of the organization.
- This individual has modified the chronological format by grouping her two terms at the Provincial Dental Association together. She clearly indicates that the position at the Regional Health Centre was a contract for leave coverage.
- Although the résumé covers only the last 11 years, it provides sufficient information for the reader. The most recent role is designated as 1998 to present, which indicates that this individual is still working with the Association.
- When horizontal lines are used in the body of the document, make sure they are light in appearance, so they do not form barriers to the eye as the document is read.

Tip: Clarity is a primary objective in résumé writing. There are no rules or conventions for many of the special circumstances you might need to describe such as taking a contract position or returning to work for a previous employer. Use your best judgment to make the facts clear.

Sample Résumé #4

NAME, CHRP

Tel: Address
Email: City, Province   Postal Code

PROFILE

Human resources professional with extensive experience in every aspect of human resources management gained through managerial and project management roles. Sees human resources management as an integral part of business planning, quality service delivery, information systems and budgeting. Strong HRIS experience. An energetic program creator, implementer and developer with proven skills in employee relations and communications.

EMPLOYMENT

PROVINCIAL DENTAL ASSOCIATION   **1996–1997 and 1998 to present**
Project Coordinator, Human Resources and Project Coordinator, Pensions, 1995 to present
Project Coordinator, Membership, 1996–1997

Business Review: Documented all HR processes and implemented new administrative procedures where necessary. Initiated and implemented documentation to simplify and control communication of employee information between department managers, HR and payroll. Provided software skills required to automate compensation reports and documented resulting process. Revisited pay equity procedures, documented processing and updated staff.

Training and Development: Developed and delivered 18 hours of process improvement training to human resources staff, a 4-hour customer service small group training session for 60 employees, and a customer focus strategy for the organization.

Pension Administration: Improved the administration of a 200-member defined benefit pension plan and ensured legislative compliance. Prepared a detailed description of the administrative system as part of a Request for Proposal for new software and programming. Created pension statement program using LOTUS.

HRIS: Reviewed HR Department's information needs and facilitated an organization-wide working group of managers and executives to identify their information needs. Prepared a Request for Information that was distributed to vendors and am currently coordinating the HRIS selection process.

Communications: Coordinated 8 staff members to answer a "Referendum Ballot Replacement Hot Line," and handled over 1,000 calls in 3 days from dentists who had not received their ballot numbers through a mass mailing. Enhanced membership process while providing frontline communications to over 300 dentists with unusual circumstances. Proposed and designed a computer-based system to track communications with several thousand dentists.

REGIONAL HEALTH CENTRE   **1997–1998**
Human Resources Manager, Contract Position, incumbent on leave

Department Administration: Supervised an HR Assistant, responsible for salary and benefit administration, meeting coordination, and workplace health and safety. Coordinated a French-language services audit and ensured that legislative requirements were met. Provided Chief Operating Officer with regular reports on the department budget, recruitment budget and employee hires, transfers, terminations and compensation changes.

Recruitment and Selection: Managed the budget and expanded recruitment process for specialized professionals and support employees.

Performance Management: Introduced the corporate office's performance management tool and process, ensuring it was successfully implemented. Advised management and employees on performance management concerns.

Job Design: Participated in a task group to re-engineer clerical support and led sessions to facilitate the change process.

Training and Development: Initiated and chaired a New Employee Orientation Committee to enhance existing one-day program. Coordinated the orientation day and developed and delivered HR's portion. Presented a video on changing work environments and facilitated an accompanying discussion period.

HRIS: Implemented a LOTUS-based HR information system and initiated the HR application of payroll report writer and register. Initiated and chaired an interdisciplinary work group responsible for the identification of staffing information needs and the drafting of a proposal for a computer system to meet those needs.

WELLNESS INSTITUTE   1994–1997
Staffing and Development Officer, Employment Equity Coordinator

Training and Development: Proposed, developed and administered a centralized staff development function, including policies, procedures, quality assurance and budget. Designed and delivered training on interviewing and selection, human rights, employment equity, zero-based budgeting and professional development. Chaired the Training Steering Committee, mandated to develop a training model. Initiated and facilitated a group process to improve newsletters. Participated in an ad hoc group to nurture the Institute's client satisfaction focus. Developed and delivered a client session on "Exploring Differences." Trained Conservation Authority's management on harassment in the workplace.

Business Review: Wrote and interpreted policy. Developed and introduced a workplace harassment policy, procedure and communication strategy used as a model by hospitals, the Human Rights Commission and the organization's lawyers.

Recruitment and Selection: Developed and implemented recruitment strategies including job descriptions, job postings, advertisements, résumé reviews, interview preparation, interviews and reference checks.

Performance Management: Oriented all employees to their role in performance management and assisted managers in the resolution of performance management issues.

Benefit Administration: Inducted all new employees into the benefit programs available to them. Assisted employees with the investigation of claims inquiries. Identified the need for and coordinated presentations by carriers at "Brown Bag Lunches."

Salary Administration: Utilized a job evaluation tool to assess job classification, and recommended appropriate new employee compensation levels. Communicated annual and incidental pay changes to payroll.

HRIS: Developed a basic HRIS with an employment equity module using dBase.

Employment Equity: Designed and implemented a communication strategy for employment equity initiatives including information sessions, staff orientation, newsletter articles and open houses. Designed and completed a workforce census with a 98% return rate. Recruited, oriented and chaired the Employment Equity Committee. Prepared timely proposals and administrative/financial reports as required by the hospital and the Hospital Association.

COMMUNITY PUBLIC HOSPITAL   1993–1994
Employment Equity Officer

Performance Management: Negotiated and coordinated "Performance Appraisal Tool Development" workshops delivered by an external consultant. Designed management and staff appraisal tools based on results of session.

Training and Development: Developed and conducted awareness sessions in response to employee needs. Topics included budgeting, payroll savings plans, career path options and employment equity awareness.

Job Design: Proposed and initiated the inclusion of physical demands analysis on all job descriptions.

Employment Equity: Developed and implemented initiatives focusing on women in the workplace. Designed a five-year strategy for the Employment Equity Committee. Ensured program costs remained within allocation. Prepared timely administrative and financial reports as required by the hospital and the Hospital Association.

EDUCATION

CERTIFICATE IN HUMAN RESOURCES MANAGEMENT   Human Resources Professionals
Association, 1999

MASTER'S OF BUSINESS ADMINISTRATION   Provincial University, 1993

BACHELOR OF ARTS   Provincial University II, 1992

Key points to note as you read Sample Résumé #5

Branch Manager

Retail and Commercial Banking

- This is a chronological résumé. The writer's background lends itself perfectly to this format because of the steady progression up the ladder of responsibility and accountability. The layout of the résumé allows the reader to clearly see the writer's progress.
- This layout has appeal because it uses plenty of white space. The trade-off is that less space is available for accomplishment statements. However, the writer has captured his background clearly and concisely. The reader sees the career highlights of a capable branch manager with a focus on business development.
- Look at the content of the résumé. The first bullet point is more of a role description than an accomplishment statement. This works in this layout where the use of italics or bold type might be confusing.
- The inclusion of quantified facts gives the reader an understanding of this individual's level of responsibility. His role revolved around the sales numbers, and without them, this résumé would be incomplete.
- Notice how the last bullet point on the first page refers to community involvement, reinforcing the claim in the profile statement. It's a good idea to place an important and convincing statement here. Readers who skim résumés will often read the last point on the page.
- The description of this individual's experience in his most recent role contains seven bullet points. The previous role is described with four; and the one previous to that, only three. This is an appropriate method of giving weight to more recent accomplishments, and it shows a progression of responsibility.
- This layout and the use of shading and columns will not scan well if older technology is being used. Also, there is a risk that the formatting will not transfer correctly through all email software. This individual should always include a plain text copy when submitting his résumé by email or to any organization that is likely to use scanning technology.

Sample Résumé #5

Name
Address   Telephone: (111) 222-3333
City, Province   Fax: (111) 222-4444
Postal Code   **email:** yourname@company.com

Profile   A dedicated and people-oriented financial services professional with extensive experience in meeting the specialized needs of agricultural and business clients. Expertise includes business development and sales management.

Committed to building outstanding customer relationships by understanding each client's financial requirements and providing customized solutions. Skilled in developing motivated teams, focused on delivering results. A proven self-starter who takes pride in creating a strong business presence through active involvement in the community.

Experience

ABC Bank   1981–2004

Branch Manager,
Town 1 & 2   1993–2004

- Managed a full-service branch and guided day-to-day operations with a staff of seven people in a community of 3,000 with a large rural base.
- Achieved 28% growth in market share over a five-year period for both personal and commercial/agri-business in both loans and deposits, through exceptional levels of customer service and judicious lending practices. This growth was achieved in spite of a recession.
- Assessed clients' requests for loans and analyzed financial information to ensure debt servicing and repayment ability. Recommended and guided the implementation of customized financial solutions to meet clients' needs.
- Managed a commercial credit portfolio of 125 borrowing relationships and 30 non-borrowing relationships. Individual client borrowing requirements ranged from $10,000 to $1.8 million.
- Introduced 80 clients to a new government initiative that provided agricultural subsidies to individuals and farm corporations to allow for continued viability during poor years. As a result, over $2 million in deposits were achieved within an 18-month period. At the time, this was the largest branch deposit volume for all the Bank's Ontario branches.
- Worked closely with Bank Mutual Funds Account Representative to provide brokerage services, investment advice and financial planning to novice

investors. Within an eight-month period, accumulated deposits in excess of $2.5 million dollars, 70% of which represented new business.
- Supported numerous local events and fundraising projects to enhance community relationships, including the solicitation of a $20,000 donation from a client to help establish Camp Wildflower for children.

Assistant Manager, Town 3   **1988–1993**
- Handled the renewal of credit lines for approximately 80 agricultural clients and acted as Account Manager for approximately 20 new borrowing relationships over a five-year period. Worked with each business proprietor to provide personalized banking services.
- Supervised the personal credit department and focused on providing excellent customer service to ensure volume growth.
- Handled day-to-day human resources issues for a staff of 10, and managed all marketing and sales initiatives for the retail business.
- Generated monthly reports for all functional areas, with a specific focus on sales. Met with Branch Manager on a regular basis to set monthly performance goals and review branch operations and performance.

Retail Loans Officer   **1983–1988**
- Perfected follow-up system with clients to ensure mortgage renewals were handled proactively. Achieved 100% retention in a six-month period.
- Generated growth in personal loans and mortgage portfolio from $20MM to $32MM by working closely with internal existing client base to develop referrals, and with external clients, including lawyers, mortgage brokers and real estate brokers to generate new business.
- Took over a portfolio of agricultural credits and increased the account base by 120% while continuing a primary focus on personal lending.

Manager-in-Training   **1981–1983**
- Recruited from university to join the Bank's structured two-year program.

Professional Development
Numerous internal training programs including:
- Management I, II and III
- Credit Analysis
- Mutual Funds
- RRSPs

Education
Bachelor of Commerce, Dalhousie University   **1977–1981**

Interests
Golf, baseball, community theatre, travel

Key points to note as you read Sample Résumé #6

Information Technology Executive
Financial Services

- This individual has successfully made the transition from long-term employee to independent consultant. His up-to-date résumé includes accomplishments from his consulting work.
- The emphasis is on the alignment of technology with strategic business goals. Quantified cost savings, meeting deadlines and increased productivity are also key deliverables at the executive level.
- Where results remain unproven, indicate projections as shown in the third bullet point.
- Timelines add impact to accomplishment statements. For instance, the phrases "had been cancelled two weeks prior to implementation" and "implementation over 18 to 24 months" demonstrate the urgency involved.
- Spell out acronyms and demystify jargon. For example, in the third bullet point "SWOT" is clarified. In the fourth bullet point "Public Key Infrastructure" is mentioned, using upper case first letters for emphasis, and in the next point, the acronym "PKI" is used. This is a subtle and effective way of ensuring the reader's understanding.
- Ongoing professional development shows a commitment to being on the leading edge. This IT professional has chosen management courses to enhance his leadership potential.
- Sample biographies, an executive summary of the résumé and a sample brochure for this IT executive are included in the next chapter.

Tip: If your targets entail looking for contract assignments, let your résumé form the core of your marketing materials. Once you've written the résumé, the other pieces flow with less difficulty. At the end of every contract, update your résumé and all your additional marketing materials.

Sample Résumé #6

NAME
ADDRESS
CITY, PROVINCE POSTAL CODE
TEL   EMAIL   WEB SITE

PROFILE

A visionary IT executive with proven expertise in aligning technical strategies to organizational goals. Applies intuitive and analytical skills to evolve programs of interrelated, realizable projects focused on the strategic vision. Successful in driving projects to implementation by building upon and extending existing foundations. Over 20 years' experience in financial services information technology software and hardware combined with extensive experience in project management of operational architectures for high availability, mission-critical systems.

PROFESSIONAL EXPERIENCE

John Smith, Principal
IT TECHNICAL AND STRATEGIC CONSULTING   2002–PRESENT

- Directed outsourcing of statement printing, selective insertion and mailing of customer statements. Project was planned and implemented to meet customer's schedule. Negotiated a competitive agreement with the preferred service provider valued at over $12 million.

- Resurrected a project to close a major data centre that had been cancelled 2 weeks prior to implementation. Working with the senior executive sponsor, and previous project participants from the involved companies, addressed the obstacles in the objectives, staffing, scope and schedule. As a result, the project was redefined and implemented on schedule and under budget.

- Contracted to translate a service organization's print business strategy and business improvement plans into a program of interrelated projects for implementation over 18 to 24 months. This program addressed three critical weaknesses—efficiency, service reputation and productivity as identified in the SWOT (Strength, Weakness, Opportunities and Threats) analysis. Cost savings will exceed $3 million annually.

TRADITIONAL BANK   1981–2002
VICE PRESIDENT, SECURITY RISK EVALUATIONS AND RESEARCH   2001–2002

- Led the team to design and implement hardware, software, secure network, operations, support and systems management for Public Key Infrastructure security used in online Internet banking and stock trading systems. The high-availability design allowed for hardware and software components to fail without any service interruption or on-site staff.

- Produced a technical strategy for security systems and secure networks using PKI. This foundation opened the secure and confidential delivery of services to customers through electronic channels and set up a virtual office for the Bank's global staff.

VICE-PRESIDENT, TELECOMMUNICATIONS AND TECHNICAL SERVICES   1999–2001

- Developed the vision for strategic computer hardware and software technology for core Bank systems. Provided framework for major migration to new software, database and hardware platforms required to support expanding business needs. The strategy concurrently addressed Y2K requirements and new functionality. Further objectives met included asset preservation, technology and operations support, capacity and performance and availability and scalability.

- Implemented tactical planning processes into Telecommunication and Technical Services to provide structure. This effectively focused the efforts of 270 staff members on pre-determined strategic goals. The resulting program of interrelated projects provided the clarity and knowledge to empower lower level decision-making. Results were higher availability and increased functional delivery.

- Refocused staff resources, creating a new support organization, without increasing the Department's $110-million budget. This provided hardware and software support for the Bank's centralized server complexes installed for data mining, Work Group support for global corporate bankers and commercial customer access to account information.

ASSISTANT GENERAL MANAGER, HOST PLANNING AND HARDWARE SERVICES   1994–1999

- Appointed a member of every Systems and Operations strategic architecture task force formed within the Bank over a 12-year period. Task forces included Operations Strategic Technical Plan, Efficiency and Effectiveness and the New Branch Platform Study. Contributed to the vision and technical knowledge regarding the hardware, software and database infrastructure that would facilitate the addition and extension of applications.
- Directed the project that integrated computer operations and technical support areas following the acquisition of Seaview Trust. The project exceeded expectations for transparency to the end users and compressed an 8-month schedule to 5 months. Savings were in excess of $8 million.
- Restored credibility to the forecasting, planning and control processes that provided the business justification to hardware, software and database assets acquisitions. The revamped methodologies introduced the concept of asset management to ensure that investments in infrastructure provided a business return to the Bank. Acceptance of the process by the Finance Department and CEO paved the way for major tape and print automation projects.
- Established closer relationships with vendors, specifically EMC, IBM, STK, Hitachi, Tandem and Amdahl, to understand their view of business drivers, and their future product directions. Advised and influenced vendors' development, sensitizing them to the needs of the Canadian banking system and Traditional Bank in particular. Scalability, high performance operability and cost effectiveness were critical as transactions migrated from paper to electronic formats.

ASSISTANT GENERAL MANAGER, SYSTEMS DEVELOPMENT RESEARCH   1989–1994

- Directed research into expert and knowledge-based systems, application development automation, and CASE (Computer Automated System Evaluation) systems. Result was the implementation of a $4-million investment in development automation and training. Accumulated annual increases in measured productivity ranging from 2 to 25 times the base.
- Led the design team of Bank and hardware and software vendors to solve the problem of the Bank's expanding network and database applications exceeding the technology's capabilities. The new design exploited the technology in an unprecedented manner. Project-managed a solution involving 7 related projects to upgrade server, host, database, telecommunication and application system software without loss of availability or stability to 1200 domestic branches.

ROLES PRIOR TO 1989 INCLUDED A NUMBER OF MANAGEMENT POSITIONS AT TRADITIONAL BANK AND TECHNICAL SPECIALIST ROLES AT ESTABLISHMENT BANK.

PROFESSIONAL DEVELOPMENT

Myers-Briggs Type Indicator, Qualification Complete
Professional Management Skills, Quality Management Group
Re-engineering, Seaforth and Company

EDUCATION AND PROFESSIONAL ASSOCIATIONS

Member, Canadian Information Processing Society, CIPS
University of Waterloo, Bachelor of Mathematics, Computer Science

Key points to note as you read Sample Résumé #7

Publishing Director
Non-Profit Sector

- This individual's duties remained substantially the same for over six years while her level of responsibility increased through challenging assignments. During this time, she held several titles concurrently. To explain these unusual circumstances, the writer has grouped the titles together and described her achievements using a functional résumé format.
- Although her achievements associated with the publication of the hymnal are quite noteworthy, they may not immediately be seen as highly transferable. For this reason, she has chosen to focus on her general publishing, management, creative direction and new media development achievements.
- A combination functional/chronological format has been chosen to highlight the transferability of skills.
- Keywords such as "electronic publishing," "new media," "CD-ROM" and "web site" are embedded in the résumé.
- Where an occupation or industry is changing rapidly due to technology, innovation or competition, it is important to note ongoing professional development. The breadth of this individual's exposure to the latest information on industry developments is truly impressive.
- This individual's association experience offers further evidence of her commitment to staying current and involved with industry issues and developments. She has included both past and present memberships to give the reader a picture of the breadth of participation. It is important to either include only current memberships or be clear that you have listed some from your past. Noting dates (e.g., "2001–Present" or "2001–2002") is a commonly used option.
- This résumé leaves an impression of an individual with multi-disciplinary publishing expertise and current skills in electronic media.

Tip: Mention on the first page the skills and functions that you most want to use in your next employment opportunity. Make sure that they stand out.

Sample Résumé #7

NAME

Address   **Res: No.**
City, Province   **Bus: No.**
Postal Code   **email:**

PROFILE

An innovative and energetic project manager with in-depth experience in planning, budgeting and team leadership gained in the non-profit sector. Skilled in print publication and resource development including multi-media and copyright experience. Takes pride in providing creative direction and out-of-the-box conceptual thinking. Enjoys complex, multi-faceted assignments where pulling together a collaborative pool of skills is essential. Fosters a lively and professional work environment that values commitment to excellence and innovation.

PROFESSIONAL BACKGROUND

PEOPLE'S PUBLISHING HOUSE (OPERATED BY DENOMINATIONAL CHURCH)

A denominational publisher, formerly Highline Press, which also includes a design and production service for all Church print, books and resources, and recently, electronic publishing.

DIRECTOR, DEPARTMENT OF PUBLISHING AND GRAPHICS	**2000 to 2004**
SENIOR MANAGER, DIVISION OF COMMUNICATION	**1994 to 2004**
DIRECTOR, PEOPLE'S PUBLISHING HOUSE	**2000 to 2004**

PUBLISHING AND MANAGEMENT

- Managed a full range of project-related tasks for the in-house creative and production department including research, setting priorities, planning the workflow, administration and evaluation.
- Repositioned front list of 12 titles annually for the professional and trade markets in North America in order to appeal to a wider audience, increase the sales of foreign rights and expand the export market.
- Led the acquisition and publishing process to acquire, produce and sell both front and back list books. Achieved net projected revenue of $177,000 per year. Supervised the Managing and Senior Editors, promotions staff and several freelancers.
- Managed a team of 11 staff members and additional freelance consultants according to project requirements, with budget implications over $2 million annually.
- Participated as one of four senior managers in a National Communication Division, which included policy setting, communication strategies, and budget development. Director on the National Executive Board.

CREATIVE DIRECTION AND NEW MEDIA DEVELOPMENT

- Developed first hymnal software CD-ROM with words and music, audio files, cross-referenced data, and personal tracking calendar. Conducted market research and handled development, production and clearance of digital rights. Revenues projected to exceed development and production costs within one year.
- Initiated concept and produced audio compact disk of spiritual music for the North American market, featuring several Canadian artists and well-known choirs.
- Created first Canadian denominational clip art software. Success of this project led to demand for a second volume the following year. Produced the first Church policy manual on disk.

- Worked on project teams with colleagues in television and video production, web site, retail sales, marketing, advertising and promotion.

Coypright Policies and Procedures

- Created copyright clearance procedures and contracts for over 2,000 individual works through 1,500 copyright holders world-wide for a new Hymn Book.
- Secured music licenses for two compact disks, and digital rights for music software product.
- Advised staff and volunteers regarding the seeking or giving of copyright permission for print, audio and electronic resources.
- Researched the creation of contracts for print and multi media through contact with copyright lawyers. Developed policies and guidelines to protect Church material both in print and on the web.

PROJECT MANAGER, SPECIAL ASSIGNMENTS   1989 to 2001

Mandate: To publish the All Seasons Hymn Book, which has subsequently sold over 280,000 copies, plus five ancillary editions and related products, which resulted in over $7 million in gross revenue.

- Designed and led full production, copyright and marketing strategy in order to produce a high quality product on time and budget, for a project with no precedent for production in Canada.
- Recognized the need for a complex information management system for all text and music entries in order to create 12 indexes, a permanent database, and royalty payment program. Directed a consultant in the creation of a customized software program to address these needs.
- Created and supervised production and design process including music engraving, art direction, print purchasing, scheduling and proofing.
- Developed marketing strategy, guided and advised on subsequent promotion and publicity.
- Coordinated development of ancillary editions and products: teaching CD, words-only and leather-bound editions, performance and history edition, and hymnal software.
- Oversaw ongoing sales, copyright issues, royalty payments, and spin-off products.
- Provided expertise and advice to two additional Canadian churches with regard to copyright and production issues for their hymn book projects.

NORTH AMERICAN CURRICULUM PUBLISHING

- Participated as one of 10 North American publishers on a Steering Committee for the development of a church school curriculum for all ages, with expected North American, first-year profits of $500,000.
- Seconded as Art Consultant for the project to advise on the creative and technical considerations for the five North American art directors.

Roles Prior to 1989 included Director of Department of Graphics and Print Production and Production Editor and Writer.

NATIONAL AND INTERNATIONAL COMMUNICATION EVENTS

- Planned and implemented major trade shows' display for book sales in New York and Toronto; book launches, signings, and event displays in Ottawa, Calgary, Kingston, Sudbury and Halifax.
- Led international launch of All Seasons Hymn Book for Hymn Society of Canada.
- Women in Communication, international event, Bangkok, Thailand.

PROFESSIONAL DEVELOPMENT AND EDUCATION

Specialized Courses: 2002–2004

- Web Publishing, Centennial College
- Essentials of Publishing Management, Simon Fraser University
- E-Commerce and the Law
- Digital Rights and Copyright Law

Additional Courses

- Copyright Law in Canada (Canadian Institute)
- School of Communication and Design, Ontario College of Art
- Publishing Management (Magazine Association of America, New York)
- Publishing Management, Production Control (Leading Seminars, Atlanta, Boston)
- How to Direct a Publishing House (Leading Seminars, San Diego)
- Management Workshop (Financial Times, Ottawa)
- Advertising and Design (New York)
- Direct mail, marketing and promotion for not-for-profit organization (Able Publishing, Chicago)
- Not-for-Profit Fund Raising (Canadian Centre for Philanthropy)

ASSOCIATION EXPERIENCE, Past and Present

Book Publishers Professional Association
Organization of Book Publishers of Ontario
Canadian Publishing Council—Trade Group
Church-Owned Publishers Association
Toronto Chapter, American Marketing Association

EDUCATION

McGill University
BA, English Specialist

University of Western Ontario
MA, School of Journalism

INTERESTS

Creative writing, watercolour painting, piano and gardening

Key points to note as you read Sample Résumé #8

Project Manager
Information Technology—Financial Services

- For IT résumés, the rules change. If the experience is relevant, the résumé may exceed the standard two or three pages.
- Career objectives are expected for IT résumés.
- The profile balances the technical content of the résumé by stressing customer service, management and teamwork skills, all of which are valued for progression to a leadership role.
- The summary of skills section uses a table format to list the individual's technical skills and organize them by type.
- The number of months of each assignment are noted for each position. IT employers want to know both how current and for what duration your experience with a particular technology is.
- This individual's accomplishments showcase a range of skills from troubleshooting and training to sales support and project leadership.
- In the education section, there is no attempt to hide the fact that the degree was not completed. Including your record of significant higher education is important even though you have chosen another route.

Tip: Do not be vague or misleading about education currently in progress or discontinued before the completion of the diploma or degree requirements. List all relevant education and use phrases such as "currently enrolled," "course completed" or "completed two years toward degree in."

Sample Résumé #8

NAME
ADDRESS, CITY, PROVINCE AND POSTAL CODE
RES: CELL:
eMAIL: WEB SITE:

OBJECTIVE

To contribute as a software engineer and project manager at a senior level.

PROFILE

An experienced, client-focused project leader, respected for delivering quality results on time and within budget. Manages and motivates people effectively, empowering individuals through positive reinforcement to be high-quality performers in demanding, multi-tasking environments. Recognized as a creative team player with unwavering commitment to quality and client satisfaction.

SUMMARY OF SKILLS

Management	Project leadership, performance management, hiring, retention, coaching, technology implementation, customer service and vendor management.
Technical	Client/Server application development. Asynchronous communication systems. User Interface design and usability.
Languages	SQL, C, C++, Visual Basic, Forth, Assembler, MagicPC
Databases	Sybase, MS Access, Btrieve, dBase III,
Development Tools	Microsoft Project, Office, Outlook, Word, Excel, Crystal Reports
Operating Systems	MS Windows NT 4.0, /95/3.x, MS-DOS
Networks	Windows NT 4.0, TCP/IP, Novell
Mini Systems	Tandem, Data General

CAREER HISTORY

Company 1   **1993–2004**
Project Leader—Client Access Systems   **Oct. 1998–Dec. 2004**
- Led a five-member team for support and integration of a vendor application for Trust and Securities clients. System was a successful amalgamation of both 16-bit and 32-bit products resulting in an application suitable for both WIN 95/98 and NT 4.0. Release featured several functional enhancements and was delivered two weeks ahead of schedule.

- Developed specifications for an enhanced client dial-up facility. Significant improvements made to speed of data transmission from Tandem hub to client workstation, thereby making the product viable for larger volume clients.
- Provided training, demonstrations and seminars for the support team on various product trouble-shooting techniques, to make the help desk and support areas more self-reliant.
- Provided technical support for product installation, help desk staff, and client training staff
- Performed analysis and code maintenance for PC-Investment Manager, an MS-DOS application, which was subsequently certified as Y2K ready. This allowed re-deployment of resources for the development of the NT replacement product.
- Developed application programs, Report Viewer, Automated Backup, Com. Stat using VB 5.0.

Senior Technical Analyst — Electronic Business Banking   May 1997–Dec. 2001
- Developed a Visual Basic client interface for Bank's 16-bit EBB communications platform.
- Created a broadcast message facility to relate important messages to the Bank clients, vis-à-vis daily data downloads.
- Converted a DOS data warehouse utility using an upgraded communication protocol. Application is certified as Y2K ready and will continue to be used into the next millennium
- Provided production support to the Bank's clients.

Technical Systems Analyst — Electronic Business Banking   Nov. 1993–May 1997
- Led development of PC Investment Manager, a DOS application written in MS C 6.0.
- Developed PC to PC file transmission utility for the EBB Umbrella.
- Converted PC Disbursement Auditor into a French-language version.

Company 2   **Feb. 1993–Nov. 1993**
Programmer
- Developed user interfaces for energy management and climate control systems using MS C 5.0
- Coded PLC communication components using FORTH and Motorola 6502 assembler.

Company 3   **June 1991–Feb. 1993**
Product Support Specialist/Software Engineer
- Provided product support for EASYL, pressure-sensitive digitizing tablet.
- Developed electronic correction algorithm-based on cubic spline quadrature, for digitizing tablet.
- Implemented algorithm in Motorola 68HC11 assembler.
- Developed graphical production control program for the EASYL using Lattice C for Amiga.

Company 4   **Feb. 1990–June 1991**
Technical Support Manager
- Supervised a two-person team, overcame linguistic and cultural barriers to deliver Japanese-engineered solutions to satisfy US client expectations.
- Designed and developed PC/AT user interfaces for a pressure-sensitive digitizing tablet and signature verification system using, GW-Basic, dBase III and Paradox.
- Provided sales support and after market support.

Company 5   **June 1986–Feb. 1990**
Programmer/Analyst
- Designed and developed general financial and accounting applications using Business Basic on a Data General Eclipse S140.
- Created Lotus 123 macros for accounting staff on IBM PC/XT.
- Developed a remote dial-in facility allowing a Commodore 64 to emulate a Dasher D-100 terminal, thereby introducing full-screen editing to Data General programmers for the first time.

EDUCATION

Bank's Internal Courses:
- Tandem Concepts and Facilities, Project Life Cycle, Managing Personal Growth and ABT Project Management.

Career Learning Centre   **1984–1985**
- Computer Programming and Systems Analysis (community college equivalent).
- Languages: COBOL, FORTRAN, RPG II, BASIC. Structured database design methodologies.

University   **1981–1984**
- Completed 11 courses in Applied Science and Electrical Engineering.

INTERESTS

Golf, tennis, music, guitar and MIDI equipment, Visual Basic computer graphics.

Chapter 11

Develop Additional
Marketing Materials

Packaging isn't everything; it's only 90% of everything.

Developing a set of additional marketing materials and stationery appropriate for your targets gives you an image that expresses confidence and professionalism. Your image will assist in conveying information to specific audiences. Your materials should have a consistent look, designed to leave a specific impression. The range of items that you might consider includes:

- Business cards
- Letterhead, either personal or using the name of your operating entity
- Envelopes and labels to match the letterhead
- Fax cover sheets
- Note cards for thank-you messages
- Memo paper for attaching an informal note to enclosures
- Biographies in various lengths
- Executive summary of your résumé
- CD-ROM containing your résumé
- Brochure describing your services
- Portfolio
- Web site

Refer to the chart on the next page to determine which materials you need.

What Do You Need?

For traditional job seekers, business cards are the only essential item. You might also consider printed letterhead, envelopes and note cards. However, these are not crucial, especially with the increasing use of email in the job market. Everything you need for job search correspondence can be produced with computer software and a laser-quality printer.

If you are looking for contract work or establishing a consulting practice, you need to have professional-looking stationery and, of course, business cards. In addition, you will need biographies and an executive summary of your résumé for inclusion in proposals. Both of these are concise summaries of your credentials, experience and capabilities. Biographies are done in a narrative style, while executive summaries retain the bullet-point style of your résumé but are condensed to a single page. Prospective clients often ask for a biography if they need approval to use your services or if they are subcontracting your services and want to present your credentials to their client. Contractors and consultants often have a brochure describing their product, service or area of expertise. Many have web sites. All of these options are described more fully, later in this chapter.

Type of Material	Job Search	Contract/Consulting Work	Small Business
Business cards	must have	must have	must have
Executive summary of résumé	helpful	must have	must have for professional services
CD-ROM containing résumé	optional	optional	optional
Letterhead	optional	optional	must have
Envelopes of quality and colour to match letterhead	must have	must have	must have
Printed envelopes or address labels	optional	optional	optional
Fax cover sheet	optional	must have	must have
Memo paper and note cards	optional	optional	optional
One-page biography	not necessary	must have	must have for professional services
Short versions of the biography	not necessary	must have	must have for professional services
Portfolio	optional	optional	optional
Web site	essential for some, not necessary for most	optional	must have

Tip: Note cards and memo paper are optional. If you are seeking contract work or consulting assignments, having them makes you look more established. However, if you don't have them, they won't be missed.

CD-ROMs containing your résumé, photo and other marketing pieces are becoming popular.

Portfolios are unique to those who create a product that is better appreciated visually. They are a necessity for some job seekers as well as some contractors and consultants. Samples of writing, web sites, art, training materials, drawings, design boards, print ads and the like should be collected and displayed online or in a binder of photographs or print materials.

For individuals launching a small business, the nature of the business and the marketing strategy will determine the need for materials. The range of possibilities is vast and more elaborate marketing and advertising plans will likely benefit from professional help. However, for all small businesses, standard stationery is a must and a brochure of some kind is probably also an essential item. The principals of a small business will need biographies if they are providing a professional service. Many small businesses develop a web site as part of their launch.

Tip: Use good judgment in deciding what additional marketing materials and stationery you need. Don't spend your time and money developing items unless they are necessary and will aid your efforts to communicate effectively with decision-makers.

Consider a Web Site

The value of having a web site varies dramatically from one industry to another. It also differs given various roles within industries. Your return on investment and the expectations and viewing habits of your target audience should be the deciding factors. You need to constantly stay in touch with your market niche and find out what your competition is doing. If your competitors have web sites, you need one. If your industry is becoming more focused on e-business, having a web site positions you appropriately. A hiring organization or prospective client that highly values the use of technology might make their decision in favour of the candidate or supplier with the more current web site, all other factors being equal.

For most traditional job seekers, designing a web site is not an efficient use of time and energy. That said, web sites are a must for many job seekers in new media companies. Web developers, multimedia designers and people working in CD-ROM production or interactive broadcasting will be expected to use their personal site as a means of demonstrating their ability to create one. Many IT, communications, public relations, advertising and marketing specialists need to establish their ability to manage the development of a web site, and as a venue for displaying their portfolio. Having your personal web site to support your job search is a growing trend.

> **Tip:** The design and programming of web sites has recently shifted from something that everyone was doing to a very sophisticated skill. If you create a web site, ensure that its quality is good.

Anyone considering an entrepreneurial venture—whether it's establishing a consulting practice or starting a small business—should have a web site. It's tantamount to being in the phone book, but the increasingly high expectation of quality and interactivity makes it difficult to know what level of investment makes sense. Seeking expert advice is a prudent step.

The varied need for web sites is exemplified by two next-door neighbours who operate sole proprietorships from their home offices. One of the entrepreneurs, a financial counsellor, has only her contact information and service offerings on a very simple web page that was created at minimal cost by her Internet Service Provider (ISP). She is convinced that her site is sufficient for her needs. If she were to provide a value-added service for her clients on her web site, she would need to develop inordinately expensive interactive models, which would undermine her commitment to personalized service. In contrast, her neighbour, a real estate agent, could not do his job without a top-quality web site. He needs real-time information and the best virtual touring capabilities to work effectively with his clients in the timing-sensitive environment of residential real estate. Fortunately, his wife has a talent for technology and is constantly upgrading her design and programming skills along with her husband's site.

Develop Your Materials at the Outset of Your Search

Developing your marketing materials before you actively approach the market is a good idea. It takes time to perfect these communication pieces, and thinking through the message you want to deliver often helps to clarify what product or service you are offering. Another advantage is that they will be in place as your marketing efforts gain momentum.

> **Tip:** Biographies are inevitably requested on a moment's notice. Having several versions prepared in advance is a good strategy. The different versions can be in varied lengths and emphasize specific strengths, skills or services offered.

The risk of developing your materials before you begin networking and marketing is that you may want to adjust your message in response to what your prospective clients tell you about their needs and interests. As you meet with people, you will pick up current jargon and develop ways of explaining your services that are generally understood in the industry.

The best strategy is to write the text of your materials before you tackle your market. Think about how you want the finished product to look in terms of style and image, but don't use high-quality, expensive production options at this point. Print your early materials on good paper using your computer and a laser-quality printer. After you have tested them with your support network and several prospective clients, and you are satisfied with the content, consider improving the quality of production. Upgrade only if you genuinely believe that a more expensive look will aid in delivering your message. Your materials must project an appropriate image, but most clients care more about the quality of your work than the amount of money you've spent on your marketing materials.

Tip: Spending time developing materials is often used as a convenient excuse for delaying marketing and networking efforts. You have to get out there and meet people. Your materials will always be secondary to your personal presentation!

Develop a Look

For a very small investment of time and money, you can create an image that expresses your style and appeals to your target audience. It can be understated and conservative or a bit more creative and flamboyant, simply through your choice of paper, colour, type, layout and other elements of design. Use the guidelines to help you with your choices.

GUIDELINES FOR DEVELOPING A LOOK

- Start by looking at other marketing materials. Collect samples of the items you need, and use the layout and design features that will work best for you. Business supply stores and print shops usually have catalogues of samples and off-the-shelf designs.
- Choose the colour and texture of your paper carefully. White is always safe because there's no problem finding matching envelopes, and it faxes and photocopies well. You can add colour with a logo or other printed design features. The texture and feel of your paper is important. High-quality paper is more expensive, but quality alone can do a lot to create an image.
- Different fonts create distinctive looks. Choose one you like and use it exclusively for letterhead design and headings. Vary your style by using (but not overusing) bold, italic and upper and lower case, but don't change the font. Be sure that your selection prints out crisp and clear in small type for labels and footers.
- Good font choices include Times, Tahoma, Arial, Helvetica and Garamond. Inexpensive software containing extra fonts is available at any business supply store.
- Your colour palette could contain any number of colours. Black or any single colour print is considered a one-colour job. Choosing more than one will increase your costs substantially. If you require fewer than 500 copies, most copy shops can produce materials digitally in full-colour fairly inexpensively. For larger quantities it is more economical to have your materials produced using four-colour (full-colour) digital offset printing.

- Use very dark colours for the text in titles, logos and headings, and only black for the main text to ensure readability.
- Ink colours look different when printed on coated, uncoated and coloured paper. Check a sample of your ink colour choices printed on your specific paper before ordering.
- Work with layout and type alignment. Specific elements such as name, date, page numbers, logo and slogan should always appear in the same place on the page. Be consistent with the use of centring and left and right justification.
- Be creative in your choice of other elements of style such as contrast, borders, lines, bullets and other symbols. Let the various design elements you choose become your signature by using them consistently.
- Having a logo is not necessary. If you decide to use one, have a graphic designer produce it. Homemade logos usually look unprofessional.
- Be sure that your design faxes and photocopies well.
- You might consider hiring a designer for assistance. Print shops and business supply stores usually provide referrals.
- If you use a designer, give them an idea of your style by showing them samples of letterhead, cards, brochures, ads or book covers that you like. Let them do their craft and then evaluate their concepts by asking yourself these questions:
  - Is the message clear to read?
  - Does it reflect my style and create the impression I want?
  - Is the content correct?
  - Is there anything else I should add before approving the design?
- Whether you work with a designer or deal directly with a print shop, you are always entitled to see a proof. Remember that you are still responsible for content, proofreading and final appearance. Colours on the proof will not match the final printed copy exactly unless you pay for a very expensive proof. Ask for a chip of the final printed colour along with the proof. Scrupulously check the layout, including a cut, trimmed and folded version of the final product if appropriate.

Tip: Never use design simply for the sake of design. Make sure that the message is clear, readable and worth reading. In the words of Shakespeare, use "more matter, less art."

There are a few essential pointers for each of the communication and marketing pieces that you decide to produce. Follow these guidelines to achieve results that will help your search.

GUIDELINES FOR DEVELOPING MARKETING MATERIALS

Business Cards

- Your name and contact information on your business card should match your résumé and other marketing materials. If your contact information might change during your job search, use a less expensive production option and plan to reprint your business cards.

- Consider giving yourself a title that explains something about your key skills or knowledge. For example, under your name you might print "E-commerce Solutions," "Human Resources Consultant," "Project Management" or "Strategic Sourcing." Don't force this. If it doesn't sound right, don't use it.
- Consider putting information, such as your mission statement or a concise outline of services offered, on the back of the card.
- Stick with the standard size. Choose a heavy stock, and use the design elements consistent with your other materials and stationery.
- Do not overcrowd either the front or back of the card.

Letterhead, Envelopes and Labels

- For most job seekers, creating personal letterhead with your computer software and using good-quality paper with a laser-quality printer is sufficient.
- White is the most cost-effective colour option. Matching envelopes are easier to find, and white faxes and photocopies well. If you choose a distinctive colour and quality of paper for printed letterhead, purchase an ample supply of the same paper for producing the subsequent pages. Matching envelopes are a must.
- Keep the design consistent on letterhead, envelopes and labels.
- Before having letterhead printed, check how it will look with an actual letter printed on it. Does it work well with the design elements and style you've chosen?
- Standard labels for letter-size envelopes are too small to accommodate a design along with the address. Use the standard stock from a business supply store or print the envelopes on your computer. Labels for larger envelopes can be printed with your design, making your larger packages consistent with your look.

Note Cards and Memo Paper

- Handwritten notes on printed cards do not suit everyone's style. However, if you are comfortable with this form of correspondence, it offers an excellent alternative when a standard business letter seems excessive. Because handwritten notes on printed cards are less common, they are noticed and appreciated.
- Blank, single-fold note cards are sufficient and can be purchased in any greeting card store. Similar cards with the words "Thank You" are also an appropriate choice.
- If you want to go one step up, have only your name and / or the name of your operating entity printed on the front of the note card. The design should be consistent with your look, and you'll need matching envelopes. You will probably need to find a specialty printer for this job. Give them samples of your other materials and check the proof carefully.
- Memo paper or pads have wider use. Your informal, handwritten note attached to an enclosure can sometimes replace a letter and gives the recipient a quick reminder of the point of interest you share.

- The print shop that produced your letterhead will recommend a size and produce these for you. Make them consistent with your other materials.
- When sending handwritten notes, write legibly and briefly.

Fax Cover Sheets

- Any standard template from your computer software is sufficient, but a personal fax sheet adds another professional touch.
- Use your letterhead design, but keep the sheet simple so that you don't irritate the recipient by using too much ink with graphics and shading.

Biographies

- Biographies in various lengths are frequently required of consultants, contractors and some small business owners, for inclusion in their own and their clients' proposals.
- Write a full biography that is 300 to 350 words in length, keeping it to one page. Write a shorter version that is approximately 100 words and a very brief one, less than 50 words. Writing the shorter version is usually more difficult, but when you need these biographies, you will appreciate having done them in advance, even if revisions are needed.
- Put your one-page biography on your letterhead, or design a special page with the same elements of style used on your letterhead.
- Write in the style of a press release. Use the third person, as if you were describing someone else.
- Include your professional credentials and a synopsis of your background as it relates to the work you are seeking. Don't go into detail, but do include accomplishments in a concise form. Name any well-known organizations where you've worked, and mention your titles. Include professional associations and designations that add to your credibility.
- One of the shorter versions might be appropriate as text for your brochure.
- Use the samples at the end of this chapter as a guide.

Executive Summary of Your Résumé

- Consultants, contractors, small business owners and even some traditional job seekers often find an executive summary of their résumé useful. It can be an introductory piece attached to a marketing letter, a document that you walk through in a meeting or an enclosure with a follow-up letter.
- Design it to match your original résumé, and keep it to one page.
- Begin with your profile statement; highlight only your key accomplishments and include employment information.
- Do not overcrowd the page.
- Do not use it when applying for an advertised position. To pass an initial screening process, your full history is essential.
- Use the sample at the end of this chapter as a guide.

Brochure Describing Your Services

- Design your brochure to highlight your key marketing points. Possible inclusions are the type of services you provide, benefits of the service, brief case studies, profiles of the principals, mission statement, quotes from clients and names of client organizations, with their permission.
- Contact information should stand out clearly.
- Writing your brochure can help clarify your thinking about exactly what service you are proposing to provide and what differentiates you from the competition.
- Draft the contents, design the layout and review it with your network. Consider having it printed professionally only after you have tested a prototype with a few clients.
- Keep the format clean, concise and consistent with your look. People are often tempted to be more creative with their brochure than they are with other marketing materials. Do not produce one that strays too far from your consistent image.
- A simple and effective format uses a standard letter-sized page with a landscape page setup, printed on both sides and folded in thirds. Print it on heavy paper or light cardboard.
- Use the sample three-fold brochure at the end of this chapter as a guide.

Portfolio

- Most individuals who have use for a portfolio are in a field or profession where the standards for these unique marketing materials are well known.
- Develop your portfolio with your audience in mind, and include a broad sampling of items. You might be surprised by what interests them.
- Know what's in it and have a plan for how you will walk your prospective client or employer through it.
- If presenting your portfolio requires the use of any technology such as PowerPoint, arrive at your destination early and make sure that everything works.
- Display every item in the best possible way. Don't take shortcuts in presentation.

Web Site

- Before starting your design or hiring a web developer, ask yourself who you want to attract to your site and what you intend to accomplish.
- Target your design to the viewing habits, needs and expectations of your audience.
- If you are not providing interactive functions or any information over and above that which is contained in your other marketing materials, your site should be fairly inexpensive.
- If you are in a technical role and need to illustrate your design or programming skills, develop your own site. If not, outsource it.
- There are many web site developers, including your ISP, who will be able to deliver a professional product at a reasonable price. Evaluate sites built by prospective suppliers before making your choice.
- Review web sites that are appealing, call the organization and ask them who developed it.
- If you prefer to do it yourself as a learning experience, community colleges offer courses on web site development. Do not let time spent on developing a web site deter you from networking and marketing.

- Avoid using graphics that frustrate the reader by taking too long to download or print.
- Be prepared to update the content on a regular basis.
- If you include your web site in any of your marketing materials, make sure the site is of high quality.

Tip: People don't have the time or inclination to read dense and lengthy materials. Say less rather than more, especially on your web site.

Sample Full Biography

John Smith

John Smith's career spans over 20 years of broad experience in aligning technical strategy to organizational goals for the Financial Services—Information Technology sector. He successfully applies outstanding analytical and intuitive skills to drive complex, interrelated projects to completion. With an excellent track record of leading specialized teams, his diverse expertise encompasses software, hardware, planning, project management and operational architectures for highly available and mission-critical systems. Committed to leveraging existing technology, John provides crucial insight to the business value of new technologies and their best utilization to maximize return on investment. He brings an ability to foster vendor relationships that moves outsourcing to the level of synergistic partnerships.

With the launch of his consulting practice, John has provided expertise in IT solutions to Integrated Processors, Regency Limited and Paradigm International. Assignments have included an 18-month program of interrelated projects to improve operational effectiveness through technological innovation with a projected cost savings of $3 million annually. He also salvaged a five-year outsourcing agreement valued at $12 million, and project-managed a data centre closure that was at risk of cancellation.

As a Vice President at Traditional Bank, John combined his accumulated knowledge gathered from previous positions in line management, technical, strategic and executive responsibilities to lead the technical strategic vision for the $100-million centralized processing initiative. He also directed the design and implementation team for a fault-tolerant and secure Internet server complex for online banking and brokerage. In earlier roles he directed the integration of computer operations and technical support following the acquisition of Major Trust Co., delivering over $9 million in savings and exceeding expectations for schedule and transparency to end users.

John's quick grasp of an organization's priorities and challenges and his ability to negotiate, mentor and lead with finesse, have made him an ideal choice to work with internal teams, vendors and senior executives in pursuit of key deliverables.

8910 Main Street, Toronto, Ontario M1X X1X

Bus: 416-555-1212   Fax: 416-555-1212   email: jsmith@isp.ca

Sample Abbreviated Biographies

John Smith, IT Technical and Strategic Consulting

With over 20 years' experience in aligning technical strategy to organizational goals, John's expertise encompasses software, hardware, planning, project management and operational architecture for highly available and mission-critical systems in the financial services sector. John is committed to leveraging existing technology and analyzing the business value of new technology to maximize ROI.

Consulting assignments with three major financial services companies have included a program of interrelated projects to improve operational effectiveness, delivering savings of $3 million annually; the successful management of an at-risk outsourcing project worth $12 million; and the refocusing of a faltering data centre closure. As a VP at Traditional Bank, John led a $100-million centralized processing initiative, implemented a secure Internet server for online services and led the technical integration of Major Trust Co.

John Smith: Visionary IT executive with over 20 years' experience in management and technical roles in financial services. Working with high availability and mission-critical systems focuses on strategic alignment of technology to organizational goals by implementing major initiatives including centralized processing, secure electronic banking solutions and acquisition integrations. Expert in leveraging existing technology and maximizing ROI from new technologies.

Sample Executive Summary of the Résumé

John Smith

8910 Main Street

Toronto, ON M1X X1X

Business: (416) 555-1212   Fax: (416) 555-1212   email: jsmith@isp.ca

A visionary IT executive with over 20 years' experience in aligning technical strategies to organizational goals in the financial services sector. Expertise encompasses software, hardware, planning, project management and operational architectures for high availability, mission-critical systems. Employs excellent intuitive and analytical skills to drive programs of interrelated, realizable projects to completion. Committed to building upon and extending existing foundations while bringing insight to assessing the business value of new technologies in order to maximize return on investment.

CAREER ACHIEVEMENTS

- Developed the technical strategic vision for a $100-million centralized processing system and led the implementation team.
- Developed the plan for centralized support, systems management and operation of an advanced 1,200 branch client server banking platform.
- Directed the design and implementation of a fault-tolerant unattended operation for a secure Internet server complex that provided public key encryption for online banking and brokerage. Achieved 100% availability.
- Led the tactical planning team to re-evaluate effectiveness of line functions that resulted in 10% reassignment of staff to support new services.
- Contributed to executive task forces to set out strategies for systems management in change control, performance and capacity.
- Handled project management of data centre relocations, technology support integration, complex technology upgrades and automation.
- Forged strong vendor relationships for effective acquisitions and influenced vendor development directions to support the technical vision.
- Refocused and restructured the implementation of a faltering project to relocate the print, insertion, cheque and operations units to two new sites.
- Project managed a five-year outsourcing agreement valued at $12 million.
- Led design team of service-based organization to produce an 18-month program of interrelated projects to improve business operations with an estimated cost savings of $3 million annually.

CAREER PATH

John Smith, IT Technical & Strategic Consulting	2000–Present
Traditional Bank, Head Office	1978–2000
VP, Security Risk Evaluations & Research	1998–2000
VP, Telecommunications & Technical Services	1995–1998
AGM, Host Planning & Hardware Services	1990–1995
AGM, Systems Development Research	1986–1990
Prior to 1986, progressive management positions with Traditional Bank.	

Sample Brochure

A professional-looking, three-fold brochure printed on both sides of a standard, letter-size page is easily produced using your computer software.

When folded for presentation or mailing, the contact information should be displayed clearly. Including a photograph is optional, but doing so adds a personal touch to the image and makes you look more established.

Pay attention to the order in which the reader will see your information. As the text unfolds, literally, a logical thought progression should roll out.

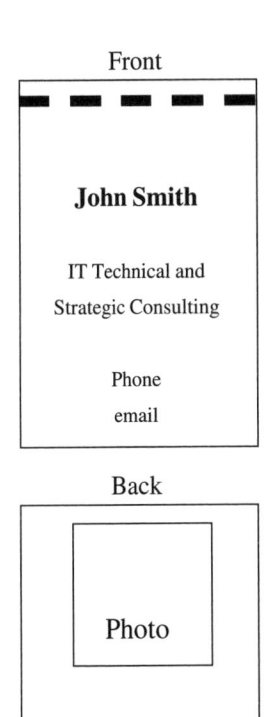

Front

John Smith

IT Technical and
Strategic Consulting

Phone
email

Back

Photo

Address:

Phone:
Fax:

The following two pages show the layout of the brochure as it would come off your printer. Reproduce it two-sided and fold neatly.

PROFILE

IT EXECUTIVE EXPERIENCED IN ALIGNING TECHNICAL STRATEGY TO ORGANIZATIONAL GOALS. APPLIES EXCELLENT INTUITIVE AND ANALYTICAL SKILLS TO CREATE PROGRAMS OF INTERRELATED, REALIZABLE PROJECTS FOCUSED ON THE STRATEGIC VISION.

SUCCESSFUL IN DRIVING TO IMPLEMENTATION PROJECTS THAT BUILD UPON AND EXTEND EXISTING FOUNDATIONS IN TECHNOLOGY AND ORGANIZATIONAL STRUCTURE TO REALIZE BUSINESS SOLUTIONS.

JOHN HAS BROAD EXPERTISE IN SOFTWARE, HARDWARE AND PLANNING, WITH EXTENSIVE EXPERIENCE IN PROJECT MANAGEMENT AND OPERATIONAL ARCHITECTURES FOR HIGH AVAILABILITY, MISSION-CRITICAL SYSTEMS.

Photo

Business: (416) 555-1 212
Fax: (416) 555-1212
email: jsmith@isp.ca

Address: 8910 Main Street
Toronto, ON M1X 1X1

JOHN SMITH

IT Technical and
Strategic Consulting

Business: (416) 555-1212
jsmith@isp.ca

BACKGROUND

John Smith's career spans over 20 years in the Financial Services Information Technology sector, advancing to executive responsibility for the support, architectures and strategies for operating software, databases and national networks of a $250-billion Canadian bank.

John's broad experience encompasses:

- applying emerging technologies for business benefit
- management of operational support for mission-critical systems
- strategic planning for transaction delivery systems
- organization integration of IT
- project management of complex initiatives

Recent research has involved:

- ☐ development productivity
- ☐ secure networks
- ☐ public key cryptography
- ☐ secure electronic transactions (SET)
- ☐ advanced systems management

SERVICES OFFERED

☑ Development of technical strategies for centralized systems supporting business directions.

☑ Articulating strategic directions for IT systems management and operation.

☑ Directing the planning, organization and implementation of highly complex technical projects.

☑ IT program development of interrelated initiatives to support business and IT strategies.

☑ Leadership in developing technical operational architectures and designs for mission-critical systems.

☑ Development and direction of projects to integrate IT operations, data centres and support organizations, following mergers and acquisitions.

☑ Outsourcing projects and development of the service management relationship processes.

GUIDING PRINCIPLES

Information Technology strategy serves the purpose of providing a business with a vision of how technology assets will support the corporate goals.

Information Technology strategy supports business solutions by enabling sound investments in technology assets that provide full value for their expected economic life.

Information Technology strategy is successful when it leverages the skills of the organization to manage, operate and support the delivery of the business function.

Availability and extensiveness of technologies are becoming critical success factors for businesses in achieving their financial and corporate goals. These vital systems require architectures, robust designs and skilled support as components of any strategy.

Chapter 12

Interview for Success

It is not always the most qualified person who gets the job;
it's the one who does the best job in the interview.

Everything you have done to this point in the career transition process is going to be put to the test during interviews. Preparing thoroughly for interviews affords you the opportunity to see if the way you describe yourself and your accomplishments substantiates your targets. It also gives you a check-point to test whether you are headed for an opportunity that fits your ideal. Once prepared, you can go into any interview, confidently expecting it to be the culmination of all your efforts.

When you have been selected for an interview, be assured that the information in your cover letter and résumé met the hiring organization's preliminary skills and experience requirements. As you enter the interview process, the audience is on your side. The interviewer is hoping that you will be the right candidate for the position so that they can successfully conclude their search and bring a qualified and well-suited person on board. The interviewer's goal will be to verify that your qualifications and experience meet the hiring specifications, and that your style, personality and other attributes will be a fit with the chemistry and culture of the organization.

Interviewing is a two-way street. While the interviewer is judging your suitability, you will be evaluating the position, the organization and the people. As you move through the interview process, you need to ascertain whether or not the content of the job meets your criteria. Both the position and the organization must also meet *your* needs and expectations regarding values, interests and career goals.

Preparation for the Interview

It's no longer enough to dress well, arrive on time and answer questions spontaneously. Today, you must understand the process and anticipate the interviewer's objectives and questions. You need to plan and practise your responses. This can present a challenge if you're out of practice. Many people haven't been interviewed for a job outside their organization for years. Even if you have changed jobs within your organization, those interviews are often merely friendly formalities.

Be cautious of being overly confident if you are experienced at interviewing others. Switching to the other side of the table requires a different mindset. There are numerous styles and approaches to interviewing, and you need to be flexible, attentive and prepared. Questions that you would never think of asking might be posed, and an unfamiliar format might be used. Don't let false confidence lead to a lack of preparation and a less-than-excellent performance.

The prerequisites for doing well in interviews include knowing your strategic advantage, having clear criteria for your ideal job, preparing an accomplishment-focused résumé and doing thorough research. If you have given any of this short shrift, go back and work on them now. If you have done your homework so far, you're ready to prepare your verbal presentation.

The Five Sound Bites

An excellent way to prepare for interviews is to create and practise a five-part script that answers the questions most frequently asked of job seekers. The five sound bites can be delivered in one piece, but more likely, you will take them apart and use them as stand-alone pieces when needed. By preparing and practicing your sound bites as a cohesive script, you create a mental checklist of the key points you want to cover whenever you have a chance to talk about your career plans. In addition to interviews, these five sound bites will be useful for networking meetings and informal conversations. The sound bites include:

• **Capsule Profile**	30 seconds
• **Key Strengths**	15–30 seconds
• **Career Review with Accomplishments**	5–7 minutes
• **Leaving Story**	30 seconds–1 minute
• **What Now?**	1–2 minutes

Capsule Profile

This is the conversational version of the profile statement you wrote for your résumé. It includes your most recent position title, plus a very brief explanation if your title would be misleading or confusing without it. The capsule profile also states your number of years' cumulative experience, the types of industries where you have worked and, if well known, the names of specific companies. It concisely describes your functional areas, level of seniority and depth and breadth of experience. Round it out with a statement of your uniqueness if that fits naturally here.

The capsule profile should be developed verbally. Do not write it out first! Try different ways of phrasing it, and keep working on it out loud until the words flow naturally. Then write down what you've said: sentence fragments, vernacular, pauses and all. Rehearse frequently without looking at your notes. This sound bite should be practised frequently so that it is virtually committed to memory.

Tip: To prepare the next four sound bites, jot down only the key points. Do not write them out in full and try to deliver them from memory. That will make you sound stilted and ill at ease. Remember the outline of each sound bite and rely on verbal practice to increase your comfort level. You will find patterns of speech and phrasing that are natural and easy for you.

Key Strengths

Name three or four of your most significant strengths in concise, bullet-point form. Open with a phrase such as, "My key strengths include …" or "I excel at …". Use single words or very short phrases to fill in the blanks (e.g., "listening and understanding my client's needs, problem solving and cross-functional team leadership"). Do not give details, explanations or substantiation of any kind. You are going for impact here, and supporting examples will follow in the career review bite.

If you did not offer a statement of uniqueness in the capsule profile, do so here. Highlight in one brief sentence how your particular combination of strengths, skills and experience work together to deliver value. This is your strategic advantage.

Tip: When you use the "key strengths" sound bite out of the context of the full presentation, offer brief supporting examples at the same time.

The capsule profile and the summary of key strengths need to be delivered together and should take no more than one minute in total. These two sound bites are a vital part of making a good first impression. They make a claim about who you are and what you can do.

Career Review with Accomplishments

This sound bite substantiates what you have said in the first two segments. It offers proof to support your claim. Introduce it by telling your listener where you're headed. Say, "Let me give you a brief overview of my career highlights. I'll concentrate on the last few years." Proceed chronologically, from earlier days to today, and walk briefly through the last 10 years of your career, touching on the dates, names of organizations, position titles, roles or mandates, key accomplishments and reasons for moving on. Do *not* use reverse chronological order; it's confusing to the listener.

Tip: As you explain your career history it's very important to bridge each move by giving a credible reason for it. This answers the unasked question, "Why did you leave that job or role?" It builds trust and holds the interviewer's attention.

Prepare for the career review by dividing your history into chapters. What determines chapter breaks is arbitrary. You could choose different organizations, jobs held within one organization, periods of time or separate projects. The first chapter should begin about 10 years ago. Mention earlier experiences only to the extent that they were significant in the formation of your core skills, interests or goals and are therefore meaningful today. Keep your listener oriented by giving dates and the names of organizations or departments.

Within each chapter, talk about accomplishments. Mention fewer from the beginning of the chronology unless they better exemplify what you would like to do next. Choose the stories for each interview carefully. Let the research you have done on the audience guide your selections. Tell the stories in their abridged form. Move from chapter to chapter quickly and lightly, like a stone skipping across the water. Let the interviewer choose where a more detailed explanation or discussion would be helpful.

For each accomplishment, use the Situation—Action—Result formula. If you do a good job describing the situation by including the starting point, mandate, challenges, issues, deadlines, magnitude, risks, etc., the rest of the story will flow. Ground your story in a solid rationale for action, so that the steps you took seem logical and prudent. Quantify the results whenever possible. Also include non-quantifiable results such as "improved communications," "model was used for other units," or "earned maximum bonus." Mention any feedback that you received and subsequent results. If you are struggling to identify results, the alternative is to explain what you learned from the experience. Keep this segment down to seven minutes, maximum.

Tip: Take the time to fully describe the situation as you tell an accomplishment story. Mention what might have happened if you didn't act. Paint a vivid "before" picture, allowing the listener to appreciate the extent of your contribution and the value of the "after" picture.

Leaving Story

For many people, explaining why they left their previous organization is a very difficult task in the career transition process. It can touch the most sensitive nerve, causing a recoil so obvious that your chance of success in the interview is ruined. The remedy involves preparation and strategic presentation.

There are three important guidelines with regards to your leaving story:
- Prepare it with utmost care.
- You broach it.
- You be comfortable with it.

The interviewer will take their level of comfort from you, and they will be relieved when it's out of the way. Most interviewers relax noticeably after you've put your leaving story on the table with an appropriate amount of detail. You have given the impression that you have nothing to hide and they don't have to worry about asking. Including it as one of your sound bites gives you a distinct advantage.

Depersonalize the story by setting it in an understandable and verifiable context. Refer your listener to well-known facts about the organization, industry, region or whatever makes sense. Talk about trends, changes in strategy or the new management focus that eroded your enthusiasm. Explain the mismatch between the organization's needs and your strengths. Work hard at making your leaving story sound like an understandable business decision that is completely acceptable to you. Keep it brief, but not too brief.

A marketing executive was hired by a highly bureaucratic, traditional organization to implement an aggressive new strategy. After three years of feeling like a pawn in the battle taking place above him, he was criticized for not fulfilling his mandate and his employment was terminated. Notwithstanding his lingering bitterness, he told his leaving story this way: "I was brought in to create a brand for the Tele-com Company. We worked on several strategies based on my earlier successes with 'Brand One' and 'Brand Two.' As yet Telecom has not chosen to move forward on any of the options. It became clear to me and to them that my approach did not match their vision. We agreed that it was best to part ways."

Invest time in developing your leaving story. Every word of it must be true. Your tone must not contain innuendo or underlying animosity, and it must not belie the positive words you've used. Practise telling your story out loud to someone from your board of advisers or support network. It is often wise to vet it through your former employer and those who will be giving references.

Never allow your leaving story to just hang there alone. After a brief but comfortable pause that implies, "You don't have any questions about that, do you?" move directly into "What now?" By sounding confident and leading your listener into your desired future, you virtually ensure that there will be no further probing or discussion of the leaving story.

What Now?

Use the final moments of your presentation to describe what you see yourself doing next. Depending on the circumstances, you can choose to stay general, speaking in terms of the skills, style and knowledge that you would like to contribute, or be specific. If you know precisely what you want to do, mention the job title, type of organization, mandate or role you hope to find and relate them to your strengths.

In an interview, make "What now?" sound remarkably like the opportunity at hand and refer back to your strengths. To be specific in a networking meeting, mention the mandate or role you seek and offer one or two hypothetical examples. Your research will allow you to tailor this sound bite to the needs of the organization and the interests of the interviewer.

Rehearse

Practising out loud is the only way to become truly comfortable with the five sound bites. After you've developed the content, put them together and rehearse them as a 5- to 10-minute presentation.

Once you've done this, you will find it easy to use each piece separately in answer to specific questions. Some interviewers will expect you to be able to talk about yourself unprompted and uninterrupted. Most will give more direction, asking targeted questions and moving the discussion through their agenda. Regardless, with the five sound bites, you are well on your way to being prepared for any interview. You are also better prepared for networking meetings and informal chats. The sound bites, used judiciously, can pack enough useful information into any encounter to interest the listener in continuing the conversation.

Tip: Use a video camera, tape recorder or your own voice mail as you practise and critique your delivery of the sound bites, especially your capsule profile and leaving story. You can have great conversations in your head, but when you actually say the words, your best approaches and phrases are easily forgotten.

WORKSHEET 12.1
Prepare the Five Sound Bites

Capsule profile (30 seconds)

_____
_____
_____
_____

Key strengths (15–30 seconds)

_____
_____
_____

Career review with accomplishments (5–7 minutes)

_____
_____
_____
_____
_____
_____
_____
_____
_____
_____
_____
_____

Leaving story (30 seconds–1 minute)

_____
_____
_____
_____

What now? (1–2 minutes)

_____
_____
_____
_____

Having the sound bites developed and rehearsed is the best general preparation you can do, but you still need to anticipate and prepare for other questions. Use the following guidelines to focus your preparation for a specific interview.

GUIDELINES FOR INTERVIEW PREPARATION

- Keep working on the research. If you haven't done so already, find out everything you can about the organization. Develop a wealth of knowledge on its products, services, strategy, structure, culture, challenges, opportunities and people.
- Get as much information about the job as you possibly can. If there is a search consultant or external recruiter involved, ask them your questions. If the interviewer makes the appointment personally, keep them on the phone for a few minutes and ask some questions about the job. Get a copy of the position description if at all possible. Be creative and determined in your research.
- Use your network to find someone who holds a similar position. Ask them in detail about their responsibilities, challenges and opportunities, as well as the key characteristics necessary for success.
- Know your audience. Search executives and external recruiters will conduct the first round of interviews for their client. Human resources staff from the hiring organization might conduct a screening interview. In some cases you proceed directly to the hiring manager. Use your research and networking techniques to learn something about each person you will be meeting in the interview process. If you can discover what's important to them, all the better.
- Plan your approach. Armed with all of the information you've collected, do the following:
  - Anticipate the key skills, knowledge and personal characteristics that could be required for the job. Think about the elements of your strategic advantage that match the requirements, and bring to mind an accomplishment story that would illustrate your expertise and attributes on every point. This takes some time.
  - Include the stories arising from your work on the previous point, and refresh your memory on at least 10 to 12 unique stories from your past. Practise telling them and keep them top-of-mind, even though you may not need to recount them all.
  - Create a brief outline of the key points you want to get across in the interview. Jot them down.
  - Go through the questions found at the end of this chapter, and plan your responses with this specific opportunity in mind.
  - Think of at least three questions that you could ask each interviewer. The individual's role will determine the suitability of the questions. Jot your questions down for review immediately prior to the interview.
  - Think of at least three reasons for your interest in the opportunity and three compelling reasons for the organization to choose you for this role. Jot them down.

- Find out exactly where you're going and plan your travel route. Think about parking, walking distance and bad weather options. You don't want to arrive late or frazzled.
- Think about the dress code for the industry sector and organization. Plan to dress one step up. If in doubt, opt for conservative business dress.
- On the night before the interview, check your outfit and accessories, consume only healthy foods and beverages and get a good night's sleep.
- Take extra copies of your résumé and your jot notes for a last-minute review. Do not weigh yourself down with an over-sized briefcase.
- Do something to control your nerves and emotions before the interview. Go for a walk, do deep breathing exercises, meditate, listen to calming music if you're tense or energizing music if you're feeling low. Call someone from your support network and have them talk you into the right frame of mind.
- Remind yourself that one of your goals is to make the interviewer's job easy for them.
- Visualize yourself doing well.

Tip: If you have trouble coming up with three convincing reasons for wanting the job, it's probably not the right one for you!

During the Interview

To gain perspective, put yourself in the interviewer's shoes. The pressure of selecting a good candidate to fill a vacant position is tremendous because hiring mistakes are costly. Choosing someone who will work well and fit comfortably with the existing group is no small task. Aside from personality issues, there's a mandate that needs to be filled, and the interviewer has limited evidence regarding your abilities and potential for the role. Perhaps reminding yourself of what the interviewer is experiencing will help you stay calm.

Interviewers have different styles, attitudes and levels of skill in conducting interviews. They also have varied knowledge of the job, the key issues and the people involved. You won't know how much information, experience, training or support the person you're meeting has. There may have been plenty of time to do adequate planning, or they might be operating on-the-fly. The interviewer might disagree with the hiring approach, or it could be their pet project. They could be a seasoned veteran at conducting interviews or a complete novice.

All of this is going to have an effect on the interview, and all you can do is be alert for clues and be prepared to adjust to the situation as it unfolds. The more calm and confident you are, the better it will go. Your body language, voice quality and ability to think improve dramatically when you are relaxed. It also helps to put your interviewer at ease and reduce tension. Remain focused on the interviewer and listen carefully to the questions. Stay in the moment by concentrating fully.

Tip: Regardless of the interviewer's level of experience and effectiveness, the responsibility for explaining your qualifications and convincing the interviewer that you are the best person for the job rests on your shoulders.

In an interview you are evaluated on much more than what you say. Some communications specialists say that body language and appearance convey well over 50 percent of the message. Eye contact, handshake, posture, walk, facial expressions, hand gestures, nods and shrugs count. Pay attention to clothing, accessories, grooming and general health. Nervous habits such as coughing, blinking, fidgeting and throat clearing detract from the message, just as a confident, courteous, friendly and poised demeanour enhance it. How you speak is important; this includes tone, volume, diction, inflection and pace. The content of your message is of primary importance, but how you say it and the disposition you project are also crucial.

Tip: When under stress, your breathing typically becomes limited to your upper chest, making it shallow and more rapid. You can counteract this, reduce your stress level and clear your mind by taking slow deep breaths.

GUIDELINES FOR CONDUCTING THE INTERVIEW

- Turn off your cell phone and pager!
- First impressions count. Greet the interviewer with good eye contact and a firm handshake that does not inflict pain. Smile and offer a pleasant greeting. Stand tall, walk with confidence and be attentive. The first 30 seconds of your interaction with the interviewer will do a lot to set the tone of the meeting.
- Break the ice by complimenting or commenting on something. The helpful staff, the decor, the location and the view are all possibilities. If none of this suits your style, try a point of common interest or experience such as the weather, the traffic, the parking, the local team's win or the headlines, as long as it is not controversial.
- As the interview proceeds, be direct and specific in your answers. Vague generalities and unsubstantiated claims are not good enough. Offer bullet-point explanations, top-line summaries, examples from experience and informed opinions. Unless it would breach confidentiality, include factual data in your examples.
- Be concise, but don't say too little. Outgoing people often say too much, and those who are too reserved need to make an effort to provide more information. Answers to most interview questions should vary in length from 30 seconds to four minutes. The most important thing is that they refer strictly to the question.
- Take cues from the interviewer. If they appear bored or uninterested, condense your answer. Their interest invites you to answer fully. Make slight adjustments in your energy level, gestures, tone, volume and pace to mirror the interviewer. Don't mimic.

- Sell your skills and abilities as they relate to the job by talking about accomplishments using the Situation—Action—Result formula.
- If you are concerned that an answer hasn't hit the mark, check it out. It's acceptable to ask the interviewer, "Did I answer the question?" or "Is there anything else that you would like to know?"
- The interviewer might be taking detailed, even verbatim notes as you speak. This can be very disconcerting, but understand that it is often part of the process. If your answers are to be scored, the interviewer will need to defend the scores with specific quotes from you.
- Keep thinking about inflection, expressions and body language as you speak. Don't slouch or assume too casual a posture in the way you sit.
- Listen for expressions, phrases and recurring themes. Pick them up and use them judiciously in your answers. Overuse will sound contrived.
- Look for opportunities to insert evidence of your research into your answers.
- Do not ask about remuneration. The interviewer will raise the topic when they are ready. The only exceptions would be your suspicion that you are well out of their range or you have another written offer with a deadline for response.
- Remember your agenda for the interview. If the interviewer's questions have not provided an opportunity to get your points across, mention them before the interview ends.
- As the interview closes, try to find the opportunity to summarize your key strengths and qualifications, and restate your interest in the job.
- When the interviewer makes it obvious that time is up, stop talking! End with a thank-you, and ask what the next steps are and in what time frame.
- Stand up when the interviewer stands. Smile, shake hands and leave.

Tip: One of the most common mistakes made in interviews is forgetting to smile. Smiling eases tension, conveys enthusiasm and indicates genuine interest. Very few people overdo smiling.

Debrief after the Interview

Before you do anything else, head for the nearest coffee shop and take the time to debrief by writing down notes about the interview. If you wait until you've made the trip home, the details of the meeting could be lost. Capture your thoughts and impressions while they are fresh in your mind. Use the following worksheet to debrief thoroughly. Your notes will help you compose the thank-you letter and will provide a valuable refresher when you return for a subsequent interview.

WORKSHEET 12.2
Debriefing after the Interview

- What did I learn about the position, the manager, the organization and the industry?

- What important details were mentioned? Sales targets? Project mandates? Relationships?

- What do the key qualifications for the role appear to be?

- How well does the position fit my skills and interests?

- What aspect of my skills, experience and knowledge appeared to be of most interest?

- Was there anything that seemed to concern the interviewer?

- What did the interviewer say about the organization's strategy, opportunities and challenges?

- What else do I need to know about the position, manager, organization or industry?

- What went particularly well in the interview?

- What aspects of my interviewing technique need more work?

- Which questions did I have difficulty answering?

- Which questions were new to me?

- What questions did I ask and what were the answers?

- What was my impression of the interviewer? The position? The company?

- What questions could I ask the next time I interview at this organization?

- What are the next steps? When do I expect to hear from them and when should I call?

Follow-up

Write a thank-you letter immediately. Ideally, you should send it within 24 hours of the interview. This gesture can make a significant difference in your chances of landing the job. Busy interviewers will be surprised and appreciative of your efforts, and by writing you can reinforce or add important information. Guidelines for writing interview thank-you letters are offered in the chapter on creating meaningful correspondence.

At the end of the interview and in your thank-you letter, expectations have been established regarding the next steps in the process. Call the external recruiter where appropriate or the interviewer on the date that was agreed, or in the absence of a specific date, call in about one week's time. Restate your interest in the position and ask how the selection process is going. If necessary, you can leave a voice mail message. Keep all anxiety and impatience out of your voice. Use a friendly and upbeat tone. Make a diary note to do a further follow-up if necessary.

Tip: By following up with tactful persistence you offer the potential employer concrete evidence of how interested you are in the job. Careful follow-up efforts will demonstrate that you are self-reliant, thorough, courteous and organized. Calling more than once a week puts you on thin ice and puts your judgment into question.

Six Different Types of Interviews

Skilled practitioners identify several types of interviews or formats for conducting interviews. The six most commonly used are described below. However, rather than adopting one particular format, most interviewers use a combination. For example, a structured interview may include some behavioural or situational questions. By understanding each format individually, you will be well equipped to handle any shift in questioning style.

The Behavioural Interview

Behavioural interviews are designed to solicit specific and detailed examples from your background that are relevant to the position being discussed. This interview format is based on the premise that past behaviour is the most accurate predictor of future behaviour. This concept and method of interviewing has become fundamental for evaluating candidates.

An interviewer's preparation for behavioural questions involves analyzing the requirements of the position, and noting the skills and attributes of individuals who have excelled in this or similar positions in the past. Doing this establishes a benchmark for each of the behaviours selected for review. Questions are designed that will draw out illustrations of how the candidate has used these skills and attributes. The questions will cover a broad spectrum of topics and will begin with phrases such as:

- "Tell me about a time when ..."
- "Give me an example of ..."
- "Have you ever had to deal with ...?"

The behavioural interview is the perfect venue for your accomplishment stories. As you would with any interview, anticipate the requirements for the job and bring to mind the stories from your past that demonstrate your qualifications on each point. Every accomplishment story can be told in a way that emphasizes the particular skill or style being questioned. You can use a story more than once by referring to it and highlighting a different aspect. The challenge is remembering and telling the stories clearly, succinctly and with sufficient detail to make your point.

Tip: In this format in particular, the interviewer will expect you to take a few moments to select, recall and think through your answer. Take the time you need. It will make a substantial difference in the quality of your answer.

In behavioural interviews that are well planned, you might encounter questions that seem to be asking for the same information repeatedly. This could indicate that the interviewer is looking for a mix of both recent and long-standing behaviours that would hold the greatest predictive value. Questions that seem repetitive might also be probing for contrary evidence. To get a balanced view of your competence, a skilled interviewer will look for both positive and negative experiences or a variety of methods and approaches to situations. Be patient with the process and vary your examples.

A sampling of behavioural questions includes:
- "Tell me about a time when you had to use your political savvy to advance a controversial project."
- "Tell me about an experience in your career that you found to be particularly frustrating."
- "What role do you typically assume when working with a team of peers? Give me an example."
- "Please give me an example of your persuasiveness."
- "Tell me about a time when you had to deal with a subordinate whose performance was below standard."
- "Please describe the most disappointing experience of your career."
- "What was the most significant decision you had to make in this past year? Tell me how you made it and what the result was."

Tip: When answering behavioural questions, be clear about why the situation was important to the organization. Explain the context, issues, obstacles and dynamics concisely yet thoroughly. What would have happened if you didn't act? Doing this will hold the interviewer's attention and allow them to appreciate the result.

The Situational Interview
The situational interview is based on the premise that intentions are the best predictor of future behaviour. The questions in a situational interview are constructed using hypothetical, but very specific, job

dilemmas, situations or case studies. You are asked to think through a problem and explain specifically what you would do under the circumstances.

Situational interviewing shifts the focus of the interview from what you have done in the past to how you might apply your knowledge and experience in future situations. If situational interview questions are well constructed, there should be no apparent correct answer, thereby limiting the risk of the candidate saying only what they think the interviewer wants to hear. You have to put yourself in the situation and be completely honest. This technique enables the interviewer to uncover a wealth of information.

The process of designing the cases used in the situational interview format is often very intensive for the organization. Several critical requirements of the job are selected. Realistic scenarios are then developed by asking experienced employees how they would respond in these situations. Their answers will elicit the qualities and skills that interviewers will be looking for in an answer. A scoring system is established to evaluate how close each candidate's answer comes to the benchmark response.

Preparation for situational interviews is difficult because the potential scenarios are innumerable and unpredictable. Sometimes they are completely unrelated to the job itself. They are designed to assess style, values and motivation as well as specific skills. Solid research, analysis and understanding of the requirements of the job are imperative. It's also helpful to review your accomplishments with a focus on how you prefer to work and in which situations you are most comfortable. The key to success is an honest, straightforward description of what you would actually do in the situation described.

GUIDELINES FOR ANSWERING SITUATIONAL INTERVIEW QUESTIONS

- As you begin your answer, state your desired outcomes.
- Be clear about any assumptions that you are making.
- Explain as clearly as possible the steps that you would take or what you would say.
- Detail how you would mobilize people and resources, if appropriate.
- Outline some of the obstacles you would expect to encounter or different directions the situation might take and explain how you would deal with them.
- Explore alternative solutions along with your primary answer.
- Give your rationale for the moves that you would make.
- Sum up your solution and explain how you would take action to prevent the situation from happening again, if that is appropriate.
- Mention any follow-up that you would do.

An early-retired bank branch manager decided that he would take a shot at fulfilling his lifelong dream of becoming a tour bus driver. He got his licence and did his research. When he had identified a company that was hiring, he landed an interview and began to prepare for it in earnest. His career transition consultant challenged him with this scenario to prepare him for situational questions: "You are returning to Ottawa along highway #417 with a full load of passengers. It's after midnight and suddenly your bus breaks down. The passengers begin to get panicky, spurred on by one individual who feels short of breath and mentions chest pains. How would you handle the situation?"

After working through his responses to this and several other scenarios, he went into the interview with confidence. A situational question similar to the breakdown story was posed, and he handled it with ease. He got the job!

The Structured Interview

Structured interviews use a pre-selected series of questions that solicit an overview of your style and background. In an effort to be equitable, every candidate will be asked the same questions in the same order. Some interviewers using this format will pose carefully constructed questions based on the job description and others will use a random sampling of their tried-and-true favourites. The structured interview could include conventional, behavioural and situational interview-type questions. A consistent characteristic of structured interviews is that the interviewer takes control of the session, leaving you little independent opportunity to deliver your convincing points.

A sampling of conventional questions includes:
- "Tell me about yourself."
- "What sort of opportunities and challenges are you hoping to have in your next role?"
- "What are your strengths?"
- "What are your weaknesses?"
- "Why did you leave your last position?"
- "Where do you see yourself in three years? In five?"
- "How would you describe your management, leadership or team style?"
- "What interests you about this position?"
- "What do you know about the organization or the position?"
- "Why should we hire you?"

You have a two-part challenge in structured interviews. First, you need to be prepared to answer the conventional questions. Your reflective work and research plus your advance preparation of the five sound bites should make this easy. Second, you must be able to interject sufficient information to prove your suitability for the position if the questions posed do not offer the opportunity. The preparation of your accomplishment stories should stand you in good stead. Use them whenever you can. If you are frustrated in your attempts to put your points forward, your chance might come when the interviewer asks a question like, "What have I missed?" or "What else should I know about you?" Another opportunity could arise when you are invited to ask questions. At that time, first make your points using a concise, bullet-point style and then ask your questions.

The Unstructured Interview

In an unstructured interview, the interviewer asks only a few pre-selected questions and offers minimal direction while you do most of the talking. The interviewer might start with a conversational approach such as, "I'll let you start by telling me about yourself," or "Tell me about your work over at Environmental Company." They might pick up on elements of what you say and use them as the basis for further questions, or they might remain silent after you have stopped speaking to see where you take the conversation. It can be a daunting experience.

Another mark of the unstructured interview is the stroll down tangential avenues. The interviewer might chat about people or events that are interesting but bear no apparent relevance to your qualifications or to the available position. The interviewer might also talk too much, making it difficult for you to get a word in edgewise. However, this could prove helpful, especially if they describe the organization or the position in depth and this interview is one of a series within the organization.

Sometimes very skilled interviewers will test your ability to perform under pressure and adapt to unexpected circumstances by using an unstructured format. They could also be using the format as a calculated method of assessing your level of preparation, research or genuine interest in the position. Unfortunately, unstructured interviews are also popular with interviewers who haven't had the time or training to prepare properly.

The challenge for you is recognizing when you need to bring some structure to the session and determining how to do that. When it appears that things won't get on track without your intervention, offer to tell the interviewer about something you believe to be pertinent. For example, "Would it be helpful if I summarized my experience at Environmental Company?" You could also use one or more of your sound bites, watching the interviewer carefully for their reaction.

Another technique for handling the unstructured interview is for you to ask the key questions and then, upon hearing the answers, offer evidence from your past that qualifies you on those points. For example, ask, "What are the major human resources challenges facing the client group at this time?" When the answer is "Retention," tell your story about implementing recruiting and orientation policies to reduce turnover by 25 percent.

Other questions that you might pose in your efforts to discover the salient points include:
- "What do you see as being the key mandate for this role?"
- "If I were successful in getting this job, how could I add the greatest value to this organization?"
- "What are the important characteristics needed to be successful in this job?"
- "What leadership, management or team style do you think would be the most effective in this role?"
- "What will the roadblocks be for the person who accepts this mandate?"

In each instance, use the answer as a lead-in for one of your main points and accomplishment stories. Be vigilant in watching for signs that the interviewer wants to reclaim control of the process. You don't want to hijack the session.

It is not easy to take control of an interview that seems to be disjointed, but the responsibility to present your background and skills is yours alone. You need to persuade the interviewer that you are the ideal candidate for the position by giving factual data to prove your qualifications, even when it is not solicited.

The Panel Interview

Panel interviews involve more than one interviewer meeting a candidate at one time. There might be a large number of interviewers or as few as two. This format was once limited to use by the public sector, institutions, non-profit organizations and boards of directors, but it has become much more widespread. Panel interviews are efficient for the organization and effective in providing an equitable venue for job candidates. They also create more internal support for the successful candidate.

The challenge for you is to determine who will be on the panel, their titles and their roles. Use your network to learn something about each member's priorities and focus, and identify the decision-makers and most influential members. It will take a lot of digging, and you may not be able to get complete information. Often, the person who is organizing the interview is an excellent source of information, regardless of the seniority of their position.

Tip: Do not let the number of interviewers on the panel affect your poise and concentration. No matter how many interviewers you face, you will still answer only one question at a time.

Sometimes you will not know in advance that you will be in a panel interview. In other circumstances you may be given a package of material about the job and the organization. You might be asked to prepare and present something for the panel. Do your homework thoroughly.

Unless they are structured solely around your presentation, panel interviews ideally use a carefully constructed series of questions, asked in turn by pre-selected members of the panel. The organization should have appointed someone as a moderator to keep the process moving smoothly. The reality is that panel interviews are not always well planned or moderated. They can easily become disjointed as individual panel members show off their interviewing styles, ask their favourite questions and pursue their own agendas. As always, prepare by anticipating the organization's needs and have your key points in mind.

Once you are in the interview, do your best to create rapport. Time will be limited and the group may want to dispense with the informalities. Use your best judgment. The questions will not differ from those used in any of the other interview formats. The following guidelines will help.

GUIDELINES FOR A PANEL INTERVIEW
- Prepare in the same way you would for any other interview, with the added task of learning something about each panel member, if possible, and preparing a presentation if required.
- Don't start the interview by making jokes about how intimidating the situation feels. Be confident and your confidence will show.
- Try to commit the names and positions of the panel members to memory before the interview. When you are introduced at the start of the session, do everything you can to remember who's who, including jotting down names as the interviewers are introduced, if that seems appropriate.
- As you answer questions, it's very impressive to call a panel member by name, but do this only if you have all their names clearly in mind. Don't make mistakes! Err on the side of caution.
- When a question is being posed, look at the person speaking as if they are the only one in the room, and begin your answer by speaking directly to them. As you speak, make eye contact with every other person, finishing with the original questioner.
- If you have done your job in discovering the panel members' individual priorities, and you have been able to catch who's who in the room, look directly at the person to whom the question really matters when you know you are dealing with a sensitive issue.

- Don't be thrown by panel members' neutral expressions. They might have been told to try to control their expressions so as not to lead or influence you in any way.
- You might see signs of internal politics and power plays as panel members vie for air time and react to one another. Take mental note of the interactions, but don't let them distract you. Remain calm and focused. Take care to continue addressing the panel members with equal eye contact.
- Do not hesitate to ask questions when invited to do so. Address your question to a specific person by looking at them as you speak.
- Don't forget to smile!
- Thank the panel as the session ends. Unless it's a very large group, close the interview by shaking hands with each person.

The Non-Interview

Outside of preparing for formal interview situations, it is crucial to understand that you are always on stage. Whether you are considering a career change or not, your colleagues, superiors and external contacts are constantly collecting information regarding your competence and style. When you are confident with who you are and what you're doing this should be an encouraging thought.

The best preparation for the ever-present non-interview is to be working at something that suits your strategic advantage and make personal and professional development a lifelong quest. Be continually conscious of how your words and actions affect others, and be clear and honest in putting your ideas forward. Even in the most challenging circumstances, you can say what you think as long as you separate the people from the issues and substantiate what you say. You don't have to be right all the time, but you do need to base your stance on solid experience, research, analysis and judgment.

GUIDELINES FOR SPECIAL INTERVIEWING CHALLENGES

When to Broach Your Leaving Story

- Be aware that the interviewer might already know your circumstances through conversation with the search firm or a few well-placed phone calls before the interview.
- If the interview starts with an open invitation such as, "Tell me about yourself," or "Tell me about your work at Entertainment Inc.," use your sound bites as prepared and rehearsed, including your leaving story.
- Don't give the impression that you are still working if that is not the case. It would be awkward to correct this misconception later, and you need to stay in control of this crucial piece of information. You do not want the interviewer to learn the truth when you are not present to explain your leaving story.
- Before the conclusion of the first interview, your leaving story must be told. Offer it at the end of the session if no better opportunity has presented.
- Be sure that you are comfortable with your leaving story through careful preparation and practice, and always include your plans for the future before you stop talking.

Questions about Weaknesses, Disappointments and Failures

- Skilled interviewers know that there is much to be learned from exploring the less successful aspects of a person's experience. Be prepared!
- Every point you make about your weaknesses, disappointments and failures must include what you've learned and how you prevent this from being an ongoing problem.
- Since most weaknesses are overused strengths, go with this premise. Reiterate one of your strengths and talk about what it's like when used in the extreme.
- Don't mention weaknesses that will ruin your chances for the job. Based on your research, decide which three to five areas you are willing to discuss. Choose characteristics that are the antithesis of the job requirements. For example, a business developer might admit to impatience and boredom with detail-focused, isolated tasks.
- Along with the preparation of accomplishment stories, think about the disappointments and failures that have advanced your learning. Be prepared to give specific examples of the difficult times, focusing on what you culled from the experience.

A general manager from an operations environment took pride in his tight control over the quality of work in his area. He would delegate responsibility reluctantly and always with excessively detailed instructions. He was often criticized for keeping too much administrative and supervisory work on his own plate. In describing his weakness, he said, "I pride myself on the quality of the output from my division. I delegate cautiously and check on my subordinates' work frequently. The result is that I'm probably slower to delegate than others. However, when my mandate changed to include both developing my subordinates and focusing my attention on business strategy, I learned to be less directive and give increasing responsibility to my people."

Handling a Series of Interviews with One Organization

- In a long series of interviews with an organization, the greatest challenge is staying fresh, enthusiastic and interested. You need to go into each interview as if it were the first one.
- Have plenty of accomplishment stories on hand. Tell the most pertinent ones repeatedly, and try to use a new story in each interview.
- Don't wear the same outfit or suit too often. Have copies of your résumé with you. Learn the names of support staff. Greet people cordially and begin to act as if you belong.
- Remember that you must make a good first impression with each separate interviewer. Be confident and relaxed. Think about how you can put them at ease by establishing rapport.
- Don't assume that the interviewers have spoken with one another, and don't take shortcuts with your answers. Be consistent and thorough.
- Know your various audiences. Before each session, use your notes to refresh your memory on the next interviewer and where they fit in the organization.
- Debrief following each interview. If you are in a series of back-to-back meetings, at the very least quickly jot down the pertinent names, facts and details that have been mentioned. Do a thorough debrief at the end of the day.
- Remember the names of previous interviewers and the distinguishing points of your conversation

with them. Drop this information into subsequent interviews, demonstrating your growing enthusiasm for the opportunity.

- To aid your understanding of the position, the organization and the key issues, ask the same questions to a number of interviewers, such as "What do you see as the major challenges facing the person chosen for this position?"
- Write a thank-you letter to every interviewer. Make them specific to each conversation because they might be circulated among the entire group.

Tip: If you are involved in a series of interviews with one organization and you have an interesting opportunity emerging with another, begin now to slow down the process with the first organization. Very carefully delay the scheduling of meetings to buy time.

Raising Your Questions

- Having thoughtful and pertinent questions to ask of your interviewers is an excellent way to demonstrate your interest in a position and gather information on which to base your evaluation of the opportunity.
- Your research should uncover areas of interest that you want to explore further. Don't hesitate to ask your questions, prefacing them with an acknowledgement that the interviewer might not be free to disclose some things.
- In an initial interview, wait for the invitation to ask your questions unless an obvious entry point presents itself. In subsequent interviews with the same person, you will be expected to have cogent questions. Do not go in unprepared.
- If the process appears to be moving toward the offer stage, and you have not had the opportunity to ask your questions and satisfy your concerns, call the person in charge of the process and ask for a meeting in which you can raise your questions.

Discussing Remuneration

- Do your homework first. It's usually possible to determine the approximate base salary range and total compensation package for the position you hope to land. The search firm or placement agency and your network are the best sources. Salary surveys will give you a general idea of the level of compensation specific jobs command in various industries.
- The interviewer will probably raise the issue of remuneration well before you are given a concrete offer of employment. However, if salary is very important to you and the issue of remuneration has not come up after several interviews, ask. It won't do either of you any good to keep the conversations going if the organization is not able to meet your needs.

A senior manager with expertise in hazardous waste management was in a series of interviews with an international firm. Both parties were excited about the obvious fit and the prospect of working together. The organization's process entailed eight interviews, several requiring officers of the company to fly in *from Europe and Asia. Unfortunately, neither the candidate nor the organization mentioned remuner-ation during any of the interviews. When the process was complete and a written offer was delivered, the base salary was set at $65,000. The candidate had been making twice that amount and could not consider taking less than $115,000. The transaction ended in disappointment for all concerned.*

- If you are asked what your salary expectations are, the interviewer is looking for an indication that you and the organization are in the same range. Don't evade the question.
  - Offer a base salary range varying by approximately 10 percent from top to bottom and indi-cate your flexibility in looking at the total remuneration package.
  - If bonuses or commissions are involved, state a range from the midpoint of your expectations up to the highest level that is reasonable for your industry.
  - Keep the conversation open by stating your interest in the position and the contribution you believe you can make.
- If you are asked point-blank what you are currently making, be honest and be sure to include everything from the excellent pension plan and the strike price of your stock options to your club memberships and parking spot. Express your flexibility in terms of the overall structure of the remuneration package and your interest in the position.

A corporate finance executive was interviewing with a major investment banking firm. His remunera-tion expectations were well within the range of what the hiring organization was willing to pay, and he was not looking for a significant increase. His interest was in working for the firm itself. When asked about his current remuneration package, he dodged the question, expressing confidence that whatever would be offered for the prospective job would be fair. He was immediately taken out of the running. The interviewer already knew what he was making and thought that if he was not prepared to be forthcoming on the issue of pay, he might be hiding something else.

Tip: Don't lie about your compensation. A surprising number of candidates do this and ruin their chance of landing a job. What you say can be verified by companies checking references.

References

When the organization is ready to extend an offer of employment to you, their last step before doing so should be a thorough reference check. This can often delay the process, but it is very important to the organization. See Chapter 18 for a thorough discussion of how to manage your references well.

In Conclusion

To be thoroughly prepared, go through the following inventory of interview questions. Some of the questions relate to your previous experience and can be answered the same way in any interview. Others are directed at the prospective opportunity, and require a specific and thoughtful answer.

An Inventory of Interview Questions

Position-Related
- What did you enjoy most (least) about your last position?
- What would you like to have done more of in your last job?
- What are the three most important things you look for in a job?
- Describe your understanding of what is required to fulfill this role.
- What objectives would you set for your first 12 months in this position?
- What aspects of your current job do you consider to be most critical to your success in this role?

Working Environment
- How would you describe the culture of your current (most recent) organization?
- What would you consider to be an ideal organizational culture?
- After working with the same organization for as long as you have, what obstacles or challenges do you anticipate in trying to adapt to a new organization?

Leadership Style
- How would you describe your leadership style? Please give an example of a specific action you have taken that would illustrate this.
- How do you stay current on what your team or work group is accomplishing?
- In what ways has your leadership style changed as you have gained experience?

Operating Style
- Please describe how you handle the following activities and give examples to illustrate:
- organizing your time
- managing your priorities
- bringing new ideas forward
- communicating to others—subordinates, peers, senior managers, clients
- managing issues
- Tell me about a work experience you have had that you found to be particularly frustrating. How did you deal with it and what was the outcome? How could you have handled it differently?
- What has been the most difficult management responsibility you have handled?

Team Skills
- What type of people do you work with best? Why?
- How do you handle conflict with co-workers? Please give me an example.
- Tell me about a time when you were on a team that was successful in accomplishing a particularly difficult task. In what ways did you participate and contribute to this achievement?
- From your experience in working as a team member, tell me about a time when the team objected to your ideas. How did you attempt to influence or persuade them to accept your views? What results did you achieve?

- Looking back on your team experiences, have you ever assumed the role of team leader? How did you act when you were the leader on various projects?

Negotiating Style

- Please give me some examples of different approaches you've used in persuading someone to help you accomplish a work priority.
- How would you approach and prepare for dealing with a complex issue requiring you to negotiate with one or more people? Please give me an example.
- Please describe a particularly successful negotiation in which you took part. What did you do to contribute to that success?
- Please describe a negotiation that did not produce the results you wanted. What went wrong and what would you do differently next time?

Decision-Making Style

- Please describe the process that you generally follow to make decisions.
- To what extent do you provide opportunities for your subordinates to participate in making decisions?
- Describe a poor decision that you made. What might you have done differently to produce a successful result?
- Tell me about a time when you changed a decision you had made or an opinion you had held, because you were persuaded that you were wrong.

Accomplishments

- What would you consider to be your most significant career-related accomplishment to date? Why?
- Name three or four of your proudest achievements.
- What would you consider to be your biggest disappointment or failure in your career to date? How did you handle it? What did you learn from it? What should you have done differently to produce a more satisfactory outcome?
- How do you define and measure success?

Personal Characteristics

- What characteristics would you say are the most important for a good manager (sales executive, senior economist, CFO, etc.) to have? Can you describe some of your accomplishments that would demonstrate how you have displayed these characteristics?
- How do you react to criticism?
- How do you handle pressure on the job? Stress?
- What did you think of your last boss? Your last organization?
- What would you consider to be your three strongest assets? Please give me an example of a time when you demonstrated these strengths to achieve successful results.
- How would you describe yourself? Tell me about some of the people or events in your life outside work that have had the greatest influence on you.

- What makes you unique among your peers?
- What areas of your skills and abilities do you feel need more work in order for you to become more effective in your career?
- How do you stay plugged in to what's happening in your current organization?
- How do you stay current on new developments in your area of expertise?
- Tell me about a time when you had to take a stand on an unpopular position or issue.
- Have you learned more from your successes or from your failures? Please give examples.
- Describe three elements of your personal code of workplace ethics.
- Why have you changed jobs so frequently/infrequently?

Chapter 13

Create Meaningful Correspondence

If I had more time,
I would write to you more briefly.

Well-written, appropriate correspondence plays a critical role in your job search. It is significant not only for its content, but also for the impression it creates. Written materials provide concrete evidence of your skill as a communicator and convey a wealth of information about your attitude, thinking skills and judgment. Career transition correspondence, whether delivered by email or regular mail, falls into five categories:

• cover letters responding to ads or job postings
• networking letters used to introduce yourself to a potential new contact
• marketing letters for contract work, consulting services or a small business
• thank-you letters to interviewers and networking contacts
• "I've Landed" letters announcing your new position

Tip: Many people use broadcast letters with attached résumés as a means of introducing themselves to a large number of prospective employers. *This one-size-fits-all approach is a poor use of your time.* Unsolicited résumés are often ignored or discarded. At best they are scanned for key words and their information is filed electronically.

Use the following guidelines to ensure that every letter you write is an effective communication piece.

GUIDELINES FOR ALL CAREER TRANSITION CORRESPONDENCE

• Allow enough time to compose and proofread each letter carefully.
• Address every letter to a specific person. Use your research skills and find out the name of the person to whom you are writing to avoid using the "Dear Sir/Madam" salutation.
• Keep every letter to a single page.
• Limit letters to four paragraphs of no more than eight lines each.
• Balance short and long sentences for variety.

- Let your personality shine through and keep the tone of your letters positive yet professional.
- Limit the use of the first person, especially the use of "I" at the beginning of sentences.
- Do not use trite phrases such as "strong communication and interpersonal skills" or other words that have lost their effectiveness through overuse.
- Use either your personal letterhead or the heading from your résumé on every letter, so that your contact information stands out.
- Close each letter with your commitment to follow-up and make a diary note to do it.
- Be meticulous about grammar and spelling. Do not rely on "Spell Check." Proofread your letter carefully.
- Keep copies of your letters where they can be easily retrieved. Use them for reference when you follow up.

GUIDELINES FOR FORMATTING A LETTER

For proper layout and paragraph formatting, use a template in your computer software or follow these rules:

- The top margin will vary according to the letterhead design. The bottom margin should be at least half an inch. Side margins should be equal and no narrower than three-quarters of an inch.
- All text should begin at the left margin.
- Place the date one or two lines down from the letterhead. Leave two to four blank lines before the inside address. Leave one blank line after the inside address before the attention line, and one blank line before and after the salutation.
- When using a reference line, centre it in bold after the salutation, leaving one blank line before and after.
- Do not indent paragraphs. Leave a blank line between paragraphs.
- Leave one blank line before the signature line and approximately four lines for your signature.
- Leave one blank line before the enclosure or cc line.

Cover Letters

A carefully written cover letter should accompany your résumé every time you respond to an ad or job posting. If it is brief, relevant and to the point, your letter can have more influence on the reader's decision to interview you than the enclosed résumé. Recruiters often give more credence to your cover letter because, unlike your résumé that could have been written by someone else, it will have been authored by you. The cover letter forms the first impression of you in the reader's mind. It builds a bridge between your past experience and the future opportunity. It should be sufficient on its own to convince the reader that you are a qualified candidate for the advertised position.

Tip: Email has not changed the importance of writing cover letters. Recruiters report that many people who use email are skipping this crucial step, but those who do make the effort significantly increase their chance of being interviewed.

Every good cover letter starts with thorough research. In addition to traditional resources, call the external recruiter or human resources department of the hiring organization and try to get a copy of the full job description. Contact your network to learn about the key people and the culture of the organization. This unpublished intelligence is often the most valuable.

Next, analyze the ad or job posting carefully. Use the worksheet that follows to record the requirements of the position, and compare them with your skills and abilities. Consider what you could bring to the position or the organization over and above the requirements mentioned in the ad, and describe it succinctly. This added-value statement will give you a distinct advantage because most people reply only in terms of the requirements mentioned in the ad.

Tip: Your cover letter should tell the reader that you read the ad or posting thoroughly, you gave it careful thought and you have a good reason for applying.

WORSHEET 13.1	
The Cover Letter	
Key Points in the Ad or Job Posting	**Corresponding Points Describing You**
Professional and Functional Skills	Professional and Functional Skills
•	•
•	•
•	•
•	•
•	•
Personal Characteristics and Values	Personal Characteristics and Values
•	•
•	•
•	•
•	•
•	•
Relevant Industry and Corporate Information You've Learned through Research	
•	
•	
•	
Added Value You Would Bring to the Position and the Organization	
•	
•	

In the heading of your letter, clearly identify the ad, posting, reference number, project name, file number or position title for which you are applying. If your application is going to an external recruiter or the human resources department, this information should stand out to ensure that your material is sorted correctly.

Tip: Suspend the use of informal email etiquette for cover letters. Most hiring managers will be put off by "Hi Susan" from someone they've never met. Stick with formal salutations, good grammar and perfect spelling, even in the casual milieu of email.

Compose a compelling opening. You want to do more than refer the reader to the ad and your enclosed résumé. Here is an example of what you should *not* write: "Enclosed please find a copy of my résumé in response to your ad in *The Globe and Mail* on May 4th for the position of Purchasing Manager." This opening generates little interest, and shows a lack of originality and effort.

Contrast the following opening to the one above: "As an experienced Purchasing Manager with a track record of consistent cost reduction and quality standards maintenance, I am very interested in the position you have advertised. Industrial Parts Company's reputation in the widget industry is second-to-none, and I would like to be a part of your service-focused team." Assume that the writer picked up the phrase "service-focused team" from a networking contact.

In the body of the letter, point out the information on your résumé that substantiates your qualifications. Highlight one or two convincing accomplishments and mention quantified results, adding explanations of their relevance if needed. Use crisp, powerful phrases and persuasive points to sell your style and skills. Express enthusiasm for the position. Explain the added value you offer and close by stating your commitment to follow up. Make a diary note so you remember to do this important step.

Tip: Don't be tempted to rewrite your résumé to fit each ad or job posting. A résumé that targets your ideal employment opportunity and a well-written cover letter should be adequate for almost every opportunity. Don't let résumé revising become the focus of your job search energies.

Do not make the mistake of using the same cover letter repeatedly, and don't compose a generic one. If a letter is tailored to one ad, it will not be appropriate for another. Customize your letter to reflect the contents of the specific ad or posting and the additional information that you collect through research. Certain phrases and sentences may transfer well from one letter to another, but avoid copying whole paragraphs without making suitable changes.

A market research specialist from a multinational consumer packaged-goods company wanted to explore opportunities with other organizations. Her interest was in either advancing her career in research or switching to a marketing role with a broader focus. She saw two ads run by a major retailer, one for a research specialist and the other for a more junior position as a marketing generalist. Her dilemma was that both opportunities appeared to be well worth pursuing. After struggling with the idea of submitting separate applications, she decided to write one straightforward cover letter that explained her interests and stated the contribution she could make to each job. She asked to be considered for both opportunities and successfully landed both interviews.

GUIDELINES FOR WRITING COVER LETTERS

Opening Paragraph
- Write a compelling opening to capture the reader's attention. Refer to the ad or job posting.
- Explain why this opportunity appeals to you.
- Write a comment that illustrates your effort to learn something about the organization.

Second Paragraph—Skills Match
- Demonstrate that your skills match those mentioned in the ad or posting by briefly highlighting one or two accomplishments.
- Describe the added value you would bring to the position.

Third Paragraph—Personal Style
- Describe your competencies and characteristics in terms that mirror the ad or job posting.
- Indicate your interest and enthusiasm for the position.

Closing Paragraph—Follow-up Commitment
- Indicate your desire to meet for an interview.
- Thank the reader for considering your application.
- Commit to following up on a specific date.

Look at the samples that follow. They illustrate good technique and the application of the principles that will help you find the work you want.

Tip: It's not easy to critique your own work. *Grammatical and spelling mistakes are inexcusable.* Have someone else proofread your cover letters before sending them.

The sample cover letter on the facing page responds to this ad.

VP Marketing and Sales
Reference # 81349

Using current and emerging marketing and promotional tools, you will be responsible for expanding market share and profitability for our major consumer product lines. Your mandate will be to continuously develop, improve and manage strategies to outpace the competition and advance our relationships with major retailers. You are skilled in direct marketing, project management, media effectiveness and business analysis. You are strategic, conceptual and analytical in your thinking and you thrive in a fast-paced, team environment.

Multi-household Products Co.
Address
City, Province Postal Code

Sample Cover Letter #1

NAME
Address
City, Province Postal Code
Telephone / Fax / email

Date

Donna O'Rourke
Vice-President, Human Resources
Multi-household Products Co.
Address
City, Province Postal Code

VP Marketing and Sales
Reference #81349

Dear Ms. O'Rourke,

Your recent ad for the position of Vice-President Marketing and Sales is of great interest to me. I believe that Multi-household Products Co.'s strong national presence in household paper products provides the ideal platform for launching your recently announced global expansion plans. The emerging Asian markets and their potential for high-volume sales hold particular promise, and I would like play a leadership role in your aggressive marketing strategies and dynamic sales initiatives.

My marketing experience began with Classic Established Co., where I spent four years in new product development in addition to several product management and sales assignments. The move to Smaller Co. as National Sales Manager in 1995 afforded me the opportunity to establish excellent relationships with senior managers at the major retail accounts in Canada. I was able to negotiate both additional shelf space and better advertising support for our household product line with Tight Co.

As Vice-President, New Products Division, for ABC Company my contributions have included the increase in specialty products sales from $750,000 to $2.5 million and the aggressive driving of Ultra-Pack Tissues to capture market share in excess of 50%. Strategies have included maximizing the emerging potential of B2B commodity buying with major international accounts.

My management style can be best described as energetic and hands-on. I thrive in a results-oriented environment that is focused on growth and profits. I take pride in motivating and inspiring individuals to higher achievements and building committed teams founded on mutual respect.

I trust you will find my qualifications well suited to your requirements. I will take the initiative to touch base with you next Thursday to discuss your needs in greater depth.

Sincerely,

Name

Encl.

Sample cover letter # 2 responds to this ad.

Manager of Accounting
The Children's Charitable Foundation

We are interested in only those candidates who are passionate about working as part of our team and dedicated to the cause of helping children. Our immediate need is for a Manager of Accounting, preferably with experience in the not-for-profit sector. The mandate is to implement a plan that will support the Foundation's restructuring initiatives. Reporting to the Executive Director, you will have accountability for all aspects of the Foundation's finances, and will be a key member of the Information Management Team. Qualified candidates will possess a professional accounting designation and a minimum of five years' experience in a similar position. Candidates will have demonstrated ability to work with external investment managers, and manage the donor database. A solid track record in change management and an ability to work closely with others are essential.

Respond in writing or by email to:

Michel Daveau
Director, Human Resources
The Children's Charitable Foundation
Address
City, Province Postal Code
email

Sample Cover Letter #2

NAME
Address
City, Province Postal Code
Telephone / Fax / email

Date

Michel Daveau
Director, Human Resources
The Children's Charitable Foundation
Address
City, Province Postal Code

Dear M. Daveau,

My commitment to helping children who are living with serious illnesses caused me to read with great interest your ad in the *National Post* for Manager of Accounting for The Children's Charitable Foundation. I have been actively involved for some time with St. Nicholas' Hospital as a volunteer member of their Foundation Committee. The opportunity to combine my personal commitment with my professional career is compelling. I understand that last year, you succeeded in raising over $12 million to help children across North America.

Through my 17-year career in accounting with the County Board of Education, I have gained experience in recommending financial controls, developing forecasts, budgeting and identifying opportunities for cost reductions. For example, by implementing controls, I was able to achieve annual savings of over $50,000 for the special education department alone. The ability to work closely with my colleagues and subordinates in a team environment is a hallmark of my personal style.

Through my volunteer work at the St. Nicholas' Hospital Foundation I have learned the importance of coordinating the database management with the accounting function. In addition, I have developed a large network of high net worth contacts. I would look forward to contributing both to the financial management and the development goals of the Children's Charitable Foundation.

I would welcome the opportunity to meet with you to learn more about this position, and how I can be a part of The Children's Charitable Foundation's plans for the future. I will call you early next week to see if we might set up a meeting to discuss my qualifications further.

Sincerely,

Name

Encl.

Networking Letters

Conducting an active job search sometimes involves writing introductory letters, known as networking letters. Their sole purpose is to aid the process of arranging meetings with individuals to gather information, leads and advice. More is said about the networking process in later chapters.

A networking letter introduces the writer, explains the reason for the contact, requests a face-to-face meeting and promises to follow up by telephone. Without a follow-up phone call, networking letters are ineffective. Few people will take the initiative to phone you and set up a meeting in response to your letter.

Use this type of letter only if it helps you gain comfort with the networking process. For some people, picking up the phone and asking for a meeting without first having sent a letter is daunting. If you are one of those people, use networking letters as part of your strategy, but remember that writing them creates a significant amount of extra work and delays your direct contact with people who are probably willing to help you. Measure the effectiveness of your networking letters by keeping track of the ones that result in meetings.

Tip: Networking letters can be used as a last resort when all other attempts to make contact have failed.

Use the following guidelines to increase the effectiveness of networking letters. A sample follows the guidelines.

GUIDELINES FOR NETWORKING LETTERS
- Target each letter to the recipient. Generic networking letters and broadcast mailings are not effective.
- In your opening sentence, mention the person who referred you. When there is a personal connection, people pay attention; their willingness to help increases and their curiosity is piqued.
- Be clear about your intention to request a meeting and state your agenda for the meeting. You should be looking for information and advice on something specific. Do not say that you would like to know what opportunities are available at the recipient's organization.
- Consider enclosing a topical article. This could form the basis for your discussion in the meeting.
- Another option is to put forward a hypothesis or mention an issue you would like to discuss.
- In some instances, a summary of your targets might be appropriate.
- Do not enclose your résumé. You are not applying for a job with the recipient, you are asking for a discussion, information and advice.
- Close with the commitment to call and schedule a meeting. Make a diary note and follow up.

A senior manager from the strategic sourcing division of a large entertainment company wrote to the VP Operations of a smaller organization in the transportation industry. He wanted to demonstrate his familiarity with emerging issues created by the expanding use of the Internet by purchasing managers.

He enclosed a reprint of a recent article from Harvard Business Review *on the topic and wrote, "This article states that e-hubs will exert increasing influence on the methods of purchasing goods and services by major accounts. My experience here at Mammoth Movie Theatres provides ample evidence that the author of the article has hit the nail on the head. I'm interested in discussing with you how purchasing managers can avoid excessive spending on the enforcement of quality guarantees while taking full advantage of discount pricing in this new electronic commodity market." When he made his follow-up call, the VP Operations was very interested in scheduling a meeting.*

Sample Networking Letter

NAME
Street Address
City, Province Postal Code
Telephone / Fax / email

Date

Name
Title
Organization
Division
Address
City, Province Postal Code

Dear First Name,

Fred Smith, Vice-President at Enterprise Inc., recently told me of your new role as Director, Vendor Relations for Interprovincial Trains Ltd. Congratulations on your success. Although we have not spoken in some time, you may recall our brief contact while I was Manager of Operations at Start-Up Inc. prior to the acquisition. My role there came to an end in May, and I am currently exploring new career options. Fred suggested that I get in touch with you.

Because of my diversified background, which includes senior roles at Marketing Plus and Stellar Inc., I am researching a range of options that include operations or project management within a pharmaceutical, health care or biotech environment.

With this in mind, I would appreciate the chance to speak with you briefly. Any information or comments you have regarding potential areas of growth within these industries would be helpful. I will call you toward the end of next week to see when a short meeting might be convenient. I'm looking forward to speaking with you and hearing about your new responsibilities.

Yours truly,

Your Name
Encl.

Marketing Letters

Marketing letters might form a part of your strategy if you decide to pursue contract or consulting work. These letters introduce your services and offer a few persuasive points highlighting the potential benefits of retaining you. Their objective is to prepare the way for a phone call requesting a meeting, ideally as the result of a specific referral. Develop a generic edition of the letter at the outset of your marketing efforts and plan to customize it for each recipient. The content of the letter will evolve as your consulting or contracting practice grows.

An indiscriminate mass mailing of marketing letters is usually a waste of effort and money. You know what happens to the unsolicited mail that you receive. A personal referral provides the most compelling reason for writing, but where you don't have a referral, use a focused approach that shows you have made an effort to learn something about the person or organization.

Review the guidelines for writing networking letters. The same tips and techniques apply to marketing letters. A quote, a copy of an article or a hypothesis based on your research are ideal ways to introduce the potential issues and challenges for which you propose to provide solutions. Include a brief description of a few of your relevant accomplishments either as part of the narrative or in bullet-point form. Do not include your résumé. You are not applying for a job, but rather making contacts that might lead to work opportunities.

Other ways to generate interest with marketing letters include enclosing your brochure or samples of your materials. However, you might prefer to reserve these for use in the marketing meeting. You could include a list of your clients or relevant quotes from clients, with their permission. Another possibility is to include an invitation for the reader to visit your web site. If you do this, be sure that your site adds something to what you have said in the letter.

Tip: Write an article for a trade journal or industry newsletter that addresses an issue where your expertise could be applied. Buy reprints of the article, reference it in your letter and attach a copy.

Sample Marketing Letter

NAME
Address
City, Province Postal Code
Telephone / Fax / email

Date

Name
Title
Company
Address
City, Province Postal Code

Dear Name,

Mark Steiner suggested that I contact you to introduce myself. My background in driving major organizational change may be helpful to you and your firm.

The leading companies in the Canadian insurance industry are undergoing some very costly, risky and potentially beneficial changes. These changes include: acquisitions and divestitures in Canada, the U.S. and internationally; outsourcing of information technology; outsourcing of business processes; and the launching of new products and services to increase revenues. These changes can be very complex, spanning multiple business functions, covering broad geographies and including both business and information technology functions.

I believe that I could assist you and your executive team in meeting these challenges by drawing on my capabilities in:
• Driving multi-million-dollar change initiatives.
• Defining quantified business cases for major organizational change and clearly articulating the benefits.
• Determining when and how information technology is appropriate to business needs.
• Turning around major projects that are not meeting expectations.
• Developing strategies and implementing them.
• Working with complex multi-business-units organizations.

I have enclosed a brief summary of my achievements at XYZ Insurance Co. and ABC Consulting Co. I will call you next week to see if we might find a time to meet.

Sincerely,

Name

Encl.

Thank-You Letters

As you search for your next opportunity, whether it is a full-time job, consulting assignments or starting your own small business, you will have many occasions to thank people for their help. A simple and effective way to show your appreciation is to put your thanks in writing. It's best to do this within 24 hours of a meeting or phone call, but don't let tardiness stop you from writing. Even if your letter is dispatched months later, it's better to send it rather than entirely neglect this important piece of correspondence.

You will want to thank every networking and marketing contact plus the person who provided the introduction. It is also important to thank every interviewer at every stage in the process, and the people who provide references on your behalf.

Thank-you letters and notes don't always need to be formal business letters. You could send a handwritten note on a blank card or businesslike stationery. Some people buy single-fold note cards with their name printed on the front. In some cases, email might be appropriate. Your choice of paper, print and delivery channel is a matter of your style and your evaluation of the recipient's style. What's most important is that you thank people every time the opportunity arises.

Tip: One drawback with using email to write thank-you notes is that most people will read the note and then delete the message rather than print it. A letter or a note is more likely to be kept in a file and looked at later.

You can show your appreciation in other ways, too. You might be able to provide useful information, leads and referrals for those who have helped you. For exceptional assistance and support from a networking contact, consider sending or delivering flowers, a gift basket or some other token of appreciation. Once you have landed, you might want to celebrate by taking a key contact to lunch.

Networking Thank-You Letters

In the networking process, thank-you notes and letters are the simplest and most appropriate way to stay in touch with the people who give you their time and support. Immediately following every networking meeting, write a thank-you letter. Be specific, mentioning what you learned that was new or helpful. If you can, offer concrete proof that you have taken advice given to you in the meeting. This might mean commenting on a recommended article or web site, or on rare occasions enclosing a revised copy of your résumé. Forwarding a revised résumé is especially important if your contact has mentioned an available position at the same time. Reiterate your intention to pursue the leads you were given and indicate when the recipient can expect to hear from you again. Be realistic with these commitments. If you say you'll do something, you must do it.

A young woman seeking an entry-level role in the human resources field kept her ever-increasing network of contacts informed every time she met with a person who was suggested by another. Her handwritten thank-you notes sat on her contacts' desks and bookshelves, reminding them of her interests and goals. What's more, her job search became the topic of conversation for a group of eight women in human resources roles who supported her efforts. It took over a year, but finally someone heard of the perfect opportunity and personally arranged the interview that led to the break she needed. Without the flow of thank-you notes, her networking contacts might have forgotten her.

Sample Networking Thank-You Letter #1

NAME
Address
City, Province Postal Code
Telephone / Fax / email

Date

Name
Title
Company
Division
Address
City, Province Postal Code

Dear First Name,

Thank you for taking the time to speak with me during this hectic period surrounding the launch of your capital campaign. Your insights regarding my explorations of the fundraising and development industry were very generous, and I appreciate your suggestion that I speak with Anne-Marie Stepanovich and Frank Oliveri.

In reflecting on our discussion, I can see more clearly how to adjust my focus and target my job search toward the smaller consulting firms. I did not know that Nubion was active in supporting so many educational institutions. I think that the combination of my years of experience in business development with Trademark Cards, plus my commitment to Acadia's fundraising efforts could be of interest to them. I will make that call today and let you know how it turns out.

John, thank you for offering your guidance and advice. I will also be in touch with Anne-Marie Stepanovich at your suggestion, and I'll keep you apprised of the outcome of that contact as well. Have a great vacation at the cottage and I'll be in touch with you early next month.

Regards,

Your Name

Sample Networking Thank-You Letter #2

NAME
Address
City, Province Postal Code
Telephone / Fax / email

Date

Name
Title
Company
Address
City, Province Postal Code

Dear First Name,

Just a brief note to update you on the status of my contact with Pat Chan and Gary DeNova. I was able to meet with each of them this week to discuss my interest in moving into the e-commerce sector. They were very helpful, and I appreciate the introductions you provided.

As you had mentioned, they have vastly different viewpoints on the challenges facing start-up businesses and it was enlightening to hear both sides of the issues surrounding growth and financing. Gary was especially helpful and I will be meeting with his Manager of Special Projects, Ghitu Das Gupta, to explore the possibility of contract work. I would welcome a short-term assignment. It would give me a first-hand opportunity to assess my fit with the culture of a high-tech environment like theirs.

I'll let you know how this next meeting turns out and in the meantime, please accept my thanks for all your efforts on my behalf.

Regards,

Your Name

Thank-You Letters for Interviews

After each interview, follow up immediately by writing a thank-you letter. This will remind the interviewer of the discussion you had and refresh their memory of your qualifications for the job. It will also differentiate you from other candidates since writing thank-you letters following interviews is a relatively rare practice.

Use your debriefing notes, and make specific reference in your letter to points that were discussed in the interview. Express your appreciation for something you learned as well as any advice or direction you received. Reiterate your strengths and relate them to the job requirements. If there is something important that was not mentioned during the interview, include it in your letter. It could be a convincing point that is necessary for your success. As you debrief you might think of things said in the interview that you would like to correct or clarify. Use the thank-you letter to revisit points that were not addressed adequately in person.

Allow your interest and enthusiasm in the job and the organization to show. Restate the follow-up steps that were set out. If nothing was said about next steps, indicate when you plan to initiate contact again. Make a diary note and do it.

Sample Interview Thank-You Letter #1

NAME
Address
City, Province Postal Code
Telephone / Fax / email

Date

Interviewer's Name
Title
Company
Address
City, Province Postal Code

Dear Name,

I enjoyed the opportunity to meet with you again this week. Thank you for making the time to meet for breakfast on Tuesday morning.

As I mentioned in our subsequent telephone discussion on Tuesday evening, I very much enjoyed meeting with Messrs. Brazeau and de Selliers. I found their perspectives on the development, priorities and future opportunities for the Caribbean Bank tremendously interesting and exciting. I especially appreciated their insights on the scope of some of the challenges that are emerging for the human resources function.

Lorraine, I feel most fortunate to have had the opportunity to pursue these employment discussions with you and your colleagues at the Caribbean Bank. Everyone I have met has been most enthusiastic about the Bank's mission and achievements and about the prospects for the future. I believe that my 10 years' experience in international recruiting in the financial services sector plus my recent experience with implementing world-wide compensation policies for Global Mutual Funds, Inc. would enable me to contribute significantly to the Bank's future plans.

Thank you again for your time and for facilitating my interviews with your colleagues. Please be assured of my very keen interest in the Bank and in the position of Director of Human Resources. I will look forward to hearing from you over the next few weeks.

Yours truly,

Your Name

Sample Interview Thank-You Letter #2

NAME
Address
City, Province Postal Code
Telephone / Fax / email

Date

Interviewer's Name
Title
Company
Address
City, Province Postal Code

Dear Name,

This is just a short note to thank you again for meeting with me on Tuesday morning. I very much enjoyed our discussion and I especially appreciated your perspective on the development and focus of the Constant Care Living Centre. The opportunities available to the organization as it establishes its business in Canada are tremendous. Your unique approach to education for families is, to my knowledge, unprecedented in this country. I believe that education is the most important factor in creating a team approach involving all caregivers of people living with Alzheimer's disease.

I would like to mention one additional part of my experience that I believe will help you understand my keen interest in pursuing this opportunity with Constant Care. Fifteen years ago, while I was the Director of Nursing at Seven Lakes Chronic Care Hospital, I developed and led a series of seminars for families to assist them in understanding the needs of their loved ones. I did this outside of my position mandate because I was, and still am, committed to making the move to a care facility as smooth as possible for both the client and their families.

My personal dedication to the needs of long-term care patients, plus my early years' experience in nursing, and recent roles in general management make the position of Director, Client Relations a step for which I am well-suited. I am very interested in joining your team and making the entry of Constant Care Living Centre to Canada an overwhelming success.

Yours truly,

Your Name

"I've Landed" Letters

When you land that next position, whether it's a permanent, full-time job or an interim contract or consulting assignment, be very careful to let the contacts you've made during your job search know where you are working and what your new role entails. Sending an "I've Landed" letter is a professional courtesy that you owe to those who have helped along the way. By closing the loop, they gain a sense of satisfaction from assisting you, and you can offer your future assistance in return. Unfortunately, in the excitement of beginning a new job, many people neglect this important step. If you have your new business cards, enclose one with the letter. If not, follow up again by sending your card in a later note. These simple courtesies are very much appreciated and they often lead to ongoing networking relationships and perhaps future business.

A senior sales and marketing manager accepted a three-month assignment with a media company that was experiencing significant growth. He wrote to each one of his networking contacts, telling them what he was doing and indicating that he would continue his search for a full-time job at the end of the contract. Two weeks before he wrapped things up with the media firm he dispatched another batch of letters, saying that he was back in the job market and would be in touch shortly. During the first week of his resumed full-time search, he made a phone call to every person to whom he had sent a letter.

Tip: It's never too late! Even if you have allowed months to pass by in the excitement of landing and starting your new job, it's still appropriate to send a letter announcing where you're working. People appreciate hearing the news.

Sample "I've Landed" Letter

NAME
Address
City, Province Postal Code
Telephone / Fax / email

Date

Name
Title
Company
Address
City, Province Postal Code

Dear First Name,

I'm very pleased to let you know that I have joined Communications Consultants, an international human resources consulting firm with offices in Montreal, Toronto, Vancouver and over 175 locations worldwide. In my role as Director here in Montreal, I will be conducting activities primarily related to professional development for executives.

My decision to join Communications Consultants was influenced in large part by their substantial experience in managing the human side of organizational change, working with leading corporations. In particular, I was impressed by their success in the areas of leadership and organizational development. I believe that my experience in assessment and coaching will complement the firm's reputation for excellence in working with executive teams.

I would like to thank you for your assistance and encouragement during my transition, especially since Trailblazer's initiatives have placed such a premium on your time. As you know, your introduction to Michel Remy was particularly helpful. His advice on 360° performance reviews paved the way for my early discussions with Communications Consultants. I hope that I will be able to repay your kindness in some way.

I will look forward to keeping in touch.

Yours truly,

Your Name

Part Four

Move into Action

Opportunity is found
where good luck and hard work intersect.

Objectives

This step involves being organized, staying focused on your priorities, building momentum, maintaining motivation and refining your targets as you search for employment. It demystifies the use of networking and provides a process for conducting effective networking meetings. The chapters in Part 4 cover:
- Putting your targets in priority order.
- Allocating time to maximize effectiveness.
- Networking effectively.
- Using search firms and placement agencies.
- The importance of newspaper and trade journal ads.
- The Internet and your job search.
- The advantages and challenges of an active job search.

Rules to Follow

- Try not to worry; never be bitter. Although it is hard to do, make sure that you are able to hide your negative feelings while you are networking and interviewing.
- Go for the buy-in. As this book and others will tell you, being out there talking to people is imperative.
- Keep asking questions aimed at clarifying your targets.
- Set up a record-keeping and diary system that works for you. Efficient information retrieval and timely follow-up are critical to the effective job search.
- Trust that the vast majority of people are pleased to be helpful. As long as you approach them in an appropriate way, they will respond positively and supportively.

Moves That Can Set You Back

- Allowing yourself to remain isolated and inactive.
- Spending countless hours on the Internet. It's the most effective black hole for time that's come along in quite a long time.
- Making networking calls or attending a networking meeting without doing your research and planning your approach.
- Failing to plan time to take care of yourself. You need to do whatever it takes to keep your energy and spirits up.
- Thinking that the only measure of success is landing a job, rather than giving yourself credit for every positive step along the way.

Chapter 14

On Your Mark, Get Set...

Plan your work and work your plan.

You are almost ready to launch an active search for employment that will require you to reach out and talk with a large number of people. To increase your confidence and help you do your best, there are a few more preparatory steps to complete. You need to prioritize your targets; give them time frames and align the resources you have developed with each of your intended targets. Finally, you need to create a sales plan establish a good record-keeping system and get yourself organized. With these steps complete, you'll be ready to go.

Refer to Appendix A. You are in the communication and sales planning phases.

Set Your Priorities: Targets A, B and C

Return to the targets you set in Chapter 8. If you have only one target, stretch your thinking and create at least two more. If you already have more than three targets, narrow your focus to only three for now. Pursuit of these targets will direct your initial forays into the marketplace. Prioritize them based on your current market knowledge and interests.

Your top priority, Target A, could be the role and market where you expect to achieve the quickest results. Alternatively, your first priority could be the target that would involve moving to your preferred geographical location, or starting your own business. It could also be the target that you are most compelled to pursue because of personal interests. Choose Targets A, B and C using the criteria that make sense for you. As your search progresses, you will refine, revise and re-prioritize your targets.

Use your strategic targeting worksheets from Chapter 8 (Worksheet 8.3) and label them A, B or C according to your priorities. Briefly state your rationale for the priority ranking you have given to each target.

The human resources professional described at the end of Chapter 8 had set three targets: a more senior HR role in the sector where she had recent experience, an HR role at her current level in a different industry and a significant change that involved both a new role and a new market. She made the latter, becoming an executive director of a non-profit organization, her first priority, or Target A. She was very committed to helping children with challenges similar to those of her niece and she wanted to either quickly eliminate the possibility of finding this sort of work, or decide to pursue it exclusively for several months. Target B became the lateral move to the health care industry, which she believed to be somewhat close to her primary interest. Target C, her most accessible option, became staying in the industry she knew best to seek a more senior role. The priority order of her targets was driven entirely by her personal interests.

In contrast to this story, many people take a more narrowly focused approach to setting their targets. Some are successful with a singular focus, landing a good opportunity without having to expand their range of possibilities.

A risk management expert with experience in implementing fraud prevention software needed to replace his income immediately. He saw his severance package as an opportunity to get out of debt, and he knew that he could land another job quickly. For him, Targets A, B and C involved approaching different companies in the market he knew very well, and accepting the highest offer available in the shortest period of time. Job content, title and future direction took a back seat to maximizing earnings and minimizing transition time.

Allocate Time to Each Target

Use Appendix B to create a detailed project plan and track your progress. Review the number of weeks left before your desired re-employment date, and plan the amount of time you can spend in pursuit of each target. Do you have the luxury of taking several weeks or even months to assess each target, or do you need to evaluate and revise your targets quickly? For each target, set a start date for actively and aggressively pursuing it. Also set a date when you will evaluate its viability and revise, drop or continue pursuing it.

A lawyer who handled supplier contracts in the legal department of a large automobile company wanted to make a major career change. When she did her self-assessment, writing emerged as the skill she most enjoyed using. In fact, she had often thought about writing a novel and made this Target A. Her personal circumstances allowed her the luxury of taking two years to complete her transition. Allocating six months to the pursuit of Target A, she took a creative writing course, began her novel and approached publishers. At the six-month mark, she decided that being a fiction writer would not provide a sufficient income. She moved to Target B, which was enrolling in a public relations and business communications course at a community college. This generated an abundance of well-paid freelance assignments, allowing her to pursue the novel as a hobby for the present and a career goal for the future.

Most people pursue several targets concurrently. Allocate a specific percentage of your time to each target each week. For example, you might spend 90% of your time pursuing Target A in the first two weeks of your search, and later reduce the allocation to 60%, while increasing the amount of time you spend on Target B or C.

Make a commitment to yourself regarding the amount of time per week you will dedicate to your search for employment. Looking for work is a full-time job. It's wise to devote 30 to 40 hours a week to it. If you need a temporary break, take one; but don't fritter your time away through the weeks that are allocated to the search.

Record your weekly time commitment and time allocation plans on each of your strategic worksheets.

Tip: The deadlines you set and the amount of time you devote to exploring each target are matters of personal priority and circumstance. Some people need only a few days to determine if their most compelling idea is feasible. Others might have a vision that will take years to develop, and their targeting work will help them identify the steps toward their ultimate goal.

A sales and marketing executive in the pharmaceutical industry worked with multinational organizations during the early years of his career. A brief opportunity to run the Canadian division of an offshore company gave him the vision of owning and managing a small company. His Target A was to immediately identify and purchase a small company; however, he recognized that his operational skills were in need of development. Consequently, he placed equal priority on Target B, a lateral move to an operational role in a medium-sized company. An opportunity aligned with Target B came along first and he accepted it, which proved to be a valuable interim step toward his ultimate goal. Five years later, he landed the employment opportunity of his choice, heading up a spin-off organization from one of his former multinational employers.

Align Your Communication Resources with Each Target

Think carefully about how your résumé communicates your fit with each target. Take one target at a time and review your written resources. Do you need to tweak or revise your résumé? Do you need additional marketing pieces such as a brochure or biography for a particular target? Be judicious about this. Don't have more résumés than the diversity of your targets requires.

Tip: Ideas for effectively tailoring written resources to different targets will emerge from research and conversations with people in your network. Listen, learn and improve your materials as you go.

Your verbal pitch in networking meetings and interviews must be consistent with the target you are pursuing. Go back to the five sound bites (Chapter 12). For different targets, you will need to change some of the content or simply adjust your emphasis. It is crucial to try out your pitch on a few people whose opinion you trust.

Consult your support network, board of advisers and, as appropriate, references. Ask them if they think each target is realistic and suitable for you. Are your thoughts too narrow and concrete, or is your thinking so broad and open that it won't be understood? Fully explain your thinking to help them understand why you are interested in a target that might surprise them. Tell them how you think you can make a contribution. You need to know if they will refer and recommend you to others for each target you plan to pursue. A first revision of your targets often comes from receiving this input.

You will often be discussing more than one target with a networking contact. It's important to be able to articulate how all of your targets incorporate a common thread. Even if they seem disparate, your targets arise from your unique history and present circumstances. When you explain your rationale clearly, openly and fully, others will understand your targets.

For each target, align your communication resources and aim them directly at the target. The figure below illustrates the process. Refer to Appendix A to chart your progress.

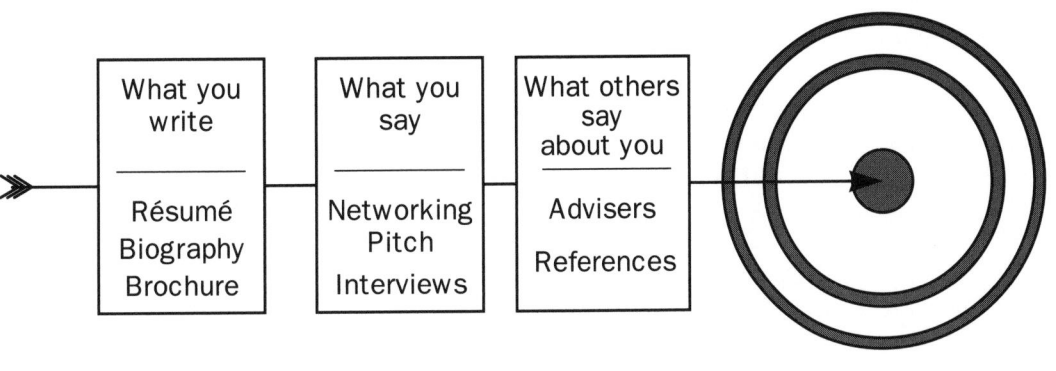

Tip: Many people begin their search with a generic networking pitch that includes their vision of their ideal employment opportunity and their preliminary market assessments. Conversations with others help them identify potential targets that are aligned with what they say and what they have written.

Create a Sales Plan

Return to your market assessment worksheets (Worksheet 8.3). Add to the lists of organizations in your target markets and key people you want to meet by doing thorough research using publicly available information. These lists will expand further as you network. Incorporate the input from your support network, and plan how you will pursue each target efficiently. Which organizations are highest on your list? Who in your network might know a board member or someone who works there? Which contacts are likely to provide valuable insights to your targets? How can you arrange to be introduced to key people?

Once you know what you want to learn about an industry or organization and whom you need to meet, networking will get you there. The next chapter deals exclusively with how to network effectively and appropriately.

Establish a Record-Keeping System

Once you are actively networking, your search for work will become a numbers game. The more face-to-face meetings you have with your networking contacts and those to whom you are referred, the closer you will come to your goal. A good system for keeping track of your activities is essential.

Choose a diary or calendar that you will use and visualize it filled with appointments. Organize your address book now. Don't get behind in recording contact information for everyone you intend to contact plus every new person you meet while networking.

Develop a method of keeping notes from each meeting. Consider using contact tracking software. *A sample networking tracking sheet* follows, which you can set up to merge with your address book for efficiency. Develop a way to measure your weekly activity level.

Sample Networking Tracking Sheet

Contact Name:		
Name: _____ Title: _____ Company Name: _____ Address: _____	Business Phone: _____ Cell Phone: _____ Business Fax: _____ email: _____	
Referred By: Name Title: Company: Phone Number:		
Date:	**Status/Comments:**	**Follow-up Plans**

It's a Dynamic Process

You have now completed the preparation phase for launching an active search for employment. Refer to Appendix A. You have reached the implementation phase. As you move forward, you will receive valuable information about your targets, learn more clearly where your strategic advantage meets marketplace needs, revise your targets, reallocate your time, set new targets, ask for more input and keep the process going until your hard work uncovers an opportunity that is right for you.

   The process is not linear. It will require you to loop back to your market assessments and targets many times. You will also fine-tune how you describe your style, skills and knowledge as you get feedback in the marketplace. You will need to remain flexible and open to new possibilities as you build momentum and become more widely networked.

An international consultant specializing in business process outsourcing recognized the need to accommodate his family's priorities and reduce his overseas travel. In his preliminary search for domestic opportunities, he discovered that one of his ex-employers was selling its Canadian operation. His Target A very quickly shifted from business development in Canada to exploring the possibility of purchasing this company. The idea of being a small business owner had been on his list but relegated to the distant future. Suddenly, it was Target A and he was into full exploration mode. The purchase eventually went to another bidder, and finding domestic assignments returned to Target A status.

Chapter 15

…GO!

Make Networking the Focus of Your Search

You seldom get what you don't ask for.

Networking is the way to access your most valuable resource—people. Networking is an organized process whereby you arrange and conduct a series of face-to-face meetings with your colleagues, contacts and individuals they have recommended as you pursue your targets. Cold calls are not part of an effective networking process.

The objectives of networking include acquainting people with your background and targets, and exchanging information, advice, leads, opinions and, most importantly, referrals. Networking does not involve asking for a job nor is it always a one-sided encounter where you are the sole beneficiary. Through networking, you often have the opportunity to share your knowledge and insights and build valuable relationships you will take into the future.

Tip: "I'm looking for work" is an unspoken message in networking meetings. Gathering information and advice about your targets should always be the formal agenda. If you carefully plan your presentation and ask pertinent questions, your networking contacts will have the opportunity to help you without feeling pressured to talk about specific job opportunities.

Why Network?
The most convincing argument for networking is that over 80% of people seeking employment find their next opportunity through their network. For those at the most senior levels of organizations, networking probably represents a 95% success rate, and for anyone pursuing a new role in a new market, it likely accounts for 99% of success. The only alternatives to networking are using search firms and placement agencies or answering ads for posted positions. Your options look like this:

Success Rates of Job Search Methods

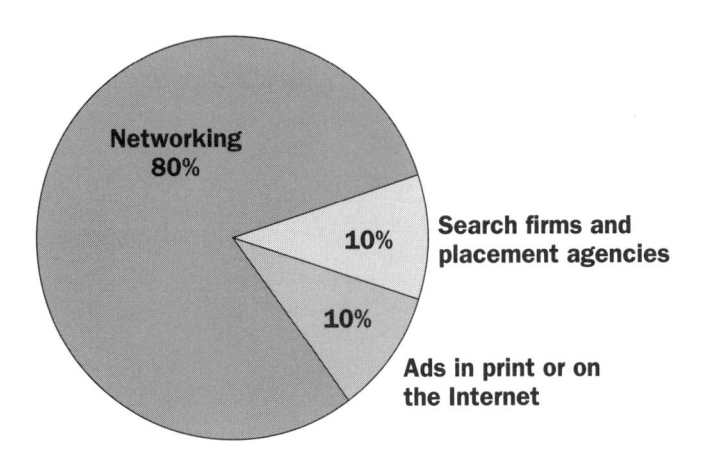

Tip: An active job seeker should divide their time and energy in proportion to the success rates of the various methods.

If you are not convinced by the success rates, consider the many additional benefits of networking. First, networking keeps you up-to-date on events, issues, ideas and opinions. It's the best way to keep track of people on the move in your target organizations and industries. Knowing what's happening is crucial. You need to become a sponge, soaking up information and opinions, reading and talking constantly about what's new.

Second, networking can give you an early advantage for an employment opportunity. When you discover an opening through networking, you may have an earlier entry into the selection process, potentially less competition for the job and the advantage of having been referred by someone known to the organization. Many job opportunities go to effective networkers without ever being advertised or posted, and networking sometimes results in an organization creating a position to accommodate an excellent candidate.

Another benefit of networking is the longer-term value of being connected to a large number of people in a wide variety of occupations and industries. In the new world of work, managers and executives alike are taking a more collaborative approach to work. Therefore, maintaining a healthy network is important for ongoing success. Networking not only enables you to gather information and advice for on-the-job decisions, it will also be invaluable if you decide to change employers, careers, industries or even launch your own venture at some point in the future. The networking process you begin now will be an important resource for you throughout your career.

Finally, networking helps to prevent you from becoming isolated and despondent during your search. People who actively network usually have less difficulty staying motivated because they are busy and externally focused. There are phone calls to be made or returned, letters to write and upcoming meetings that require preparation. Networking is a way to keep going when optimism wanes. People who diligently network find work.

Networking Is a Mutual Exchange

The information you gather through networking can flow both ways. Even in the short term, your own experience and the knowledge you gain as you network can be of great benefit to others. As well, your ever-expanding list of contacts might contain a key name for someone else. If employment opportunities are mentioned that are not suitable for you, perhaps you have met someone who would be a qualified candidate. In the long term, you will have the chance to return the favour for some of the people who helped you.

If you are no longer employed, you have the unique advantage of being a free agent. Most people will be more generous with their information because you are not representing anyone except yourself. They will tend to talk about their organization, its strategies and challenges with less reserve, while at the same time you will be free to discuss many topics more openly.

Tip: Be careful that you do not betray confidences or give away sensitive information in networking meetings. If you are indiscreet about a person or organization, you will be seen as untrustworthy. When discussing confidential information or highly competitive subjects, talk only about information that is in the public domain.

If you are unemployed, you have the luxury of time to read. Most busy people have a stack of magazines and trade journals weighing down their briefcase. If you can point out the useful and interesting pieces in recent literature, you will have done your networking contacts a favour. Be prepared to give a synopsis of the articles and books you are recommending. Get reprints of exceptional material.

A change management consultant who was in the process of building her own practice read a pivotal article in Harvard Business Review *about communicating change to front-line employees. She made a point of mentioning the article in networking and marketing meetings during the first six months of building her venture. She also purchased a supply of reprints and found that almost everyone who heard her synopsis and accompanying interpretation wanted to read the article for themselves. Sending a reprint gave her another welcome point of contact and a topic for further discussion.*

Steps to Effective Networking

The secret to effective networking is targeted planning and a singular focus on each person you intend to meet. Everything must be tailored to the individual, from deciding when you are ready to make the contact to planning the telephone message, arranging the time and venue for the meeting, planning how you will open the meeting, how much of your background you describe, which targets you mention and what questions you ask. It's obvious that you would handle a meeting with your boss from 12 years ago differently than you would handle one with an industry expert or key decision-maker you have not previously met. There is no universal plan, agenda or script that works for every networking meeting. You must plan and use your judgment for each one separately.

Develop a Comprehensive Networking List

This list is broader than the one you compiled in the market assessment and sales planning exercises. It captures *everyone* you know, including the names of key people you previously identified as being valuable contacts. Do not exclude anyone assuming that you could never get a meeting with them or that they couldn't help you. First, they might surprise you, and second, they might be able to introduce you to others who could be helpful. Use the following Personal Network Chart to jog your memory and think as broadly as possible. For the moment, don't make judgments or do any analysis; just record as extensive an inventory of names as you can.

A career transition consultant was working with a group of warehouse workers in a light industrial park. These men were very skeptical about the value of talking with everyone they knew about their need to find work. However, when each one was asked how he got his most recent job, it was networking all around. Shortly after this discussion, a woman who operated a catering truck arrived. Having heard that the warehouse was closing, she wanted the men to square their accounts with her. They jokingly asked her if she knew of any job openings. The next day she returned to tell the group that a warehouse down the road was hiring. Several applied and two men landed jobs through that serendipitous networking opportunity.

Tip: Consider contacting people who have successfully completed a search somewhat similar to yours. They might have information, contacts and leads they would be glad to share.

Personal Network Chart

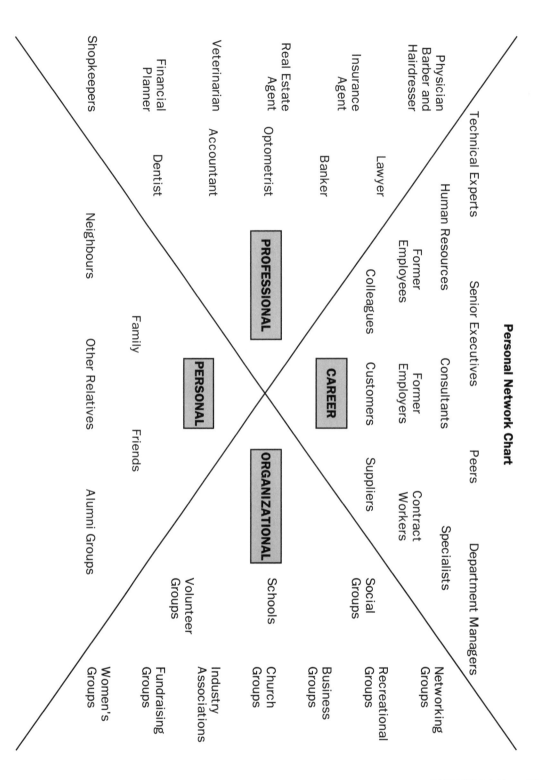

Technical Experts

Physician
Barber and
Hairdresser

Human Resources

Insurance
Agent

Lawyer

Banker

Senior Executives

Real Estate
Agent

Former
Employees

Optometrist

Colleagues

Veterinarian

Accountant

Customers

Former
Employers

Financial
Planner

Dentist

Consultants

PROFESSIONAL

CAREER

Peers

Suppliers

Contract
Workers

Family

PERSONAL

ORGANIZATIONAL

Specialists

Department Managers

Friends

Neighbours

Other Relatives

Alumni Groups

Volunteer
Groups

Schools

Social
Groups

Recreational
Groups

Networking
Groups

Shopkeepers

Women's
Groups

Fundraising
Groups

Industry
Associations

Church
Groups

Business
Groups

Categorize the List

To make your list manageable, you need to sort the names. These three categories are usually sufficient:

Category 1 Include the people you know well and feel comfortable approaching. This will include your original support network, board of advisers, references, colleagues from the workplace and perhaps some additional friends and family members. These are the people you will contact first, as you gain comfort with the networking process.

Category 2 These are people less well known or less accessible to you. Also include people who would know *of* you and might be willing to meet with you without an introduction. You will contact the people in this category as your confidence and competence at networking increase.

Category 3 Include people you know are beyond you in seniority or expertise, making them seem inaccessible to you. Also include people you know who seem busy, aloof or otherwise unapproachable, and those you haven't met, for whom you need an introduction or referral.

Return to Your Targets and Plan Your Calls

Deciding on what order to make networking calls is not a random or haphazard process. You want to pursue your targets as efficiently as possible while increasing your confidence at networking. At the outset, call only people from Category 1. Tell them that you want to talk about your targets and search plans, and ask their advice on both. Later in the process, when you are calling people from Category 2 or Category 3, you will need to be more specific in your approach.

> **Tip:** Match your list of names to your targets. Approach people from Category 1 who might advance your pursuit of Target A first. Move to other categories and targets as your confidence grows and your clarity regarding specific targets increases.

Being fully prepared before making a call is a large part of networking success. You don't want to make key calls too early in the game, yet you can't wait too long after having been offered a referral before making the contact. Also, it is important to consider the appropriateness of the referring person. It is best to be referred to key decision-makers and influential people by someone they respect. Sometimes it's prudent to intentionally arrange one meeting ahead of another, based on your expectation of what you might learn, and how that information could be useful in subsequent meetings.

   Before you pick up the phone, use these guidelines to be sure you're ready.

GUIDELINES FOR PREPARING TO MAKE AN INITIAL CALL

- Focus on one person at a time.
- Decide who to call next based on the following:
  - Your readiness to meet with them, including how comfortable you have become with the networking process and where you are in pursuing your targets.

- • Your level of confidence that the person who referred you is the best one to provide the introduction.
- • How recently their name was suggested to you. It's better to make the call while the suggestion is fresh so that you can let the referring person know that you are following their suggestion.
- • In what way you anticipate the contact to be helpful.
- Once you've chosen a name, do your research. Review what you learned about this person from the referral source or in what context you know them personally. Research their organization, the industry or anything else that will give you clues as to what you might discuss with them.
- If they are from an industry less familiar to you, get copies of recent issues of newsletters or journals from their industry to see what topics are current.
- Surmise what might interest them from your experience, knowledge and research.
- Before planning what you will say on the telephone, create a preliminary agenda for the networking meeting.
- If you know them, how will you bridge the gap from the last time you've spoken with them?
- If you don't know them, what will you say about the person who referred you? Why did they suggest that you make this call?
- Why are you asking for this meeting? What is it that you want to learn from them?
- In the meeting, what key questions might you use to invite them to take the floor?
- Script the telephone call to set up the meeting.

Tip: Remember that you are not making cold calls but rather following up on the leads given to you by someone else in your network. Contacting people you know and using their referrals is the best way to network.

A communications and public relations specialist was looking for a new job when market conditions were particularly slow. She asked for a networking meeting with the VP of Communications at her husband's firm. In that meeting she was given the names of contacts at four organizations that were suppliers of communications services to the firm and valued their relationship with the VP of Communications. She called the contacts and found that using the VP's name was magical. Meetings were immediately arranged with the four contacts, and she was able to offer them valuable insights into her husband's firm's culture. Although there were no immediate openings at the suppliers' firms, she was given 14 new leads. Three months later, one of those leads resulted in a contract assignment that eventually led to a full-time job.

Tip: Don't feel that arranging networking meetings over lunch is necessary. It's usually easier to schedule a brief meeting in the contact's office than to arrange a lunch date. Also, a series of networking lunches can become very expensive. If you suggest lunch, you need to be prepared to pay.

The Phone Call

The purpose of your telephone call is to arrange a face-to-face meeting that will last approximately 15 to 30 minutes. It seems very short, but this is the amount of time that most people are readily willing to commit. In stating the reason for the meeting, be honest, brief and enthusiastic. Do not attempt to conceal your purpose in an effort to intrigue them and do not hint at potential benefits they might glean from the meeting. You are asking for information, advice and leads regarding a specific occupation, industry or organization. If your contact receives any immediate benefit from the meeting, it will be a bonus.

Tip: Face-to-face meetings are much better than meetings conducted over the phone. In person you will usually receive more information. You also significantly increase the likelihood of getting additional leads and referrals, and have a better chance of being remembered by your contact.

GUIDELINES FOR REQUESTING THE MEETING

- Make your initial calls during regular business hours. However, if you do not connect after a week or so, try calling either before or after hours when it is more likely that the person you want to meet will pick up their own phone.
- Stand up while making the call, to help you sound more confident and businesslike. Smile and it will transmit through your voice. Speak more slowly than usual, especially when you give your name and phone number.
- Use the feature that allows you to review and re-record your message.
- Have your diary in hand and be prepared to suggest a few dates and times.
- Be prepared for each of these three possibilities:
  - Speaking directly with the person you hope to meet.
  - Leaving a message on their voice mail.
  - Speaking with your potential contact's administrative assistant.
- Use the same basic script, adjusting it slightly for each different audience. Practise out loud before placing the call.
- Clearly state your name and the name of the person who referred you.
- Indicate that you would like to arrange a brief meeting, no more than 15 to 30 minutes, and then explain the purpose of the meeting in one or two sentences. Plan your wording carefully. Don't be vague and don't say too much.
- If you reach the contact person directly, try to avoid having the meeting on the phone. Reiterate your willingness to come to their office and be prepared to schedule the meeting for the distant future if the individual is exceptionally busy. If they are insistent about having the discussion on the spot, you'll have to comply. Go through your abbreviated sound bites, ask your questions and ask for referrals.
- If you get voice mail, explain everything as briefly as you can, suggest a time that would work for you and close by saying how much you would appreciate their willingness to meet. The message should take 30 seconds, maximum.

- After leaving a voice mail message, make a diary note to follow up within a week. The second voice mail message should simply remind them of your name, the referring person and the request for the meeting.
- Speaking with the person's administrative assistant can often be the best alternative. Although it is their job to act as a gatekeeper, you might be able to get to know them and make them your ally in arranging a meeting. You can ask them when your chances would be best to speak with their boss.
- If you are having trouble connecting either through voice mail or the administrative assistant, persist by trying once a week. Don't harass, but sound upbeat and confident in the fact that arranging the meeting will happen eventually.
- When a meeting is arranged, restate the time and place as a means of confirming the commitment. Make sure you know exactly how to get there before you hang up.

A successful networker used a telephone script that went like this: "Hi, Mr. Radomski, I'm Janet Newman. I met with Frank Cheng yesterday to talk about the retail investment business, and he suggested that you would probably be able to help me. I spent the past 12 years with Worthy Asset Management Company, where I held a series of positions focused on internal controls and policy. I am currently exploring possibilities for my next career step. My expertise is in risk management and I am interested in understanding how different organizations manage compliance issues. Would you be able to meet with me briefly at your convenience? I am available every afternoon for the balance of this week and anytime next week."

Most people are willing to schedule a networking meeting if they are approached in a straightforward manner and the proposed agenda is credible. Chances are they know first-hand about the challenges of a job search, either because they've been through it or they know someone who has.

Tip: Every time you leave a voice mail message for any reason, make it a habit to slowly and clearly state your phone number right after your name at the beginning and again at the end of your message, allowing the listener to pick it up at either point.

Further Research and Preparation for the Meeting

Now that you have the meeting scheduled, celebrate! You've leaped over a high hurdle. Move on to prepare thoroughly for the meeting.

Note anything that was said in the phone call, and review what your referral told you about the individual whom you are going to meet. Knowing their role, priorities, issues and challenges will help you plan an effective agenda for the meeting. Develop realistic objectives for the meeting that will advance the pursuit of your targets.

Think about what you will say about the person who referred you. Be exact in your plans for describing yourself and your background. Remember that you have a short time to accomplish a lot. Practise the four-minute version of your sound bites using a timer. It's easy to talk too long. Formulate three to five open-ended questions that you can use to invite your contact to take the floor. These are called "over-to-you" questions. An inventory of suggested questions is found at the end of this chapter.

Continue your research on the industry and the organization, including a last-minute check for press releases on an Internet newswire. If you have up-to-the-minute information about your contact's organization, they will be impressed with your level of preparation and realize that you are serious about your networking efforts.

A marketing specialist who became an expert networker made a habit of checking for press releases on the newswire immediately before leaving for every networking meeting. Many times, doing this enabled him to direct discussions to current topics. Once, he was able to initiate an animated conversation about revolutionary marketing approaches following the recent change in government regulation on the advertisement of specific products. His contact was unaware that a press release on the topic had been issued by his organization. The networker reported that his "over-to-you" questions were so up-to-the-minute that he sounded like a soothsayer. The meeting resulted in introductions to several more networking contacts.

The following worksheet is similar to the one used for preparing your five sound bites in Chapter 12. For networking, you need to add information explaining what you are doing to pursue your Targets A, B and C, plus the "over-to-you" questions. It's crucial that you invite dialogue. Finally, every meeting should end with your request for additional referrals. The worksheet offers a sample dialogue to guide you in preparing for networking meetings.

WORKSHEET 15.1
Prepare a Network Meeting Dialogue

Build Rapport (30 seconds–1 minute)

Greetings, handshakes and card exchange should be accompanied by a very brief conversation aimed at breaking the ice. "I appreciate your taking the time to meet me. I understand that (refer to a point of common interest or the person who introduced you) _____

_____."

"I asked for only 15 minutes of your time, and I want to stick to that, so let me get right to the point."

Capsule Profile and Career Review (3–4 minutes)

"If I may, I'll give you a quick overview of my background and current interests as a means of explaining why I wanted to meet with you. I'm a (title or professional designation) _____.

I've spent the last _____ years in the _____ industry. In the past 10 years, I have worked with or in (name the organizations, projects, people or whatever makes sense for this context) _____

_____

_____.

Most recently, I was (title)_____ of (division or area) _____ with (name of organization plus explanation of its business, if necessary) _____

where I (role or mandate) _____. One highlight for me was (mention a significant achievement relevant to this meeting and include the result) _____

_____.

I also had the opportunity to (mention more relevant achievements or experiences) _____

_____and _____."

Leaving Story (30 seconds–1 minute)

"My role at _____ came to an end as a result of _____

_____."

Or: "I'm looking for other opportunities because _____."

What You Are Looking For (30 seconds)

"Ideally, I would like my next role to entail or utilize (describe the aspects of your Targets A, B and C that are relevant to this meeting) _____,

and I'm also looking at _____.

Another option would be _____."

What You Are Doing About It (1–2 minutes)

"What I've done so far is (mention research, networking activities, and interviews)_____

_____ and _____ .

"I would appreciate your advice on _____ (or your option of) _____

and some feedback on my approach to _____."

Three to Four "Over-to-You" Questions (10 minutes)

"I understand that (lead into your questions by mentioning the referring person or something from

your research) _____ and (ask your most pressing "over-to-you"

question)_____?"

(At this point listen and watch the time. Ask your subsequent questions only if time allows)

_____

_____

_____?"

Optional: Ask for Feedback on Your Plans (1-2 minutes)

"How plausible do you think (reiterate Target A, B or C) _____ is?"

"How would you suggest that I approach _____?"

"Is there anything else you think I should keep in mind?"

Ask for Additional Referrals

"Who else do you think I should be talking to?"

"Please tell me more about them."

"Would it be appropriate for me to mention your name when I call?"

Closing

"I'll stay in touch and let you know how things go. You've been tremendously helpful and again, I
appreciate the time you've given me."

Tip: This is one time it's not advisable to telephone ahead and confirm the meeting. Doing that opens up the possibility of a cancellation.

Conduct the Meeting

Review the advice on preparing for an interview. Many of the principles apply to networking meetings as well. Put yourself in the shoes of the contact person, and be aware that they are probably unsure of how they will be able to help you. It's important to think of ways to put them at ease. Being well prepared and willing to take over the agenda is the best way to do this. This does not mean that you do the talking. You ask the questions and listen.

During the meeting, take responsibility for the time. If you asked for 15 minutes, you must try to stick to it even though it's a very short amount of time. Mention the originally agreed time limit up front, allowing your contact to either confirm that the meeting must end within the allotted time or invite you to stay longer than originally agreed. If the time can be extended, you can relax a bit and explain your background, skills and interests in more depth. However, if you have prepared well, you should be able to turn the floor over to the other person within five minutes and have enough time to get answers to your key questions before time is up.

Every networking meeting needs to be handled as if it's the most important interview you will have in your job search. You never know which meeting will be the one that generates the lead to the ideal employment opportunity for you.

Tip: Do not hand your résumé to your networking contact during the meeting. You are not asking for a job or even job leads. Some people don't take a copy of their résumé along to ensure there is no risk of appearing to be asking for a job. The résumé can always be enclosed with the thank-you letter, if requested.

Ask for Referrals

Every networking meeting should include your request for suggestions of people who might be able to offer information and advice. It's best to ask toward the end of the meeting, after you have explained your background and targets. Sometimes you will be comfortable asking for a specific referral, for example, "If you know Fernando Circosta at International Design, I would appreciate an introduction to him," or "I'm interested in finding out more about Town Travel Corporation. Is there someone there you could suggest?"

When you are given referrals, record the names and contact information. Try to find out enough about each person so that you understand why they are recommended and in what way your contact expects them to be helpful to you. Ask if you can use your contact's name when you call. Express your gratitude for these leads and commit to keeping your contact informed as you make the new contacts.

A general manager, who was quite introverted, found himself in the job market during the worst years of a recession in which his industry was particularly hard hit. He realized that he would have to make networking the central focus of his job search activities, and there was almost nothing he could have dreaded more. His career transition consultant had assured him that before he conducted his 200th face-to-face networking meeting he would find the work he wanted. The general manager discovered that thinking of networking as a "numbers game" helped to keep him motivated, and he measured his success by the number of new referrals he was given. To keep track, he kept a growing stack of contacts' business cards, which he counted regularly. At any given moment, he knew exactly how many cards he had in his "meeting completed" pile, which had grown to 168 by the time he got an excellent job offer. His success was the result of persistently being out there talking with people.

Debrief and Write a Thank-You Letter

After every networking meeting, debrief in writing as you would following an interview. Use the Sample Networking Tracking Sheet from Chapter 14 to record the relevant facts. Write a thank-you letter within 24 hours if possible, and mention something specific from the conversation that was particularly helpful to you. Close by stating your intention to follow up, and as always, make a diary note to do it. File the information in your record-keeping system so that you can retrieve it for future meetings, interviews or other opportunities.

Follow Up

As soon as you can, contact the people whose names you have been given. If you don't feel ready to make some of the calls, use your judgment, but remember that it often takes a long time to set up a meeting. If you plan the phone calls very carefully, make them and arrange a meeting, your confidence will probably build by the time you have the meeting.

Every time you contact someone to whom you have been referred, thank the person who referred you. Send a brief email message, handwritten note or letter, or leave a voice mail message. This simple courtesy accomplishes three very important things:
- It demonstrates that you value the leads given to you.
- It lets the referring person know that the contact has been made.
- It keeps your name top-of-mind with the referring person, thereby increasing the likelihood that you will be remembered when additional networking opportunities or job leads arise.

....

Tip: When someone gives you permission to use their name as a reference for a networking call, they *want* to know when the contact has been made. Your career plans often become a point of mutual interest between the referring person and the new contact. You must keep your contacts up-to-date on your activities.

....

Once you have had an initial networking meeting, followed up on all of the leads given to you and expressed your gratitude appropriately, you need to find more ways to stay in touch with your networking contacts. Think of how you can become a blip on your contacts' radar screens! It doesn't take much. A 30-second voice mail message giving a quick update on your progress will do it. A greeting card during the holidays or verbal regards delivered by a mutual acquaintance also works. Use the following guidelines to generate more ideas.

GUIDELINES FOR STAYING IN TOUCH WITH NETWORKING CONTACTS

- Make your networking follow-up efforts unique to each individual. There is no universal plan that dictates the frequency or form of subsequent contact.
- For your original support network and board of advisers, monthly contact is probably a minimum. For others, the minimum could be as long as six months. Use your judgment.
- Use voice mail, email, handwritten notes or letters to stay in touch. Brief messages are best.
- Do not put all your networking contacts on a mass mailing list using your email software. Your contacts will be annoyed to receive regular messages that are not personally relevant.
- When you have heard an interesting speaker or read an informative article or book, send a quick message about it to those whom you know would be interested.
- If there is a speaker you would like to hear, think of inviting someone in your network who would be interested in attending with you.
- When you have an upcoming interview or networking meeting and you know that someone in your network could provide valuable input, phone them and ask specific questions. Most people respond to questions such as, "I'm meeting with Heather Speigle next Tuesday, and I wonder if you know how long she's been at Engineering Consulting Company and where she worked before joining them?"
- Send your congratulations when you learn of a contact's promotion, transfer or change of employers.
- Similarly, if a mutual acquaintance receives a promotion or changes jobs, check to see if your networking contact has heard the good news.
- Remember personal details that are mentioned in networking meetings. If you know that a contact has just returned from vacation, ask about it in your next message or conversation. Try to keep track of family concerns and special occasions if your contact has confided in you.
- Schedule the occasional breakfast or lunch with your key contacts, if your budget can handle it.
- Most importantly, keep your contacts up-to-date on your job search activities, especially if your Targets A, B and C change.

Tip: The year-end holiday season and July and August are excellent times to have networking meetings. Because so many people are away, those who remain in the office often have more time and are less likely to feel pressured than at other times of the year.

Make Networking a Way of Life

Don't make the common mistake of neglecting or forgetting your network once you've landed. Stay in touch at least twice a year and look for opportunities to be helpful. Be proactive in offering your time and talents in some way that you know would be appreciated. Lead a seminar in an area of your expertise for your contact's direct reports, contribute to a fundraising effort, suggest candidates for a job opening and introduce others from your network. There will be many opportunities if you look for them.

Raise your industry profile by joining and participating actively in professional associations. By becoming involved in committees and special projects, you will be able to work with and get to know people that you would not otherwise meet. Accepting a position on the executive will also expand your range of contacts and develop your reputation.

Consider volunteering for a charitable, recreational or political organization that reflects your values. When you contribute your time to a cause or activity that means something to you, you usually meet like-minded people. Get to know the organizers and executive boards of these groups. Contacts from your non-working life can be more valuable than your work-related network when you need advice and assistance for problems on the job or during times of career transition.

Attend business and social functions. Become more active in your community. Take courses, attend conferences and sign up for workshops and seminars. Be proactive in introducing yourself in these situations. Ask questions of people you meet and learn what they do. Share your own background and look for areas of mutual interest. It's a small world, and you'll often be surprised by the connections you share with the people you meet.

Tip: How many times in your life have you made the effort to contact someone and then thought, "I wish I had waited three more weeks before I made that call"? More often, you wish you had made the call sooner. Don't procrastinate.

GUIDELINES FOR SPECIAL NETWORKING CHALLENGES

When Someone Offers to Take Your Résumé to Someone Else

- Occasionally a networking contact will offer to take a copy of your résumé and pass it around for you. At best, this offer is well-intentioned, and the individual will do what they say. At worst, it's a brush-off. Regardless, there is no assurance that your background, skills and career plans will be introduced properly by what someone else says about you.
- When someone is passing your résumé around, it can be a deterrent to your networking efforts by causing awkward overlaps that make you appear desperate.
- Letting someone else hand out your résumé precludes your opportunity to follow up.
- It's better if you maintain control of the process. Thank the people who make such offers, and ask if they would be willing to give you the names and allow you to make the approach.
- Sometimes there will be a good reason to let a contact go ahead and pass your résumé around. More often, you will be given a list of referrals for follow up.

- Ask if you might use the referring person's name. Try to find out as much as possible about each potential new contact.

Breaking Out of Concentric Circles

- Once you have been actively networking for several months, you might find that you're beginning to hear the same news and the same names repeatedly. This means that your networking is moving in concentric circles and you need to break into other networks.
- To expand your horizons, explore an entirely new idea with your existing contacts to see if additional referrals are available.
- Contact people in organizations who supply the industry that interests you.
- Take a trip to another city and network there for a week. This takes careful pre-planning and a willingness to relocate.
- Choose another industry that holds your interest and ask your existing networking contacts to introduce you to someone in that industry.
- The executive directors of industry associations are often quite generous with information and referrals.
- Ask your stock broker to provide an introduction to an industry analyst. They have in-depth knowledge of the influential people within an industry.

Getting in Touch with Category 3 Contacts

When you sorted your inventory of names, you put some people in Category 3 because you either didn't know them or you thought that they were inaccessible to you. Also, as you conduct networking meetings, you are given more Category 3 names.

- Make it a goal in your research and networking conversations to find out as much as possible about these individuals and their organizations.
- If one of them is speaking at a conference or making a public presentation, make every effort to be in the audience. Ask a thoughtful question from the floor if the opportunity arises.
- Find out who knows them, and try to arrange meetings with their acquaintances.
- Think strategically about who would provide the most persuasive referral. If you can use the name of someone who is very important to the person you want to meet, your chances of being granted a meeting are much higher.
- Be direct in telling your networking contacts and board of advisers that you are looking for an opportunity to meet these people. When you know that someone has the ability to introduce you, ask them if they would feel comfortable doing so.
- Even though some people seem so distant that they are barely on your radar screen, someone you know will know them. That brings you closer to the opportunity to be in touch.

After researching recent changes in health care, a facilities and technology manager from a large urban school board wanted to see if his skills might transfer to the health care sector. To assess his marketability, he set up a networking meeting with a senior manager at a large urban hospital. He used the meeting to verify what he had learned and gather more specific information about the impact that cutbacks within the health care industry were having on his area of specialty. During the conversation, he received excellent advice on repackaging his experience to align it more closely with the health care industry. He then drafted a résumé using this advice and forwarded it to his contact for feedback. The contact was impressed with both the résumé and the serious interest of the facilities manager, and offered several valuable leads for contract and consulting work.

An Inventory of Questions to Ask in Networking Meetings

These questions are intended to direct your thought processes, not to be rhymed off without considering the specific individual and the circumstances of the networking meeting. Your best questions will arise from your research. When you preface a question with a statement such as "I read about your recent acquisitions in Chile," your contact will be more inclined to give you useful information.

- Review the research questions on trends, industries, organizations and people listed in Chapter 9. They are excellent networking questions.
- Ask your networking contact to describe their background and experience:
  - What is your history in this organization?
  - What were your previous roles?
  - Where were you before you joined this organization?
- Ask about your contact's current role:
  - How is the organization structured and where does your department fit?
  - How is your department structured?
  - What is your mandate?
  - What issues do you think you'll be tackling in the next 18 months?
  - What might be a next step for you?
- Ask about the industry and the market:
  - How would you define your organization's competitive advantage?
  - Where do you think _____ is headed?
  - What is your attitude toward _____?
  - What skills are most in demand in this industry … in your organization?
  - Are there any books or management theories that are popular in this organization or industry?
  - Which search firms and placement agencies does your organization use?
- Ask for feedback on your plans:
  - Do you think that my skills and experience would be seen as transferable to _____?
  - What do you think of my prospects for moving into the field of _____?
  - What sort of position might someone with my background aspire to in this industry?
  - Who else should I be talking to?

Chapter 16

The Internet, Ads and Search Firms

*Passive search techniques
add value when used effectively.*

Notwithstanding the importance of getting out there and talking with people, you must also search the Internet for postings, look for ads in print media and approach search firms and placement agencies. You need to understand how to best employ these methods and include them in your search strategy. They cannot be ignored, but invest your time in them only in proportion to their effectiveness. Do not become discouraged if they don't generate quick results.

Using the Internet

The Internet is a powerful tool for corporate recruiters and executive search professionals, giving them the ability to collect many more résumés than traditional methods allowed. The cost efficiency of online postings, email receipt of information and electronic filtering for first-level sorting has caused the Internet to eclipse conventional newspaper advertising. The huge benefit to the job seeker is the increased number of advertised positions in the public domain and the efficiency of electronic matching technology.

The Internet has not, however, magically transformed the arduous task of the job search into a cakewalk. There are no guarantees of effortless success, especially for those who have reached more senior levels or work in specialized, non-technical areas. However, you must not overlook the opportunity to see what's out there. Using the Internet as an effective part of your search requires selectivity and discipline. You must stay focused on your targets; otherwise, the vast array of information and advertising can be distracting and very wasteful of your time.

Web-based recruiting through career sections on corporate web sites has grown tremendously in the past few years. Virtually all major corporations and many small ones have web pages designed to attract qualified candidates and promote the organization. On your targets' web sites, you can access the list of posted positions and apply directly using the specified protocol. Another advantage is the glimpse you get of your targets' overall hiring needs. You can learn a lot about the challenges and opportunities facing an organization and glean valuable information for planning your approach in networking meetings and in preparing for the interviewing process.

Tip: Web site career sections do not necessarily list all of the positions available in an organization. More senior positions are seldom posted and opportunities in the planning stages are never posted. Networking is the only way to find unadvertised opportunities.

There are thousands of job boards in cyberspace, some claiming to have hundreds of thousands of advertised positions. There are sites covering all industries, professions and levels. They may be Canadian, North American or global in scope. There are also specialty sites devoted to specific fields such as IT, biotech, the arts and non-profit organizations. Most industry and professional associations have career sections on their sites. It can be overwhelming. Make the initial, albeit substantial, investment of time to identify the ones that have a number of postings at your level, in the industries and locations that interest you.

Select a few, perhaps eight at most, and register using their job notification service or personal job search agents. These electronic agents are search engines within the site that you create using keywords and job titles that apply to you. They locate matches between your information and their job postings, emailing their findings to you on a regular basis. Open a separate, free email account for this purpose to protect your privacy. At the end of your search, you can cancel the email account when you delete your search agents.

Creating effective search agents requires yet another substantial investment of your time. The major job boards invite you to have multiple agents. Discovering which job titles and keywords generate appropriate responses may take a few weeks of intuitive work. You need to check the postings emailed to you by your electronic search agents against your independent search for relevant postings on the board. This way you will discover if the information you registered captures the right postings. Persist! This feature of the Internet job search repays your effort tenfold.

An architect, who moved into general management and advanced to the executive level in a major real estate company, discovered that listing the word "architect" with Internet job search agents was not helpful. The information technology industry has usurped the word, using it to describe the creators of systems and programs. At the same time, he learned that virtually no jobs requiring architects, the ones who design physical structures, are listed on Internet job search boards. Through trial and error, he discovered that using the words "executive" or "leader" in combination with "real estate" generated the desired matches.

Tip: Once you have done your research, selected the job boards that are appropriate for you and registered several search agents, do not spend more than 10 percent of your ongoing search time and energy on Internet job boards. Let the electronic agents take care of the search for you, emailing you information about possible matches. You should carry on with your networking activities.

Internet job boards also offer you the opportunity to post your résumé on their site. Once posted, your résumé is available for employers to peruse, often using sophisticated search technology. Presumably, employers will contact you and invite you to apply for appropriate jobs. It seems an attractive proposition, but there are significant drawbacks. There have been many incidents of identity theft. Databases containing online résumés and job seekers' email addresses are sometimes sold or stolen. The consequences to you could be significant.

Important: If you choose to post your résumé on any Internet venue, you will probably receive unsolicited email and phone calls in response. Those contacting you might offer to conduct your job search for you, put you in touch with a number of companies or place you in a prime job within a short period of time. These offers may have a number of motives such as seeking payment of a fee for which you may obtain no benefit, or persuading you to make an investment in a new business such as a franchise or pyramid selling scheme. Use due caution in responding to these offers.

Ads in Newspapers, Newsletters and Trade Journals

Traditional venues for job ads are still important. Until the Internet totally replaces print material, you must read the daily newspapers plus the industry journals and newsletters faithfully. You will find that many ads in the print media are also posted on Internet job boards and on organizations' web sites.

   As you peruse newspapers and magazines, be sure to keep your eyes open for appointment notices and other news items that signal a change within an organization. It's good information for your networking efforts and can offer early signals of upcoming vacancies.

A sales executive from the hospitality industry read that a conglomerate had bought several world-class cruise ships. Recognizing that the acquisition could create the need for additional senior managers, he called the president of the acquiring company and explained his interest. The president was in Spain on holidays, but when he picked up his messages, he was so impressed that he returned the call personally, arranging a meeting for his first day back in the office.

The two main sources of job postings—print ads and the Internet—should be considered as one because they represent identical strategies on the part of the employer. They simply use different delivery channels. In each case, the employer has decided to advertise the available position to a broad market and collect as many résumés as possible. You will be one of hundreds or thousands responding to the posting. Your chance of being selected for the interview process is no better for jobs posted on the Internet than for traditional print ads.

Search Firms and Placement Agencies

Search firms and placement agencies play an important role in the active job search; however, don't make the mistake of thinking that you can register with a few well-chosen ones and then sit back and wait for results. These companies have no vested interest in finding you a job. They work for their client organizations and are focused on you only to the extent that you meet the criteria for one of their current assignments. If you are not a suitable candidate for any of the positions they are seeking to fill, they will keep your information in their database for an amount of time that varies from six months to a lifetime. Policies vary. Therefore, it's up to you to keep in touch and ensure that your qualifications stay top-of-mind with them.

Tip: Once your information is on file with a search firm or placement agency, you must continue checking their ads and Internet postings. When you see an ad that matches your interests, either call your contact or resubmit your application. Don't assume that you are in the process automatically.

Having said this, most search consultants are very interested in getting to know a large number of people and keeping track of their careers. It's their business to know who's who in the industries they serve, and they are conscious of the logical career moves that an individual needs to make in order to climb the ladder of success. Therefore, getting to know a few search consultants should be a part of your active job search plan. You will need a good networking introduction in order to meet them unless you are being considered for one of their assignments. An introduction from someone in one of their client organizations is often effective.

Tip: Researchers are the hidden treasures in many search firms. It's their job to compile the initial list of qualified candidates for an assignment. They are usually more accessible than the consultants and partners of the firm, and will often take the time to talk with you over the phone. They are an invaluable source of information once you have formed a relationship with them.

Search firms, also known as executive search firms or headhunters, differ from placement agencies in that they typically work exclusively at the senior management, professional and executive levels. Positions with starting salaries of less than $100,000 probably do not warrant their services. Search firms are usually paid on a retainer basis. Their fees are typically based on a percentage of the position's base or total cash compensation for the first year. With a retainer-based firm, fees are payable whether or not the search firm identifies a candidate who is successful in being hired by the organization. Once you have been identified as a candidate for one of their assignments, they will work very hard to help you.

Most search firms advertise the positions they are filling on their web sites, making it easy for the job seeker to evaluate the suitability of a particular firm. Many search firms also offer a confidential résumé posting service where hiring organizations may peruse candidates' résumés. Some search firms require you to fill out a lengthy online questionnaire as a way of registering with them. Many have linked their web sites to Internet job boards. Before posting your résumé on a search firm's or placement agency's site, read their privacy policy.

An operations manager from a major utility company, who became a legend of the active job search game, asked most of the people he met through his networking efforts to identify the search firms and placement agencies their organizations used. Doing this narrowed his list of firms for ongoing attention and contact, making this part of his job search as efficient as possible.

Placement agencies often specialize in specific market niches. The jobs they fill cover the whole spectrum from full-time to temporary, seasonal or contract opportunities. They typically work on a contingency basis, being paid only when one of their candidates is hired. Although some agencies, particularly in the United States, charge an additional fee to the candidate, this is not a common practice in Canada. Placement agencies are interested in you only to the extent that your qualifications fit one of their current assignments.

Regardless, do your research and find the placement agencies that are active and respected in your industry. Keep in touch with a few carefully chosen ones either by checking their web sites regularly or by calling occasionally to see if there are any new possibilities.

GUIDELINES FOR USING SEARCH FIRMS AND PLACEMENT AGENCIES

- Do not expect these organizations to find a job for you. No more than 10 percent of your job search time and energy should be spent with them unless you are actively in consideration for one of their assignments.
- Use your network and do thorough research to determine which search firms and placement agencies typically have assignments that match your skills and interests. Check their web sites regularly and try to develop a relationship with someone in the firm.
- Some employers do not post their openings on their own web site but rather use a select group of search firms and placement agencies for all their hiring needs. Find out which firms are used by the organizations that are of interest to you, and stay in touch with them.
- If you approach a company directly for a position that has been contracted out to an agency, expect to be redirected to the agency. If the hiring organization proceeds independently, a dispute over the fee could ensue. You might be caught in the middle and ultimately lose your chance at landing the job.
- If you approach more than one placement agency, you might find yourself being presented for the same job by several firms. This is a problem. You must immediately decline the opportunity with the firm that was second in bringing it to you.
- Search consultants and placement agency representatives are expert interviewers. They will probe your background using a full range of interviewing techniques, particularly behavioural interviewing.
- In the initial interview with a search firm or placement agency, the name of the hiring organization will probably be withheld. This is done to maintain the confidentiality of the search so that neither an incumbent nor the competition will be prematurely alerted to changes.
- Once you are being considered for a position they represent, your consultant should be very helpful in providing inside information on the hiring organization. Talking with them should allow you to complete a large portion of your research.
- Your consultant should offer you feedback from each interview, with tips on what areas of your expertise should be highlighted in subsequent interviews.

- Always remember that the consultant is working primarily for the hiring organization. If there are several finalists for a position, the consultant will probably have input in the selection. It is important that you continually manage your discussions with them as if you are being interviewed.
- Placement agencies and search firms will either help you with salary negotiations or negotiate for you. Stay involved with this aspect of the process.
- Hiring processes are often protracted, especially at more senior levels. If you are seen early in the process by the hiring organization, you may be a benchmark candidate, meaning that you appear to be ideally suited for the job and all subsequent candidates have the challenge of testing out above you. Although the wait can be disconcerting, you're in a good position unless you have other opportunities that need to be resolved.

Passive Search Techniques to Avoid

The ease with which you can distribute data through cyberspace has given rise to many job seekers blasting their résumés, unsolicited, to numerous prospective employers. Do not waste your time doing this, and do not pay a fee-based résumé distribution service to do it for you. It merely creates résumé spam, the scourge of corporate recruiters. It's the current equivalent of an old technique, the broadcast distribution of your résumé and generic cover letter by mail. This search method was, and still is, ineffective.

Beware of organizations that charge you a fee and promise to find you a job. Often, they represent you only by distributing your résumé, with minimal targeting and no follow-up, to vast numbers of hiring organizations. Your money is seldom well-spent on such services.

Chapter 17

Keep Your Search Active

When the going gets tough,
just keep going.

An active employment search is just that—active! A passive search is reactive. It concentrates on the techniques that do not require a proactive approach to people and new ideas. This doesn't mean that a passive job search will be unsuccessful; it simply means that you are relying on circumstances and events outside your control to bring opportunities your way. Active job seekers go out and find new possibilities through creative thinking, probing research and an open-minded exploration of their targets. They talk with as many people as possible in carefully planned and appropriate ways.

The following chart compares and contrasts the characteristics of the two approaches. Locate yourself on the chart and think about what you need to do to shift your attitude and activities to the "active" column.

Job Search Factors	Active	Passive
Attitude of the job seeker	• Feels in control and confident • Willing to take up the challenge • Tries new approaches and techniques • Open to feedback and suggestions • Enthusiastic, highly motivated	• Feels victimized, blames others • Unwilling • Inflexible • Defensive • Despondent
Focus of the search	• Seeks external contact • Involved and engaged • Focus is on the job search • Interested in people • Has targets A, B & C in place	• Turned inward • Isolated • Scattered energies • Interested in inanimate resources • Willing to take any job available
Scope of search	• Looks at a variety of industries • Seeks out unfamiliar organizations • Thinks creatively about roles • Goes out to find new possibilities	• Stays with known industries • Has a limited list of organizations • Seeks to stay with known roles • Closed to new possibilities
Hours dedicated	• Works at the job search full-time • Spends 30 to 40 hours per week on dedicated job search activities • Sustained effort	• Spends 10 to 20 hours or less each week on the job search • Counts all Internet surfing time and reading the comics in the 10 hours • Sporadic effort
Methods employed	• Spends 80% of time actively networking • Follows up on all leads regardless of how unlikely they seem • Creates and follows a plan for using agencies or search firms • Answers ads and Internet postings • Posts résumé on Internet job boards • Plans time for self-care to keep energy and spirits high	• Answers ads and Internet postings • Posts résumé on Internet job boards • Contacts a few agencies or search firms without follow-up • Sends out broadcast letters with résumé attached • Sends out networking letters without personal follow-up • Networks with only a few close and well-known colleagues and friends
Resilience	• Manages to depersonalize rejection • Generates activity on many fronts • Recognizes and guards vulnerabilities • Persistent	• Takes rejection personally • Puts all eggs in one basket • Remains unaware of vulnerabilities • Stops trying after setbacks
Measures of success	• Every plan implemented and every short-term goal attained is counted as a success and celebrated • Finds an ideal opportunity	• Uses only one measure: landing a job

The Employer's Point of View

Stand in the employer's shoes for a moment. When you have a vacancy to fill there are three objectives:
- Find the person with the right skills, and the right fit for the position, the team and the culture of the organization.
- Fill the vacancy quickly.
- Minimize the cost of the search.

The major risk in hiring is the employer's limited access to information about a candidate's past performance and ability to deal with people. For this reason, hiring someone known to the interviewer or recommended by a trusted colleague or employee substantially minimizes the risk.

An experienced hiring manager will usually follow these steps in this order:
- Search for an internal candidate using personal observations and knowledge plus internal networking.
- Consider individuals outside the organization who are known first-hand.
- Follow formal internal job posting procedures.
- Use an external network of contacts to identify appropriate candidates.
- Check the organization's database of external résumés.
- Place the posting on an Internet job board or advertise using traditional print media.
- Use an executive search firm or placement agency.

Tip: Even when policy requires that all vacancies be posted internally, the informal networking and selection process is still active and powerful. If the best candidate is someone known or recommended, but who is outside the organization, executives will often find a way to hire them.

A CFO from an established communications organization was interested in making a move to a media company. He researched the industry and identified three companies that appealed to him. Using his network, he was able to meet with the CEO and founder of one company. He explained his professional skills and background, and was explicit about his interest in joining the founder's team. Although there was no immediate opening, the founder had been thinking about upgrading his management team in preparation for an acquisition within 24 months. That networking meeting was the catalyst for advancing the founder's plans. The CFO was hired, the acquisition successfully completed and the CFO launched a new phase of his career that was more closely attuned to his interests.

Your Point of View

As a job seeker, you want to have your potential candidacy identified as early in the selection process as possible. To achieve this you must be in touch with many people in numerous organizations so that your name will be raised for consideration during the initial steps of a search.

Ironically, most people prefer to focus their energies where the decision-makers least prefer to conduct their search. It's easy to surf the Internet, register on a few job boards, answer ads, talk with a search firm or two and believe that the best opportunities will eventually come your way. Excellent opportunities are often filled before they get to agencies, the Internet, newspapers or trade journals.

A senior retail executive got past his initial reluctance to network and quickly transformed his passive job search into a very active one. His weeks were filled with one meeting after another and all of his time outside meetings was devoted to preparation and follow-up. One day he got a phone call out of the blue from the CEO of a small manufacturing company. The CEO said, "I'm looking for a new VP of Operations, and the last five people I talked to mentioned your name! I don't know who you are, but I've got to meet you!" Although the job was not a good fit, their meeting generated a long list of new contacts and the CEO's ongoing support.

Barriers to the Active Job Search

Fear of Rejection

The primary barrier to conducting an active job search is the fear of rejection. Looking for employment can be one of the more daunting experiences that life has to offer. What you do for a living can be such a large part of your identity that it's difficult not to take everything connected with your search personally. Who would want to compound the stress of looking for a new opportunity with the small setbacks of phone calls not returned, meetings refused and polite brush-offs from those you approach for help? Of course, the answer is "No one!" It's easier to stay hidden behind your computer or busy with résumé revisions and broadcast emails than to brave the world of networking.

Those who master the techniques of the active job search don't entirely eliminate their feelings of fear and vulnerability; rather, they reduce them through good planning, research, well-crafted scripts, appropriate approaches to people and, most importantly, a strong support system. You need to acknowledge what will be most difficult for you and work hard to get yourself through it.

Introverts and Extroverts

Another often-cited barrier to conducting an active job search is the intrinsic difference between people with outgoing personalities and those who are more reserved and quiet. This distinction is important, and the issue is actually quite complex. Even naturally extroverted people might withdraw into a shell when they are experiencing the stress of a job search. Confidence is the critical factor. Regardless of your personality type, if you can muster the confidence, you can do what's needed to conduct an active job search.

Unquestionably, the job search methods that generate better success are easier for people who prefer an extroverted approach. Although there are distinct advantages throughout the career transition process to the introverted approach, the employment market consistently gives greater rewards to extroverted activities. Job seekers who are more introverted need to mimic extroverts, at their confident best, and those who are too outgoing can learn to rein in their effusiveness by observing their introverted colleagues.

Introverts tend to do an excellent job of thinking through their search plans and techniques before enacting them. This is advantageous in the early stages of career transition because it usually results in quality work in the more individual tasks of planning strategy, doing research and conducting a career assessment. In later stages, it can translate into good record-keeping, administration and follow-up, although many extroverts are also very well organized.

Extroverts are more inclined to talk about their job search before they plan it fully. These are the people who prefer to verbally form their strategy and do their research by asking questions of other people. Naturally drawn to action, extroverts risk interacting with their network too soon, confusing or tiring important contacts. However, they are usually more natural marketers who promote themselves and their experience with greater ease. Developing rapport with new contacts comes more easily and conversations flow with less effort.

In the networking process, virtually everyone has difficulty making telephone calls, particularly to people they don't know well. Making these calls can make you feel like you're asking someone to give up their valuable time to help you, a privilege that you think you don't deserve. As well, most people dislike appearing needy and when you are networking, you truly need information, advice and leads. For these reasons, making initial calls to ask for networking meetings is the crucial test of confidence for extroverts and introverts alike. The only way around this barrier is to trust in others' genuine willingness to be helpful, and plan an approach that is straightforward and credible. Remember that you will likely have something to offer them in return, if not now, at some point in the future. Tackle one call at a time, plan it carefully and give yourself full credit—even a reward—for making the call. Once a meeting is arranged, preparing for it and conducting it is a far easier task.

Introverted activities such as doing the research and developing targeted questions will help lower anxiety levels for both introverts and extroverts as they prepare for networking meetings. Showing reserve in meetings by listening attentively and not overstaying your welcome is also an introverted trait that is recommended for all. At the same time, introverts need to act more like extroverts and relate to networking contacts with their own expression of enthusiasm.

Tip: Don't let your natural preference for introversion or extroversion become a barrier to the active job search. Intentionally manage your behaviour to achieve a balanced approach, and remember that confidence is by far the more crucial factor.

Maintaining Motivation

An active search generates its own momentum and motivation. The law of inertia applies: objects, or in this instance, search activities, in motion tend to stay in motion. The notable reward for asking people for information, advice and leads is that you get what you request with encouragement as a bonus. Obviously, information, advice, leads and encouragement motivate you to initiate more meetings, which return additional information, advice, leads and encouragement, and so on.

Even with an active search underway, everyone has ups and downs as they go through the process. This is especially true for those with target markets that are quite specialized, very small or in a phase of consolidation or inactivity, resulting in a longer search. A protracted search is challenging for even the most optimistic individuals. Mood swings still need attention even though they are not as exaggerated as they were at the outset of the career transition process. Good coping techniques are crucial as the weeks go by.

Coping well entails recognizing your emotional needs and taking steps to manage them. Your method of dealing with your emotions is unique. You might need more time to yourself to recharge your batteries, or maybe you're the sort of person who seeks contact with others for a boost. Depending on your style, either working harder or backing off a bit might help you. Some people can talk themselves into a positive frame of mind, while others benefit from motivational books or inspiring speakers. Your support network and professionals such as your doctor, counsellor or career transition consultant can be excellent resources for the long haul.

Tip: Worry is a misuse of imagination!

The guidelines found in Chapter 3, for coping with the emotions accompanying loss and change, can also help sustain your motivation throughout your search for work. Regardless of the source of stress, the same techniques work. In addition to reviewing those strategies, use the guidelines that follow for more practical tips.

GUIDELINES FOR STAYING MOTIVATED THROUGHOUT THE JOB SEARCH
- Put a structure in place for your job search activities. Set business hours for yourself just as if you were expected to report to the office.
- Don't let hobbies, volunteer commitments, household chores, renovations or other activities unrelated to the job search take over your schedule.
- Have a plan with daily goals and objectives. Make them reasonable so that you can end each day by congratulating yourself on a job well done.
- Build stress-reducing activities into your daily schedule. Plan to go for a walk or a workout every day after you've completed your tough calls.
- Organize your day to accommodate your mood swings and energy levels. For example, if early afternoon is always a low time for you, don't make initial networking calls at that time.
- Use your high-energy moments as springboards for tackling the more daunting tasks. When you are feeling up, get tomorrow's calls out of the way early. Tackle the list of thank-you letters or get that cover letter finalized and dispatched.
- When you are feeling down, cut yourself some slack and seek out those things that you know will help restore your equilibrium.
- Keep weekends as time off for you and your loved ones.
- Do a weekly performance review. Since you are effectively paying yourself, evaluate whether or not you have earned your pay. What percentage of your time has been spent on the activities that are known to generate success?
- Counting the number of networking meetings you conduct each week is a good measure of the success of your search efforts. Between scheduling, doing the preliminary research, planning

your agenda, attending the meetings and following up with thank-you letters, six to eight networking meetings each week will keep you very active in the job search.

- Celebrate every success. Give yourself a reward for accomplishing your daily or weekly goals. Make the reward something that is healthy, fun or vitally interesting to you.
- Build some volunteer time into your weekly schedule. Helping someone whose needs are different from yours can be an excellent way to keep things in perspective.
- Remind yourself that your family and friends like you because you are *you*. It wasn't your identity as Vice President of Whatever at Previous Co. that held their affection and admiration.
- Keep the active job search going full speed ahead even when you are in the final stages of negotiating with an organization. It's devastating to have an opportunity that you really want fall through and have nothing else on the go.

A communications and public relations officer was feeling quite despondent at the outset of her job search. Although she was not usually in the habit of watching golf tournaments on TV, she tuned into the British Open. The announcer was talking about what factors differentiated the champions. He said that it had very little to do with physical build, natural athletic ability or a unique swing, but rather that it was the athlete's focus, determination and strength of character to sustain the long, arduous training that produced winners. She wrote down what the announcer said and began to think of each bit of research, and every phone call, letter and meeting as another practice swing. With this in mind, she knew she could do it, and she did. She landed a job that suited her to a tee!

There is work out there for people with your skills and abilities! If you are not finding opportunities, you need to have a look at the search techniques you are using. Are you truly engaged in an active search or are you allowing passive search methods to take up more than 20 percent of your time? Call on your board of advisers and ask networking contacts for an infusion of fresh ideas. When you apply creative thinking, and look at your situation from a different perspective, new paths often appear. Sometimes the change that is needed is simply a change in your viewpoint.

Refer to Appendix A one last time. You have worked your way through the steps of a targeted search for employment. If you keep at it, the outcome will be positive for you.

Outcomes

An active search, one with 80% of your time and energy allocated to networking, will result in two vitally important outcomes:

- An aware network to keep you informed
- Employment opportunities

An aware network will help you understand the marketplace, provide more contacts and alert you to opportunities. As you learn about market realities and the pragmatism of your targets, you expand your network and pursue new opportunities. One of them will be the right one for you.

Keep this proverb posted where you will see it often.

When nothing seems to help, I go and look at a stonecutter hammering away at his rock, perhaps a hundred times without so much as a crack showing in it. Yet at the hundred and first blow it will split in two, and I know it was not that blow that did it—but all that had gone before.

—Jacob Riis

Part Five

Cross the Finish Line

Perseverance yields success.

Objectives

This final step takes you across the finish line and back to the starting point. It offers guidelines for getting off to the best possible start in a new role and recommends lifelong career management techniques. The chapters in Part Five cover:

- Managing your references well.
- Analyzing and aligning an employment offer with your key criteria for job satisfaction.
- Evaluating a remuneration package.
- The principles of win–win negotiations.
- Saying "No" to an offer without burning bridges.
- Planning what you need to achieve during the first 90 days on the job.
- Building good relationships at your new organization.
- Adapting to a new culture.
- Guidelines for ongoing career management.
- Goal-setting for the long term.

Rules to Follow

- Choose your references carefully. Prepare them through direct communication.
- Review your priorities and think about trade-offs as you evaluate your job offer.
- Think of negotiations as an opportunity to understand the interests of the other party.
- When starting a new job, eliminate as many extraneous responsibilities as possible so that the first 90 days will include ample time for planning and reflection.
- Remember to listen more than you talk.
- Adopt aspects of the new culture that will be noticed, such as the dress code, use of buzzwords and attendance at social events and opportunities for informal camaraderie.
- Get things done early in your tenure and be sure that your boss is aware of it.

- Keep noticing and recording your accomplishments.
- Keep your résumé up-to-date.
- Always have short-term and long-term learning goals.
- Value each job for being one step along your career path rather than thinking of it as one step up the ladder.

Moves That Can Set You Back

- Neglecting to deal openly with potential negative references.
- Negotiating too hard for concessions that your prospective employer is loath to make.
- Failing to understand exactly what you were hired to do.
- Arriving at your new job loaded down with old baggage.
- Thinking that this new job will be yours until you retire.
- Failing to start considering your next moves now.

Chapter 18

Close the Deal

You can't negotiate after you're hired.

Once you've nurtured a lead into a solid employment opportunity, finalize the offer with professionalism. Your references now play a leading role in helping you bring the transaction to a successful close. Manage their involvement carefully. At the same time, scrutinize the opportunity and the offer. You want to go in with your eyes wide open, or back away for valid reasons. When you discuss your questions and requests for amendments with your prospective employer, be conscious that your negotiating style will be on full display. You are setting the stage for the new relationship, and you want to establish trust, openness and goodwill.

References

From the beginning of the transition process you will have been in touch with the people who can now provide a reference for you. Some may have been part of your close support network, giving you counsel and support along the way. Others will be more distant, but presumably willing to step in and contribute to your success at this point. There may still be others whom you feel would not be inclined to give you a positive reference. You must manage the involvement of every potential reference carefully and respectfully.

GUIDELINES FOR MANAGING REFERENCES

- Be thoughtful about the people you select as references. Their experience with you and your work should be relevant to the position.
- If you are currently employed, the hiring organization should not expect you to provide references from within your organization until an offer of employment has been extended and accepted. The offer can be conditional upon final reference checks.
- Call each person before offering their name to the prospective employer. Describe the position, explain why you are interested in it, how it complements your experience, skills and strengths and how you expect to add value. This will allow them to decide whether or not they feel comfortable providing the reference and it will help them in preparing for the conversation.
- Gain explicit permission from each person before giving their name to your prospective employer. Tell your references when to expect a call and who will be calling.

- When you are offered the job, immediately call your reference providers with the good news.
- At the conclusion of the process, thank them in writing regardless of the outcome.

Managing No-Reference Policies and Negative References

There is growing reluctance on the part of organizations to provide references for former employees due to fear of legal liability. The confirmation of name, title and dates of employment is about as far as many will go. Some will also confirm salary. If your former employer has a no-reference policy, former co-workers and bosses who have since joined other companies are appropriate alternatives provided they have worked with you in the not too distant past. If you are stuck, you might approach trusted colleagues who are still employed with the organization; ask if they would consider offering a personal reference that does not represent the organization or speak to work-related issues.

Tip: A novel way of dealing with no-reference policies is to script your leaving story and provide it to those who will be contacted in the reference checking process. Ask them to merely confirm its truthfulness when someone calls and relates the story as part of a reference check.

Potentially negative references must be handled with care, particularly if one of them is your most recent boss. It's best to deal with this honestly and openly. Contact the individual who concerns you and tell them where you are in the process of finding new employment. Describe the role you hope to land and how you believe you can make a contribution. Be honest about how you described the reason for your departure, your contribution, your strengths and areas in need of development. If there are particularly sensitive issues, consider putting your thoughts in writing before making the call. Have a trusted member of your support network vet the content of your message.

When you call, be brief and dispassionate. Seek to understand what is being said, and negotiate a way to acceptably express each point to your prospective new employer. If your potentially negative reference refuses to have the discussion or remains recalcitrant, pre-empt their remarks by explaining to your prospective employer what they are likely to hear from this person and why. Remain dispassionate. Respectfully provide your explanation of the situation before references are checked.

Evaluate the Offer

By the time you receive an offer of employment, there may be no question in your mind about accepting it. On the other hand, you might have some serious thinking to do.

The first step in conducting an in-depth evaluation of a written employment offer is to return to the reflective work you did at the outset of your career transition. Review the criteria you established for the ideal employment opportunity. Next, use the worksheets in this chapter for a thorough analysis of the position, the people and the organization. Finally, use intuitive questions to bring to the surface underlying issues that go beyond concrete facts.

Following these steps will be particularly helpful when you have more than one opportunity to consider. Even if you have only one written offer, surmise the terms of your possible alternatives and use the evaluation worksheet to score them. This can help you decide if it's worth taking the risk of losing one opportunity while waiting for another.

Tip: Don't think of this as an all-or-nothing exercise. Your objective is to develop a list of things to negotiate and rank them in priority order. Even if an offer seems acceptable, you might find ways to improve it.

Not all factors in an employment opportunity are of equal importance to you. First, establish the weighting for each, using a scale of 1 to 3, the higher number being the most important. Rank each element of the position, the organization and the offer with a score from 1 to 5. The final score for each factor combines the weighting and ranking.

Category	Factor	Weighting (A)	Ranking (B)	Score (A x B)
Job content	Degree to which your key skills will be engaged Elements of your style that will be useful Use of your knowledge Incorporation of your interests Match with your non-negotiable values and motivators Overall challenge Realistic performance expectations Alignment with your previous experience			
Job-related factors	Title Travel required (+ or -) Physical environment Resources available			
People	Fit with boss peers subordinates clients external contacts			
The organization	Reputation of the organization Positioning and direction of the industry Vision and values Ethics and principles Your compatibility with culture			

Future prospects	Direction of the industry			
	Appropriate career direction			
	Professional development opportunities			
	Positioning for next steps (internally)			
	Positioning for next steps (externally)			
Relocation issues	Suitability of housing			
	Quality/accessibility of schooling			
	Comparability of disposable income			
	Opportunity to build equity or wealth			
	Quality of business life			
	Quality of family life and opportunities for your spouse			
	Social relationships			
	Balance between work and personal priorities			
	Proximity to the "action"			
	Ease of settling in			
	Overall comfort			
	Distance from home and extended family			
Remuneration	Base salary			
	Variable pay*			
	Equity			
	Benefits			
	Pension			
	Vacation			
Perqs	Car			
	Club memberships			
	Parking			
	Other			
Non-compete or Non-solicit	Restrictions on future activities if you resign			
Exit clause	Contracted amount of pay in lieu of notice			
Total Score				

* Variable pay includes bonuses, commission, profit sharing and long-term incentives. Be sure that you understand when your eligibility begins. There can be a waiting period of several months with no retroactive payment.

Intuitive Factors to Consider

- People are on their best behaviour during the interview process, and the organization will have been putting its best foot forward. If there is anything about them that does not sit well with you now, be forewarned that it's not likely to get any better.
- What is your gut feeling about this offer of employment? Are you genuinely pleased and looking forward to the job?
- What were your issues and questions at the beginning of the interview process? What early reservations did you mention to your spouse or partner and members of your support network or board of advisers? Has everything been addressed to your satisfaction?
- How will your colleagues and peers react to the news? Can you sincerely present this as being a good move for you?

An engineer was applying for a job in an aerospace firm. She arrived early and sat in the reception area observing her prospective colleagues as they came and went. They scurried past with heads down and eyes focused on their feet. No one spoke. She landed the job and accepted it, but quickly found the work environment oppressive. In hindsight, the clues had been there from the start, but because she wanted the job, she had not allowed herself to be honest about what she noticed.

Negotiate the Deal

The foregoing analysis should give you a clear picture of the positives and areas of concern regarding an employment opportunity. You need to be clear about how important the job is to you before opening negotiations. Don't feel that you must negotiate an offer of employment. If it's acceptable, take it as it is!

The salary and benefits have probably been negotiated to some extent prior to the organization making an offer. At this point, you are not likely to be able to achieve a significant increase in base salary, but there could be more room for improving the terms of variable pay. Think of remuneration and perqs as a composite, and don't get stuck on any specific point in isolation. If the organization cannot give you concessions in one area, they might have flexibility in another. Go for the best overall deal. If relocation is involved, comparable disposable income and the opportunity to establish equity in property must be considered as a part of the overall package.

Tip: If you come to a stalemate in negotiating remuneration, ask for an early review of both performance and remuneration. If agreed, ask that the offer letter be changed or sign it back noting the change. This precaution will give you some protection if the individual negotiating on behalf of the organization is no longer in the same position when the time for the review comes around.

Asking for a broader scope of responsibilities, a different job title or a different reporting structure may be met with a definitive "No." However, the more senior the role, the more competitive the market or the less bureaucratic the organization, the better your chance of success. Sometimes organizations will shape a role to fit an individual who brings a rare combination of skills and knowledge to the deal. Proceed with caution when negotiating factors that go beyond remuneration. Know your position well.

A senior executive from a large financial institution learned through a networking contact that a US-based custodial services firm was considering expanding its business into the Canadian market. After a thorough round of interviews with the organization, the executive was given a verbal offer. His job was to establish and manage the Canadian business. Six months went by, during which time the executive and the organization negotiated not only compensation, but also authority, responsibility and autonomy. Much discussion ensued over the non-existent job description until the executive finally wrote one. Always confident that with the proper mandate the venture would be a success, he kept a very low profile so that other opportunities would not find him in the interim. Finally he moved ahead on finding office space and identifying capable support staff for the start-up. He used his activities around building the infrastructure as leverage to bring the protracted negotiations to a successful close.

Use the worksheet that follows to list and prioritize your negotiating points, and then use the guidelines that follow the worksheet to plan and implement successful negotiations.

WORKSHEET 18.2 **Analyze Your Negotiating Points**			
Negotiating Points	**Terms of the Offer**	**Terms Desired**	**Priority**
Base Salary			
Variable pay: signing bonus			
individual performance bonus			
profit-sharing plan			
long-term incentive			
Equity: stock purchase			
stock options			
share ownership programs			
Benefits: life and disability insurance			
medical and dental coverage			
Employee Assistance Program			
Pension plan or group RRSP			
Vacation time			
Car			
Parking			
Memberships: clubs			
professional associations			
Professional development opportunities			
Conference and convention attendance			
Executive coaching support			
Exit clause			
Non-compete clause			
Non-solicit clause			
Title and position with peers			
Work Arrangements: part-time schedule			
telecommuting			
flexible schedule			
job sharing			
Business development or sales targets			
Duration of initial mandate or time to first review			
Opportunities for sabbaticals			
Equipment: laptop, cell phone, pager			
home system connection			
Internet connection			
Product or service discounts			
Leave policies: sick days			
personal days			
parental leave			
compassionate leave			
Start date			

Tip: Have an employment lawyer review the offer, especially if it contains complex variable pay arrangements, equity, options, a non-compete clause or an exit clause. Don't finalize the deal on the back of an envelope or rely on a verbal agreement. Sign back the offer just as you would with an offer to buy a house.

GUIDELINES FOR NEGOTIATIONS

- The best time to negotiate is when you have a written offer of employment in hand. The organization clearly wants you to sign up, and it will be interested in a speedy resolution of the process. This puts you in one of the best negotiating positions you will ever have.
- Don't let this advantage go to your head. Every organization has a maximum tolerance level, and you don't want to push it too close to that line. These negotiations will have an effect on your ongoing relationship with your new employer.
- Know your position:
  - Before negotiations begin, use the worksheet "Analyze Your Negotiating Points" and make a complete list of the points you would like to improve or add to the offer.
  - Establish your minimum acceptable level for each of the negotiating points listed above and know your priorities. If the existing terms of the offer are not close to your minimum levels of acceptability, it's going to be an uphill push, and you need to be thinking about alternatives.
  - What might you be willing to trade off (e.g., variable pay for base salary)? Think about equivalent values. If you are in a period of life where your cash-flow needs are great, higher base salary might be much more important than it is for someone closer to retirement.
  - What is non-negotiable for you?
- Know your alternatives:
  - What other opportunities realistically await you if you cannot come to a satisfactory agreement on this offer? You don't want to drive too hard a bargain if there is no fallback position. Even if you win your points, you risk tainting the relationship.
  - Keep all of your other job search initiatives going.
  - If you are waiting for offers from other organizations, evaluate those opportunities and see how they would score in comparison to the offer in hand. This will give you clarity regarding the wisdom of stalling to see if something better comes through.
- Learn as much as you can about the organization's position. Use your network, ask the search or placement consultant, check with your career transition consultant or ask the individuals conducting the final interviews.
  - What does an average remuneration package contain for your peers in this organization?
  - What are the standard compensation levels and where does your position fit?
  - How are incentives and equity ownership terms usually structured?
  - What is the range for performance bonuses at your level?
  - How much authority and flexibility does the person negotiating the deal have?
  - If flexibility is limited in some areas, is there more in others?

- Get comparable industry data. Know what others are paying for people like you in similar positions.
- Enter the negotiations with the intention of finding a resolution that leaves both you and the organization feeling like winners.
- Negotiate in person if at all possible. Negotiating over the phone or through a third party is not as effective.
- Begin by affirming your interest and enthusiasm for the opportunity. Confirm items where you are in agreement, and enumerate the items to be discussed in order of priority.
- For each item, explain your interest or point of view and the rationale behind it.
- Listen carefully and ask probing questions.
- Focus on the rationale for the organization's responses to your requests, not just the answers. Find out what policies or practices make it difficult for them to meet your needs.
- Remember that you are always communicating with your body language and voice, as well as your words. Reaffirm your enthusiasm for the position where appropriate throughout the process.
- If you relent on one point, make sure that you get something else in return.
- Your goal is to build an amicable working relationship with the people in the organization. Do not give in too soon and do not create a problem for yourself by insisting on having a better deal than they can afford.

Stalling Techniques

Although it may seem a nice problem to have, it's not easy to delay accepting one offer while waiting for another that you would prefer. Anticipation and early prevention, as discussed in the interviewing chapter, are the best remedies to this situation but may not always be possible. If you find yourself struggling for ideas, use these guidelines.

GUIDELINES FOR DELAYING AN OFFER WHILE WAITING FOR ANOTHER

- If you haven't been given an offer in writing, ask for it before you start negotiations.
- Find credible reasons to meet with specific individuals before indicating your willingness to enter negotiations. Perhaps a key person was on holidays during the round of interviews, and you would like a chance to meet them. Ask for another discussion with someone that you have already met to ensure that your understanding of the mandate is clear. Indicate that you want to present your ideas about how to handle the mandate to see if they are acceptable to the organization.
- Negotiate slowly.
- Return phone calls on the same day, but do it late in the working day to delay the process. Keep your cell phone turned off as if you are busy in meetings.
- Have your lawyer review the contract.
- Ask for one more weekend to review the offer with your spouse or partner.
- Ask for an extension.

Tip: Be very careful with these delay tactics. You do not want to send a message of waning enthusiasm in case you do finally take the job. Also, the community is very small, and you might be found out.

When you are in this situation, do everything you can to speed up the process with the other organization. If there is a search firm or placement agency involved they might be able to help as long as you trust them to do so tactfully. Be honest with the organization you would rather join. Don't deliver ultimatums, but let them know about your dilemma.

Saying "No"

When you decide to turn down an offer, do so with great care. Be honest about your reasons and state them in a way that depersonalizes the message. If you are joining a competitor of the organization you are turning down, or think that you might do so in the near future, focus your reason for refusing the offer on a characteristic or issue that is a known point of differentiation between the two organizations. Try to steer clear of sensitive issues.

A business developer was offered a job by an entrepreneurial firm that had a small but healthy niche in a localized market. Although the offer was tempting, he decided that it would take a mandate with larger scope to interest him. After three months, he joined a competitor to the entrepreneurial firm and assumed responsibility for nationwide business development. He was promised an international mandate following a successful orientation period. His reputation with his competitors remained intact because his reason for turning down their offer was consistent with his reason for accepting the other.

When you go through a round of interviews that results in an offer of employment, a significant relationship is established between you, the organization and the people you have met. Regardless of the outcome, it is important to preserve those relationships. You might have opportunities to work with them in the future, either as a fellow employee or through joint ventures or partnerships. Write letters of regret and sincere thanks to each one of your interviewers.

Saying "Yes"

Once the ink is dry on the offer, contact each person you met in the interview process and let them know that you are pleased to be joining the team. Call the individuals who provided references and let them know the good news. Follow up with a formal letter of thanks. Begin to draft your "I've Landed" letters, and have them ready to send the first week on the job.

After your thank-yous are made, prepare yourself for the first 90 days on the new job.

Chapter 19

Prepare for the First 90 Days in Your New Job

*First impressions
are lasting impressions.*

Success in your new position will depend on your ability to get things done, your skills at building relationships and your flexibility in adapting to the new culture. It sounds simple, but the challenge is real. Once you have successfully negotiated your deal and know your starting date, focus your thinking on how you will handle the crucial first 90 days on the new job. Create a plan to immediately deliver results and shift your status from "new kid on the block" to "familiar face."

Know Exactly What's Expected of You

The mandate presented to you during the interview process will inevitably need further explanation and clarification at the outset of your employment. Job descriptions are seldom fully comprehensive and objectives are rarely documented in advance of your joining. In the first few days, meet with your boss and anyone else who will evaluate your work. Now is the time to find out exactly what's expected of you. You cannot wait until the end of the first 90 days to be clear about your goals and the activities that will lead to attaining them.

Gather information from multiple sources. Make an effort to meet with every stakeholder associated with your mandate. Include colleagues, team members, direct reports, support staff, internal resource providers, front-line salespeople, external suppliers and, most importantly, clients. Target your questions to get to the heart of the issues. Take notes! Find out if the people whose cooperation you need share the priorities given to you. If your mandate does not match the key stakeholders' needs, you have a problem. Raise your concerns with your superiors early and propose a solution.

A market research specialist joined a small entrepreneurial firm with a reputation for providing excellent customized service to its major corporate clients. The methodologies used by her new employer were creative, costly and radically different from traditional research methods. Selling them required extensive explanation with top-quality demonstrations to convince prospective clients of their value. The owner of the firm told the new employee that achieving her established sales targets would be dependent on scheduling and conducting numerous face-to-face meetings with clients. He identified four performance markers. They were: develop a list of at least 25 qualified prospects; schedule and conduct one introductory meeting each week; use the established follow-up guidelines to take the client through the sales cycle; and submit PowerPoint files from product demonstrations to the internal quality review team. With such clear performance markers in place, there was no mistaking the firm's expectations.

Tip: Go for some quick wins. If you can solve a problem, contribute to a project, suggest a novel approach or make a sale during the first 90 days on the job, it will be noticed and appreciated.

Identify the Support and Resources You Need

The support and resources available to you were, no doubt, discussed to some extent during the interviews. Once you are on the job, you need to check out who and what is available, determine their suitability for the task and develop an inventory of what's needed. Make sure that your list is reasonable and affordable. Present it tactfully and only after you have built a relationship with your boss. Have a fallback plan in place in case your requests are denied or delayed.

Your co-workers and subordinates are probably your most important resources. If you are the manager, evaluate your staff quickly. Look for factual evidence of their abilities and delegate as much responsibility as you can without sacrificing quality. If performance problems are present, deal with them immediately. When you put the right people in the right jobs and give them the training and supervision they need for the task, *your* chances of success increase dramatically.

If you do not have managerial responsibilities, be sure to learn how your co-workers' responsibilities relate to yours. Take the initiative to understand the materials, systems and processes that are already in place and use them to the full. When you need resources, ask. Chances are good that they are there for the asking.

Tip: New employees who busy themselves reinventing the wheel waste valuable time and irritate co-workers. If the resources you need are available, use them as they are. Opportunities to suggest improvements will arise in good time.

Look at your own skills and capabilities. Honestly evaluate your strengths and weaknesses as they relate to the tasks at hand. Reflect on the most difficult and daunting aspects of the job, and make a commitment to yourself that you will get the help you need. Whether it's technical support, strategic thinking, planning, communication, implementation or detailed follow-up, there is most likely something that is best shared with someone better suited for the particular task than you. Do not shirk responsibility, but don't leave your Achilles' heel exposed.

Finally, arrange your other responsibilities so that you can concentrate fully on your mandate. During your orientation to the organization, your new colleagues might solicit your help with their projects in a well-meant attempt to bring you on board. Handle this with diplomacy, being careful that fulfilling your mandate is not jeopardized, and that you are not overstepping the boundaries of your role. Distractions also come from outside the organization. Previous responsibilities, family issues, volunteer commitments and even poor health can sabotage the first 90 days. Plan ahead, be cautious and keep your personal calendar clear to make the best possible start.

Make a 90-Day Plan

The scope of what needs to be accomplished will come into focus as you do the above analysis. With this information, create a 90-day plan to keep yourself on track. Establish specific, measurable, realistic, time-limited goals. Document the steps to be taken toward your goals and create an inventory of the resources needed. Give yourself realistic deadlines. Use the worksheet on the next page to aid this process.

Tip: During your first 90 days, create a six-month and one-year plan for the attainment of the goals that the organization has outlined for you and your own development goals. Outline the steps to implementation and make a diary note of checkpoints.

WORKSHEET 19.1
Setting Targets for Your First 90 Days in the New Job

Goals	Steps to Implementation	Resources Needed	Deadlines

A very capable executive was hired as CEO of a major financial services company. His plan for the first 90 days of his tenure was to develop a five-year strategy to improve shareholder value. He conducted exhaustive interviews with his executive team and many of their direct reports for an in-depth understanding of internal operations. He met with external advisers, business partners and major clients to gain a view of their forecasts and expectations. By the end of the 90-day evaluation period, he had written a 200-page document containing summaries of the information he had collected, his analysis and his goals for the next five years. Priorities and implementation steps were laid out. The board was duly impressed. At the end of the five-year period the company was sold at a substantial premium. His copy of the plan, now dog-eared and tattered, stood as a record of the value of using the first 90 days to set things up.

Build Good Relationships

You are joining an established group of people and your presence will change the dynamic. Enter with caution and a willingness to understand each individual. Take the time to learn how the group interacts before you barge into the process. Regardless of your role, they have a set way of doing things and it's best to ask, "How can I help?" rather than saying, "I suggest that we do it this way!"

Ask questions. When you are first engaged in discussions or problem solving, wait until you understand each person's assessment of the situation before forming your own. Find out what's been suggested and tried in the past. When asked for your opinion, offer suggestions rather than delivering edicts. Use phrases such as, "Here's an idea," or "Has the possibility of doing such-and-such been considered?" If you are the one in charge, your opportunity to take the lead will present itself. Spend your early days listening to the collective wisdom of your team and colleagues.

Get to know your most important customer—*your boss*. Become an astute observer of how they prefer to communicate and make decisions. Note who they trust, and seek to understand why. Analyze the challenges and issues that are putting pressure on them, and learn what performance markers lead to their success. Find ways to make a direct contribution to their success.

Build a network inside the organization. Take the initiative to meet your boss's peers. This is especially important in an environment of constant turnover. If your boss changes jobs before your capabilities are widely known, you will need another advocate quickly. At your peer level, seek out and introduce yourself to people across the organization, especially those associated with your mandate or department. Clarify their roles, and learn how their areas operate and interact with yours.

Tip: If you are shy and reserved, make a conscious effort to initiate contact and conversation. Shyness is often mistaken for unfriendliness or arrogance. Remember to smile.

Find a mentor within the organization. This should be someone who can point out the potholes and land mines before you run into them. A mentor is usually someone who has been around for a while and can give you tips on communicating. They can steer you through the decision-making channels and tell you who's who. It's probably best if your mentor is not in the immediate chain of command above you. They need to be willing and able to act as your confidant, free of any conflict that would arise from having influence over your future.

Understand the decision-making process in the organization, and learn to communicate effectively through the appropriate channels. Listen to stories about initiatives that have been proposed and were accepted or rejected. Observe others going through the process of getting something approved. Float your hypotheses in confidence with a few trusted co-workers and ask what it would take to get a green light. Think about everyone whose work would be affected by your proposals and share your preliminary ideas with them. Ask what they see as the benefits and drawbacks. Listen carefully to their responses, and do not immediately try to defend your position or influence theirs.

Adapt to the Culture

In Chapter 4, you did an analysis of the cultures you have experienced in the past. Use that reflective exercise to guide your observations of this new environment. Notice how things get done, how people interact and what is valued. As mentioned earlier, be aware that the stated norms are not always practised. In the first 90 days on the job, make it one of your goals to understand both the main tenets and subtle nuances of the culture.

Leave all signs and habits of your previous organization behind. Purge your briefcase, golf bag and T-shirt drawer of any evidence that you have worked elsewhere. Do not decorate your new office with anything bearing your previous organization's name or logo. Guard against discussing how things were done at your previous place of employment. Your new colleagues do not want to hear, "Over at Old Co., we did this."

Leave all of your baggage behind. This includes frustration with your previous employer's policies and bureaucracy, suspicion of motives, disrespectful treatment of subordinates, an entitlement mentality or anything else that was destructive, yet prevalent, in your previous organization. You have a clean slate—don't write old lines on it!

To succeed, you need to become comfortable in the new culture quickly. This does not mean completely suppressing your unique personality and approach. Remember that the interviewers were pleased with your personal qualities. However, you need to adapt your style and modify your behaviour somewhat to the new environment.

Use these guidelines to remind yourself of the basic rules for adapting to a new workplace:

GUIDELINES FOR ASSIMILATION INTO THE NEW CULTURE
- Observe how information is communicated.
- Notice how meetings are conducted.
- Learn how decisions are made.
- Listen for commonly used jargon and buzzwords, and begin to integrate them into your vocabulary.
- What interpersonal qualities are respected and admired?
- Watch how people interact. How do they dress? How do they use humour?
- How do your peers conduct themselves in day-to-day operations and in meetings, and under stressful circumstances?

- Go to meetings well-prepared to contribute and participate, but sit back and watch the group dynamics first.
- What are some of the corporate legends and anecdotes? What do they indicate about behaviours, values and ethics?
- Why have long-term employees stayed with the company? Why have others left?
- How does the corporate mission statement apply, or not apply, to day-to-day operations?
- On what basis have people been promoted? Why have others been dismissed?
- Who are the rising stars of the organization and what identifies them as such?
- How formal or informal is the workplace?
- What clues do you pick up from the way the offices are furnished and laid out?
- What are the guidelines for dealing with clients or customer complaints?
- How are special events handled? Promotions? Celebrations? Sales goals? Casual days?
- Pay attention to the small things. Learn how to use the electronic filing system, and know who makes the coffee and orders the stationery.
- What discrepancies do you see between what is said and what is done?
- Remember that many of the organization's important rules and regulations will be the informal, unspoken ones. They won't be written down in the handbook. You have to discern them through observation.

A training and development specialist left an organization where the terms "programs," "seminars" and "participants" were used. In her new role she had to consciously adopt the terminology used by her new organization and refer instead to "workshops," "hands-on learning" and "clients." She knew that as long as she used the old references, she would be labeled as one still learning the ropes, rather than being accepted as part of the team.

Tip: If the culture is a poor fit for you, or your values do not match those of the organization, it will be obvious within the first 90 days. Don't fool yourself hoping that everything will work out for the best, or expect either you or the organization to make significant compromises. Start planning your exit now, even if you need to wait some time before finding the right opportunity.

Build reflection time into each day. If you charge ahead too quickly, you are likely to miss the important clues that are right in front of you. Notice the minor, seemingly unimportant comments and unexpected events. Think about what you should be learning from them. The small things are almost always signposts for more crucial issues. To pick up these subtleties and understand the dynamics, you need to carve out time for reflective analysis. Continue to call on your support network or board of advisers throughout this crucial period, to help you understand your new environment.

WORKSHEET 19.2
Do a Daily Review During the First 90 Days

- What introductions did you initiate today?

- What did you learn about the people you met? Make note of their role, challenges, communication style, level of influence and demeanour, and of any personal factors you have observed or been told.

- Who do you want to meet tomorrow?

- What new information do you have about your boss?

- Are you on track with getting things done?

- What steps did you complete toward the implementation of your goals?

- What needs to be done tomorrow to stay on track?

- What new feature of the culture did you observe today?

- What did you do today in an attempt to fit into the culture?

Restart the 90-Day Clock

The energy and enthusiasm that typically accompany a new job make it easier to do all that is necessary during the first 90 days in a new organization. Once you are acclimatized it's more difficult to recognize that each significant change in the organization signals a new beginning. Every time you have a new boss, mandate, structure or goal, you need to implement some of the same 90-day techniques in order to ensure a smooth transition. Major changes in your job should signal a new 90-day period to build relationships with the boss and co-workers, adapt to the new communication and decision-making styles, understand the values and get done what's important given the recent change.

Of equal importance to understanding that the first 90-day trial period happens again and again is realizing that you need to be consciously renewing your career management efforts throughout your entire working life. In this new world of work, it's always time to think about future options and next potential moves.

Chapter 20

Start Planning
Your Next Moves Now

If you don't know where you're going,
you'll end up somewhere else.

—*Yogi Berra*

Once you've successfully been through the career transition process, you can be confident in the knowledge that your skills are employable in another work setting. Career change will likely never again present the same degree of emotional challenge for you, and the skills you've acquired in relation to planning, research, writing a résumé, networking and interviewing will be there to serve you for years to come.

But you're not finished with this process yet. As soon as you've settled into your new role, it's time to put a revised plan in place. It should build on the one you've been following and focus on moving you even closer to your ideal employment opportunity. It might entail further development in this new role, attaining another role within your new organization or choosing to move externally. Don't allow yourself to become fed up with your job, and don't wait for something beyond your control to create a career crisis for you. Start managing your own career *now*.

Notice What You Like Doing

Focus on your accomplishments! At this point, instead of looking back over your career to surface memories of past experiences, *pay attention to your achievements in the present*. They do not need to be grandiose, out of the ordinary or recognized and rewarded by your employer. They might not be part of your specific responsibilities or mandate, but they will flow from your strategic advantage. The key criteria are that they give you a sense of pride and make work worthwhile for you.

Noteworthy accomplishments arise from situations where your creativity finds expression. Everyone has creative potential, not just inventors, musicians and painters. For a teacher, there is creativity in finding a technique that unlocks a door to learning for a struggling student. For a manager, it could be enlivening a workplace with humour and encouraging words. For a consultant, it could be finding the unexpected solution to a client's problem. Satisfying work offers regular opportunities for you to make enjoyable contributions.

Record your accomplishments. Start a journal and jot down the pertinent facts, describing the situation, your actions and the quantifiable results. Doing this will make revising your résumé a much simpler process. If you cannot name on-the-job accomplishments on a regular basis, you need to put career change plans in effect as soon as possible.

Revise Your View of Career Progression

It's old-fashioned to think that each new job should be one rung higher on the bureaucratic ladder than the previous job. It makes more sense to strive for a spiral career in which you might change occupations and/or employers several times, learn new skills and stay vitally interested in your work. This kind of career progression entails finding a role that more closely fits your strategic advantage and offers a work arrangement that better suits your lifestyle.

Professions and occupations evolve as trends come and go, and market conditions change. People often move forward by directing their search for new opportunities toward the leading edges of their profession. In the new world of work, one path leads to another.

A woman who originally trained as a librarian left the school system behind and worked for an industry association that operated a busy reference library. The exposure to numerous business people afforded her the opportunity to transfer her research skills into the consulting field, working on projects where extensive research on the client's competitors was crucial. Through this she was at the forefront of business trends and was well positioned to use the first electronic databases developed by the major newspapers. She shifted her focus to concentrate on electronic information collection and retrieval, and did product development work, looking for early applications of the databases for market research. Following her interests, she launched an entrepreneurial endeavour, providing a leading-edge market research technique to a number of blue-chip corporations.

Lateral moves, project-oriented assignments and working as an independent consultant, contractor or sole proprietor are all options for the new worker. With far too many managers vying for the few openings in the executive suite, not everyone with executive capacity will get there. Be content with satisfying work, a great group of colleagues and reasonable remuneration. These things typify the enlightened view of career progression for everyone.

Keep Your Network Healthy

Perhaps the only concept mentioned in this book as frequently as accomplishments is *networking*. The importance of staying in touch with people who helped during your career transition has already been emphasized, and a variety of ideas for doing this have been described. Don't wait until you're looking for another employment opportunity to give them a call.

Expand your existing network by intentionally seeking out people who are involved in activities, occupations, industries or organizations that interest you. Broaden your perspective beyond the boundaries of your current organization and industry. The more people you know, the easier it is to keep up-to-date on trends. Initiate conversations and be eager to learn what others find interesting, amusing, problematic and exciting.

Don't burn bridges! Try to make every client, supplier, peer, subordinate and superior your ally. You don't have to like everyone, but it's important to develop a reputation for being open-minded and reasonable. Try to find a way to get along with everyone, even with those who are the least magnanimous. Everyone you meet might someday be in a position to either advance your career or set it back.

Find a mentor outside your current organization. In the same way that an internal mentor helps you through the decision-making maze and communication avenues within your organization, an external mentor can guide you through the power channels of your industry. Your mentor should be at a more senior level than you and ideally have more years of experience. Go to your mentor for advice on professional development and career direction as well as challenges and opportunities that arise on the job.

A young woman who was starting her career in commercial real estate was unhappy with her current employer and looking for a new job. She had gotten to know a senior executive in a large real estate development company because they were active members of the same volunteer service organization. When she was offered an opportunity to join an individual in an entrepreneurial real estate venture, she checked her prospective employer's reputation with her friend, the senior executive. Immediately stepping into the role of mentor, the executive warned his young colleague that she ought to steer clear of the opportunity. He knew the entrepreneur well and was certain that if she took the job, she would quickly find that her values and the entrepreneur's were mismatched.

Tip: Your mentor should be someone with whom you feel comfortable sharing your values. It's important to have someone who can remind you of what's truly important to you when you are in danger of deviating from your values.

Be Committed to Lifelong Learning

Keeping your professional and functional skills current is rudimentary. It's your responsibility to see that you get the training you need. If everyone is using a new project management process, take a refresher course. If business process outsourcing is revolutionizing your functional area of expertise, attend conferences and seminars where industry leaders are speaking about it. When your profession moves toward requiring additional credentials or designations, don't let yourself fall behind. Do what's required for accreditation, even if you could teach the qualifying courses yourself.

Explore learning opportunities outside your area of expertise. Do this especially as it relates to your longer-term plans. In addition to learning from traditional resources and networking, arrange an experiential learning opportunity. People often have mistaken ideas of what other occupations would be like, and the easiest way to dispel these notions is to give it a temporary try. If you are currently employed as an accountant and you think you'd like to own and run a little bookstore as a step toward retirement, get a part-time job in one now.

Major career shifts often involve retraining. This is possible only if you have the patience for going back to the classroom, sufficient financial means and very supportive loved ones. However, for some people in mid-career, the realization that they have become what they are because it was expected of them can inspire a courageous decision. If you will be studying to embark on a radically different second career, do extensive research on the options available for your education, and network diligently to ensure that you will be pleased with the educational institution you choose. In mid-career, you don't want to waste your time taking courses that are poorly taught, too elementary or unnecessary.

Tip: When exploring institutions of higher education, find out what philosophies, theories, social mores, theologies or political convictions they espouse. They may claim neutrality, but there will be a bias, and if it doesn't match yours, you're likely to be unhappy.

A woman who was a stay-at-home mom until age 38 entered the world of paid work as an administrative assistant at an international development agency. In that role she was in frequent contact with a group of clergy who encouraged her to further her education and ultimately became her role models. She enrolled part-time and took 10 years to complete her bachelor's degree, following which she studied full-time for her Master of Social Work degree. She entered private practice at age 50. Two years later she decided that her ideal would not be fulfilled until her work directly involved her spirituality and deep religious convictions. She prepared for parish ministry and was ordained at age 56. Fourteen years later she retired from full-time ministry and began a part-time practice as a spiritual director. She never let her age deter her quest for lifelong learning or her commitment to making a contribution through her profession.

In addition to keeping up to date in your field, learn about something that truly interests you with no economic or professional goal in mind. Interesting people usually have some hobby or pastime that fully engages their curiosity. Become an expert in Renaissance cartography, or grow prize peonies. Study Mayan archeology or become knowledgeable about every wine-producing region in France. Understand the nuances of the toughest green at every golf course on the professional tour. These are the sorts of things that offer personal enrichment and enliven your time away from work. If there's nothing like this in your life, it's time to change that.

Tip: Capitalize on the exploding opportunities for learning over the Internet. Everything from graduate degrees to advice on hang-gliding is readily available.

GUIDELINES FOR GOOD CAREER MANAGEMENT
- Set realistic, measurable, time-specific goals for personal development, lifelong learning and career progression. Map out the steps to implementation and the resources needed.
- Build time into your daily and weekly schedule, to chart your progress toward these goals. It's best to record your progression in writing as if you were doing a performance review. As a minimum, think them through as you commute or exercise.

- Carve out time at least once every five years to redo the long-term reflective exercises in Part 2 of this book. At the same time, review your previous reflections and take notice of what has changed and what has remained the same. The constants probably hold important clues to your ideal work in the longer term. Revise your vision statement of the ideal employment opportunity for you.
- Look at every job, assignment or new piece of business as a temporary stop along the way. This is your journey toward your goal. Be content to move forward in stages.
- Come to grips with non-stop change. It's important to recognize and understand your unique reaction to change, and to develop effective coping techniques. Resilience and flexibility are valued in the new world of work.
- Keep your résumé up to date. This provides impetus for recording your accomplishments and equips you to respond to any employment opportunity that arises.
- Keep your five sound bites ready to go. Have a 30-second, 2-minute and full 10-minute version prepared so that you can give quick updates to networking contacts or present your background and capabilities to a new boss or prospective employer.
- Don't look to anyone else to take responsibility for your professional development and career progression. Keep your long-term direction under your own control, using those who traditionally manage careers—your boss, the organization or the industry associations—as input providers.
- Identify opportunities to advance your career and put yourself forward to take assignments that point toward your desired future. It's surprising how few people step up and tell their boss that they want a specific opportunity.
- Train your replacement! Make yourself available for the next move by preparing one of your subordinates or co-workers to step into your shoes. This will also earn you an excellent reputation for developing people.
- Maintain balance in your life. Don't sacrifice your personal relationships for the sake of the job. It's much easier to adjust to an unwanted career change when work isn't everything to you.
- Don't focus on your age; rather, look at how many productive years you have to go. As mentioned earlier, trend-predictors suggest that you will retire in stages, moving into full retirement at a much later age than previous generations.
- Get the important people in your life on board with your long-term plans. Share your dreams with them and involve them in the planning.
- Help your spouse or partner with their career planning. If your ultimate ideal employment opportunity requires a radical change of any kind, your life partner will probably need to make adjustments as well.

Tip: When your phone rings and someone asks for 15 minutes of your time for a networking meeting, schedule it without hesitation.

Extend Your Timeline

This is not a formula for longevity; it's the completion of the reflective exercise in Part 2 where you created your historic timeline. Pick up at today's date, and record your vision for the chapters of your life that are yet to come. Set goals for your career progression, work arrangements, continuous learning, personal enrichment and finances. Predict how your personal priorities are likely to change.

Given the speed of change in this environment, set 18 months as the time frame for the first chapter, and then project three years ahead; five years; and on to retirement. Don't worry if retirement is six or 36 years away for you. It's always helpful to have a picture of what you want to be doing at the end of your working days.

Tip: Pipe dreams are useful as long as you keep exploring what would be required to make them a reality.

Use the final worksheet to extend your timeline and create a picture of a future that's worth the effort it will take to get there.

Personal priorities

Career goals

Work arrangements

Learning goals

Personal enrichment plans

Financial goals

Today   18 months   3 years   5 years   Retirement

Keep a Balanced View

Having a comprehensive vision of the future that includes a realistic picture of your ideal employment opportunity in the longer term is a good strategic move. Whether your current circumstances allow you to pursue these goals right away or require you to postpone them in favour of a purely pragmatic approach to the job search, having this vision gives you a sense of direction and purpose.

There are also cautions regarding visions of future employment. If they are completely unattainable, they can set you up to feel discouraged and inadequate. They can also rob you of the ability to enjoy and make the most of present opportunities. Your long-term plan needs to be tempered with realism if it's going to be helpful. It should be a plan that you are continually taking steps to implement, even if it will take many years to fully achieve. Ensure that your vision of the future offers some present-day activity that keeps you motivated and gives you a feeling of accomplishment.

Another factor that needs to be kept in balance is the search for individual meaning and purpose through work. Many people use a time of transition to think about how their work can serve a purpose that transcends self-interest. Some speak of contributing to the ultimate good of society, while others say they want to leave a legacy, make a difference, fulfill their destiny or serve a divine purpose. These are enormously complex issues, going far beyond what any job or work environment alone can provide.

Take a practical view that seeks to encompass four very important facets of life. They are:

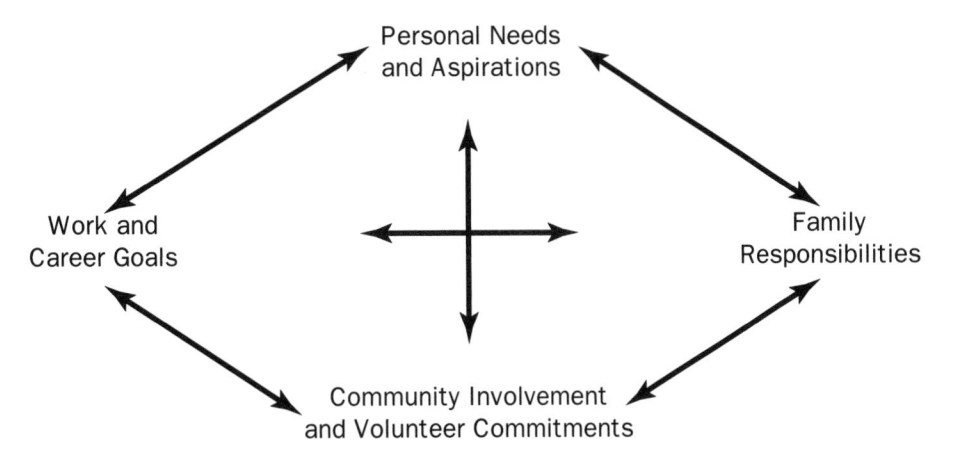

It's not healthy to let any one of these areas become the only focus of your time and energy for extended periods of time. Ideally, they should co-exist in harmony, and there should be no need for you to pretend to be a different person when you move from one role to another. The key is to keep striving for balance.

If your working life is to deliver its fair share of that balance, you need to find work that utilizes as many aspects of your strategic advantage as possible. When you achieve this, even for a short time, your work will make an appropriate contribution to your sense of meaning and purpose, and you will have a degree of contentment, knowing that you don't need to grasp for more.

You know the new rules and all the right moves. Now it's up to you to put yourself in the game and be a winner on your own terms.

Recommended Resources

What You Need to Know Before You Start

Bridges, William. *Creating You & Co.: Learn to Think Like the CEO of Your Own Career*. Reading, Massachusetts: Addison-Wesley, 1998.

Bridges, William. *Managing Transitions: Making the Most of Change*. Cambridge, Massachusetts: Perseus Publishing, 2003.

Johnson, Spencer, M.D. *Who Moved My Cheese?* New York: G.P. Putnam's Sons, 1998.

Moses, Barbara. *Career Intelligence: Mastering the New Work and Personal Realities*. Toronto: Stoddart Publishing, 1998.

Moses, Barbara. *The Good News About Careers: How You'll Be Working in the Next Decade*. Toronto: Stoddart Publishing, 2000.

Goleman, Daniel. *Emotional Intelligence: Why It Can Matter More Than IQ*. Toronto: Bantam Books, 1997.

Goleman, Daniel. *Working with Emotional Intelligence*. Toronto: Bantam Books, 2000.

Part One — Get Your Head in the Game

Borysenko, Joan. *Minding the Body, Mending the Mind*. Toronto: Bantam Books, 1987.

Burton, Mary Lindley and Richard A. Wedemeyer. *In Transition*. New York: HarperCollins, 1992.

Jukes, Jill and Ruthan Rosenberg. *Surviving Your Partner's Job Loss: The Complete Guide to Rescuing Your Marriage and Family from Today's Economy*. Toronto: Murray Axmith & Associates Ltd., 1993.

Loehr, James E. *Stress for Success*. Toronto: Random House of Canada, 1998.

McKenna, Elizabeth Perle. *When Work Doesn't Work Anymore*. New York: Dell Publishing, 1998.

Posen, David B., M.D. *Staying Afloat When the Water Gets Rough: How to Live in a Rapidly Changing World*. Toronto: Key Porter Books, 1998.

Stearns, Ann Kaiser and Rick Lamplugh. *Living Through Job Loss*. New York: Simon & Schuster, 1995.

Part Two — Develop Your Strategy

Butler, Timothy, and James Waldroop. *Discovering Your Career in Business*. New York: Perseus Books, HarperCollins, 1997.

Ibarra, Herminia. *Working Identity: Unconventional Strategies for Reinventing Your Career*. Cambridge: Harvard Business School Publishing Corporation, 2003.

Moses, Barbara. *What Next? The Complete Guide to Taking Control of Your Working Life*. London: Dorling Kindersley Publishing, 2003.

Schaffer, William A. *High-Tech Careers for Low-Tech People*. Berkeley, California: Ten Speed Press, 1999.

Sher, Barbara. *I Could Do Anything—If Only I Knew What It Was*. New York: Dell Publishing, 1995.

Smye, Marti. *Is It Too Late to Run Away and Join the Circus? A Guide for Your Second Life*. Toronto: Key Porter Books, 1999.

Tieger, Paul D., and Barbara Barron-Tieger. *Do What You Are*. New York: Little Brown and Company, 2001.

Toombs, Garth. *The Purple Book of Career Strategies: Exploring Options and Opportunities*. Edmonton: Garth Toombs & Associates Inc., 2001.

Career Assessment Testing Web Sites

www.testingroom.com
www.keirsey.com
www.careerleader.com

Part Three — Gather Your Resources

Résumés

Asher, Donald. *Asher's Bible of Executive Résumés*. Berkeley, California: Ten Speed Press, 1997.

Enelow, Wendy S. *1500+ Key Words for $100,000+ Jobs*. Manassas Park, Virginia: Impact Publications, 1998.

Enelow, Wendy S. and Louise M. Kursmark. *Expert Résumés for Managers and Executives*. Indianapolis: Jist Works, Jist Publishing, 2003

Montage, William E. *Best Résumés for $75,000+ Executive Jobs*. Toronto: John Wiley & Sons, 1999.

The Riley Guide. www.rileyguide.com.

Rice, Craig. *The $100,000 Resume*. Toronto: McGraw-Hill Ryerson, 1998.

Whitcomb, Susan Britton and Pat Kendall. *eResumes: Everything You Need to Know about Using Electronic Resumes to Tap into Today's Job Market*. New York: McGraw-Hill, 2002.

Contracting/Consulting/Small Business

Beich, Elaine. *The Business of Consulting: The Basics and Beyond*. San Francisco: Jossey-Bass Pfeiffer, 1999.

Block, Peter. *Flawless Consulting: A Guide to Getting Your Expertise Used*. San Francisco: Jossey-Bass Pfeiffer, 1981.

Boyd, Sandra. *The Hidden Job Market: An Insider's Guide to Finding Rewarding Contract or Temporary Work.* Toronto: McGraw-Hill Ryerson, 1998.

Carroll, Jim, and Rick Broadhead. *Small Business Online: A Strategic Guide for Canadian Entrepreneurs.* Scarborough, Ontario: Prentice-Hall Canada, 1998.

Lord, David. *Guide to Self-Employment*—National Business Employment Weekly *and the* Wall Street Journal. Toronto: John Wiley & Sons, Inc., 1996.

Wood, Donald M. *Handbook for Canadian Consultants: Turning Your Expertise into a Successful Small Business.* Toronto: McGraw-Hill Ryerson, 1999.

Interviewing

Adams, Robert L., ed. *Adams Job Interview Almanac.* Holbrook, Massachusetts: Adams Media Corporation, 1998.

Ball, Frederick W., and Barbara B. Ball. *Killer Interviews.* Toronto: McGraw-Hill Ryerson, 1996.

Beatty, Richard H. *The Interview Kit.* Toronto: John Wiley & Sons, 1995.

Drake, John D. *The Perfect Interview.* Toronto: American Management Association, 1997.

Hirsch, Arlene S. *Interviewing: Effective Techniques to Help You Answer Tough Questions and Make a Great Impression.* Toronto: John Wiley & Sons, 1996.

Krannich, Caryl Rae, and Ronald L. Krannich. *101 Dynamite Answers to Interview Questions.* Manassas Park, Virginia: Impact Publications, 1999.

Yate, Martin. *Knock 'Em Dead 2003: Great Answers to Over 200 Tough Interview Questions, Plus the Latest Electronic Job Search Strategies.* Holbrook, Massachusetts: Adams Media Corporation, 2002.

Writing Letters

Besson, Taunee. National Employment Weekly *Cover Letters.* Toronto: John Wiley & Sons, 1996.

Enelow, Wendy S. *201 Winning Cover Letters for $100,000+ Jobs.* Manassas Park, Virginia: Impact Publications, 1998.

Yate, Martin. *Cover Letters That Knock 'Em Dead.* Holbrook, Massachusetts: Adams Media Corporation, 2002.

Part Four — Move into Action

Baber, Anne, and Lynne Waymon. *Great Connections: Small Talk and Networking for Businesspeople.* Manassas, Virginia: Impact Publications, 1992.

Balzano, Fredrica J. *Why Do Extroverts Make All the Money? Networking Made Easy for Introverts.* Lincolnwood, Illinois: NTC/Contemporary Publishing Group, 1999.

Barabasi, Albert Lazio. *Linked.* Braintree, MA: Perseus Publishing, 2003.

Boothman, Nicholas. *How to Make People Like You in 90 Seconds or Less.* New York: Workman Publishing, 2000.

Makra, Kevin. *The Canadian Job Directory: The Ultimate Guide to Canada's Hidden Job Market.* Toronto: SEN Publishing, 1998.

Marler, Patty, and Jan Bailey Mallia. *Networking Made Easy.* NTC Publishing Group, 1997.

MacKay, Harvey. *Dig Your Well Before You're Thirsty.* New York: Doubleday, 1997.

Mediacorp Canada Inc. *Canadian Directory of Search Firms 2000*. Toronto, 2000.

Mediacorp Canada Inc. *Who's Hiring 2000*. Toronto: 2000.

Part Five — Cross the Finish Line

Behan, Beverly. *Jumping Ship: How to Navigate Your Way to a More Satisfying Job or Career*. Toronto: Stoddart Publishing, 1999.

Burdett, John O. *New Role, New Reality*. Toronto: Executive Forum, 2000.

Ciampa, Dan, and Michael Watkins. *Right from the Start*. Boston: Harvard Business School Press, 1999.

Deep, Sam, and Lyle Sussman. *Smart Moves for People in Charge*. Reading, Massachusetts: Perseus Books, 1995.

Dubrin, Andrew J. *Personal Magnetism*. New York: American Management Association (AMACOM), 1997.

Fisher, Roger, and William L. Ury. *Getting to Yes*. Boston: Houghton, Mifflin Co., 1981.

Frankel, Lois P. *Jump-Start Your Career*. New York: Three Rivers Press, 1997.

Hartman, Julia. *Strategic Job Jumping*. Rocklin, California: Prima Publishing, 1997.

Held, Vera. *How Not to Take It Personally: 10 Action Strategies for Communications Success*. Toronto: McGraw-Hill Ryerson, 1996.

Harvard Business Review. *Harvard Business Review on Managing Your Career*. Cambridge: Harvard Business School Publishing Corporation, 2002.

O'Connor, Lona. *Top Ten Dumb Career Mistakes...and How to Avoid Them*. Chicago, Illinois: NTC/Contemporary Publishing Group, 1999.

Watkins, Michael. *The First 90 Days*. Boston: Harvard Business School Press, 2003.

Appendix A

Strategic View of
Targeted Employment Search Process

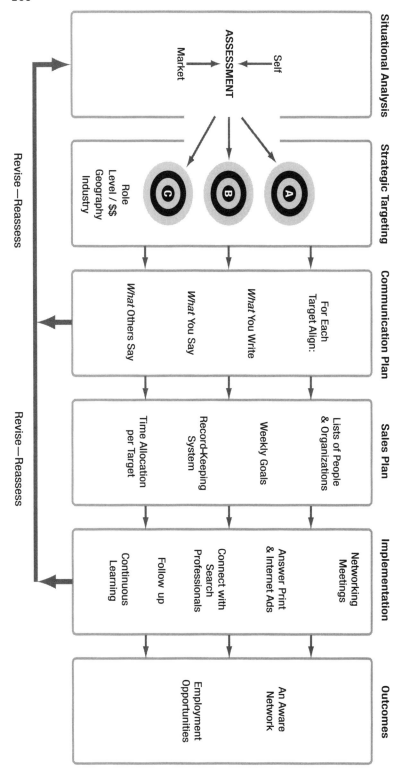

Situational Analysis

Self → ASSESSMENT ← Market

Strategic Targeting

Role
Level / $$
Geography
Industry

(C) (B) (A)

Communication Plan

For Each
Target Align:

What You Write

What You Say

What Others Say

Sales Plan

Lists of People
& Organizations

Weekly Goals

Record-Keeping
System

Time Allocation
per Target

Implementation

Networking
Meetings

Answer Print
& Internet Ads

Connect with
Search
Professionals

Follow up

Continuous
Learning

Outcomes

An Aware
Network

Employment
Opportunities

Revise—Reassess

Revise—Reassess

Appendix B

Sample Search Activities Project Plan

Task	Week of	Feb 02	Feb 09	Feb 16	Feb 23	Mar 01	Mar 08	Mar 15	Mar 22	Mar 29	Apr 05	Apr 12
Get Your Head in the Game												
Financial plan, legal advice, sign off												
Inform family, friends, close contacts												
Build support network, consider references												
Develop Your Strategy												
Self-assessment												
Market assessment												
Set strategic targets and get input from advisers												
Gather Your Resources												
Résumé and other written materials												
Verbal pitch — five sound bites												
Correspondence preparation												
Move into Action												
Sales plan, record-keeping system												
Search firms, ads, the Internet for all targets												
TARGET A—time allocation								80%	80%	80%	60%	60%
Research, align resources, input from advisers												
Active networking												
Assess target, revise if necessary												
TARGET B—time allocation								20%	20%	10%	20%	30%
Research, align resources, input from advisers												
Active networking												
Assess target, revise if necessary												
TARGET C—time allocation										10%	20%	10%
Research, align resources, input from advisers												
Active networking												
Assess target, revise if necessary												
NEW TARGETS—time allocation												
Research, align resources, input from advisers												
Active networking												
Assess target, revise if necessary												
CROSS THE FINISH LINE												

Family Ski Trip

Preferred Date for Re-employment

Acknowledgements

Writing this book has been a team effort from the beginning. I am privileged to have had the experience and wisdom of so many capable colleagues on which to draw.

I am indebted to those who brought their creative ideas to this second edition, especially those who suggested and worked with me on the new, targeted approach to the search process. For fear of omitting some, I offer my thanks to all.

My special thanks goes to everyone who contributed to the first edition. It has been rewarding to know that our collaborative work has helped so many people.

I am also grateful to everyone in the KWA Partners organization, Canada's quality leader in career transition services. Their generous support has made this second edition possible.

And finally, my gratitude goes to John Knebel, my partner in business and life. His extraordinary effort to take care of everything else as I wrote has been deeply appreciated.

Index